A WINTER
IN
INDIA AND MALAYSIA

A WINTER
IN
INDIA AND MALAYSIA
AMONG THE
METHODIST MISSIONS

M. V. B. KNOX

GYAN

Published by

GYAN

Gyan Publishing House
5, Ansari Road
Daryaganj, New Delhi-110002
Phone: 011-47034999, 9811692060
E-mail: books@gyanbooks.com

Distribution Network
gyanbooks.com
India, USA, Canada, UK, Australia

ISBN: 978-93-7097-626-9 (PB)

First Published, 1852

2nd Impression 2025

Printed at: Gyan Press, Delhi.

A WINTER IN INDIA AND MALAYSIA
Author M. V. B. KNOX

Mission Bungalow at Bareilly.

A WINTER

IN

INDIA AND MALAYSIA

AMONG THE

METHODIST MISSIONS

BY

REV. M. V. B. KNOX, Ph.D., D.D.

WITH AN INTRODUCTION BY

BISHOP JOHN F. HURST, D.D., LL.D.

NEW YORK: HUNT & EATON
CINCINNATI: CRANSTON & STOWE
1892

PREFATORY NOTE.

THESE letters are sent out with a hope that they may do some good for missions. It is also with the purpose that the fugitives may not be wholly lost that they are gathered into book-form, since gaining the facts they contain and writing them out were both pleasant and profitable to me. They were mostly written during the months of my passing through those sections of which they treat in a tour of the world. Should any income accrue from their sales it is dedicated in advance to a certain field of mission work. I gladly acknowledge the valuable aid of Rev. Joseph H. Gill, for several years a missionary in India, in reading and correcting these letters. Also I here express my thanks to the editors of those periodicals in which many of them were printed in allowing this use of them from their columns.

M. V. B. KNOX.

INTRODUCTION.

THE author of *A Winter in India and Malaysia* is a busy pastor, and a faithful student of men and countries. His lines of study had reached out widely, and for years he had utilized his spare time in a careful examination into the progress, the life, and the achievements of the great nations of history. As his studies advanced he became keenly sensible of the need of a personal visit to distant nations yet in the darkness, or at best in the gray dawn of a new period. He saw India and Malaysia with the eye of a careful observer. He seems to have become absorbed, the farther he journeyed, in the missionary feeling, until in time his missionary passion overpowered all else. In describing the life, architecture, and countries of India and Malaysia he never once forgot the supreme need of the Gospel, or failed to appreciate the invaluable power of his own ecclesiastical body—the Methodist Episcopal Church—in sending a strong missionary force of men and women to hasten the coming of the glad day of universal evangelization.

Dr. Knox's *A Winter in India and Malaysia* is so well written, so full of life and movement, and has so sprung out of the very experience and needs of the pastor at home, that they who read will hardly cease until they reach the end. Those who are asked to make contributions of money for missions must know why the appeal is made. They must see the object, the true need. The author of this work aims to bring the country to us here at home, that we may better understand the absolute need of bestowing our best gifts of missionaries and gold for its redemption.

I cordially recommend this work as a most valuable addition to our literature of the East. It should be circulated throughout the country. It should have a place on the pastor's table, in the Sunday-school library, and in the Christian homes in all parts of our land. Many of its pages abound in matter entirely new to our American readers. The book, however, is mostly to be prized for its intense and beautiful loyalty to the kingdom of the Christ.

JOHN F. HURST.

WASHINGTON, D. C., *September* 1, 1891.

CONTENTS.

A WINTER IN INDIA AND MALAYSIA

AMONG THE

METHODIST MISSIONS.

LETTER I.

STREET SIGHTS IN BOMBAY.

One is partly prepared to see India if he has passed through Egypt and Palestine on his way here, as I did, but even then he feels that the East of India is different from the East of Egypt and Syria. The Arabs are not Hindus. The former are a much finer, larger race in person, and are more filthy than the people here. The sight of hundreds of coolies on the wharves, busy unloading and loading the great ships, their bare slender legs and their brown bare arms and shoulders impress one that Bombay is Oriental and at the same time warm. The glare of the sun, even in the morning and the winter-time, also intimates the great heat. As I first cast a glance from the *Somerhill's* deck upon England's busy traffic in Bombay, and the great, strong paraphernalia necessary for dock work, there came a sense of loneliness thinking of the great city and greater country all unknown to me. Once on shore, the tram-cars, the roadway built and carried on by a New York syndicate, suggested that with these and railways my task of getting over the land would not be very hard after all. An admirable net-work of street-cars runs all through the city, and in these one finds all classes and races, Europeans, Hindus, Mohammedans, Parsees, and others. Caste yields to travel. All these Indian cities have the old native part and the newer English part, the former dirty, squalid, the latter with wide, clean streets, ample grounds, and strong, fine buildings. It is so in Bombay. The "Fort" or southern part of the island has most of the English establishments, the Malabar Hills in the west part having the rich Parsee residences and some English, while the rest of the city has mostly natives.

The native portions have their poorer and their better streets. Many Hindus and Mohammedans are rich, and for native houses have good ones well situated in yards and gardens. It is as impossible to call the streets, homes, and clothing of the rich characteristic of the Hindu life as it is to call that characteristic alone where the coolie is stark naked save a limited breech-cloth, and who lives among squalid lanes in dirtiest houses of one room only for the whole family. It takes these extremes and all the gradations between them to show the life here. All the streets swarm with people, so numerous are they in this country. It was my fortune to be taken by the missionaries through some of these streets in the denser part of the city. Smells arising from bad drainage, from cooking native foods, from the native worship, from the natives themselves, and from unknown sources, crowded upon one's olfactory nerves. It was well if he had learned to be around old tanneries and bleacheries. In many cases the mats or blankets that may have covered the entrance from the street to the single room occupied by a family were removed for the day, and thus glimpses of coolie homes were obtained without having to enter them. A light bamboo bedstead or two were sometimes to be seen, on which some rags lay, a copper kettle for cooking, a bit of mud fire-place in one corner, with no chimney for the escape of smoke, save into the room, an earthen floor, or one a grade higher made dry with a plastering of bullock-dung, not a chair or bench, and for dishes possibly three or four copper or brass ones of peculiar shape and many purposes. With one of the ladies in charge of the native Christian work I went into some of the homes of those reached by the beneficent ministries of the Gospel. More cleanly homes, better clad families, and more comfortable arrangement of beds, benches or chairs, dishes and other household utensils, were to be distinguished. Christianity touches the whole life.

On getting into an Oriental city one is impressed by the exceedingly varied and many-colored costumes. White is apt to predominate. Peoples in hot climates are inclined to adopt that color as a guard against the excessive heat. Here one sees persons clad all in white, from the white turban to the white pants on his legs, or the white cloth that by a peculiar folding covers the loins and hips, reaching to the knees. Even the breech-cloth of the coolies once was white. But this color is not absolute. The better classes often wear several colors. One will have a red or green turban, a purple or black jacket, and then white pants, with his feet encased in red slippers. Women go in blue, white, or green chuddars. Bright colors, if white is not used, are apt to be assumed. With a street full of such costumes under a bright Indian sun the effect is fanciful. At any time one might think every body was out-doors, but on second thought he knows that the harem-kept women of the better classes are never seen on the street.

Mingling with these moving masses of humanity are such grotesque carts and wagons that to stop and gaze at them is a Yankee's first impulse. Carts, carriages, cabs, all are strange. Now and then a tony carriage may roll by that was brought from England or even America, but nearly all are native. For eight annas, about sixteen cents, one can ride to almost any part of the city in a good four-wheeled cab, or "ghari," but always with a poor, miserable horse, for the Indians do not know how to take care of horses. For two or four annas, if you are democratic and independent enough to break your Western caste, you can have a ride a mile or two in a bullock-cart. Only remember that if some European sees you he will think you are lowering yourself by riding in that way. But then for a Yankee such a ride for a trial is a fine one. I climb into one, cushioned, small, covered with white cotton-cloth, the driver perched forward on a bit of seat, as much surprised as the European sitting near by in the street-car. But two other Yankees, both missionaries, share the odium with me. Away we go. The small, white, hump-shouldered bullocks strangely yoked and harnessed to the diminutive cart, urged into a smart trot by the driver, are as sharp as horses in shunning other carts and the thronging crowds that part one way and the other at the cries of our Jehu. If the bullocks do not go fast enough he can, from his place, easily catch one by the tail and give it a twist. Bullock-driving by voice, stick, and hand-pushing is a science. After all, if one rides quickly and safely and cheaply through a great city, why bother about the manner?

The shops to be seen in Bombay defy description as much as the masses of people in the streets. In the native quarters they are generally open entirely on the side toward the street, like a porch, and then in a space eight or twelve feet square are piled the goods, cloths, or food, or shoes, or chinaware, or iron, while the seller sits cross-legged or on his haunches ready to wait on you as you approach the front of his room. You do not enter, since the salesroom is three feet above the street, with no steps to go in, and there is no room for your great shoe-clad feet. He is always barefooted. The stores in the newer parts of the city are more like those in America. In the native shops the work or trade of the occupant goes on openly, instead of being done in the back rooms, as among us. Tailoring, cooking, shoe-making, blacksmithing, and the like, progress. In front of a confectioner's I saw three native women pounding some spicery or other in a mortar. The pestles were each about four feet long and two inches in diameter, the mortar large and deep. Standing around it, they threw the pestles alternately into the mortar, by a deft rhythmic order, so one did not bother the other; and further, each woman changed hands at every throw, now the right, now the left, the whole combining to make an interesting sight.

The many temples and mosques in Bombay show the Indians to be a religious race. In addition to these, images and emblems are set up in little recesses in the walls of the streets and houses, being always strewn with red ocher and oil. In front of one small image in a temple contiguous to the street, at which a young priest stood officiating, was a narrow tank into which the oil poured over the god ran, and this the priest, dipping out, sold again and again. Dirty, frowsy, hideous fakirs are every now and then to be met, willing to accept alms from the Western man as well as from their own people. One kind of a religious beggar had a high conical hat made of peacock's feathers, and to attract to alms had a clanking instrument made of steel springs in one hand, with which he kept up a rude melody as he droned a nasal song. A mendicant bag hung over one shoulder to receive the gifts of the people. Another had a conch-horn that he blew, which he said conveyed salvation to all who heard. I heard it! Once I saw a man who under some vow was measuring his length along the dust and dirt of the pavement.

Several times I saw men going about with an instrument on their shoulder like a rude harp with one string. They would utter some cry and twang this single tight string. Our missionaries told me it was a cotton-cleaner, and later I saw it in operation. The use of cotton in quilts, pillows, coats, pants, and caps is very extensive, and naturally it gets both dusty and hard packed. A pile of this packed or freshly washed cotton will need to be "picked," or fluffed, which the men with these instruments do, by snapping this string most dexterously through a little of it at a time. The rhythmic hum of this tight string makes a noise heard half a block away.

I went into the Crawfurd Market, centrally located in Bombay, thus getting a glimpse of the multitudinous productions of India. Here were oranges, sweet, delicious ones; pomegranates, apples, grapes, a few lingering mangoes, out of season and poor; pine-apples, pumalos, allied to the orange, but vastly larger; custard-apples, lemons, limes, bananas, and many other fruits. There were beautiful flowers; rich, creamy-looking native sweet-meats; of vegetables, besides many that I did not know, were cucumbers, squashes, egg-plant, potatoes, sweet-potatoes, and yams as large as pumpkins. A part of the great market was devoted to birds, where could be obtained pigeons, quails, parroquets, bulbuls, and others. One of the most interesting kinds was the Java sparrows, hundreds of the lively little dark fellows, in a cage, brightly marked with blood-red, bronze, and other colors.

Liquor-shops, many and increasing, carry their curse more and more, in spite of Hindu and Mohammedan religious objections, into the homes and lives of these people. The blessings of Western civilization are attended by cursings. Satan ever appears among the sons of God.

LETTER II.

MY FIRST EVENING IN BOMBAY.

HAVING fallen into the hands of the missionaries, and telling them I wanted to learn all I could about their work here, they have already given me some fine views. First I went with A. W. Prautch to some street-preaching, which is peculiarly hand-to-hand work among the natives. As we came to the corner where the agreement had been to hold the service we found that one of the native Methodist preachers was already speaking. Forty or fifty were gathered about him listening attentively to his earnest words. I noticed two tall, finely dressed Hindus listening, who wore on their foreheads the painted spot indicative of the devotee of some god or other in their pantheon. As the preacher ceased, to give way to another, the taller of the two Hindus spoke a few minutes, the import of whose words, as told me by Mr. Prautch, was that God, who made all things, as the preacher said, must have made sin, so if God was the author of sin he was not the good and holy God described. To this challenge the next preacher, a native also, under the auspices of the Anglican Church, responded in proper arguments as interpreted to me. What surprised me was the absorbed stare of those who listened. Two or three with a peculiar kind of crooked saws on their shoulders stopped a while to hear, then passed on. Several women also stood during the whole half hour, eager listeners, while numbers of the group about were boys from ten to fourteen, whose great dark eyes, wide open, showed that they were drinking in the truth. One man, with a big bundle of wood on his head, stood nearly all the time among the crowd. I noticed especially a group of three or four young men, sixteen or so, naked to their waists, standing eager to hear, their hands clasped over each other's brown shoulders in attitudes like some exquisitely fashioned bronze group, which, indeed, they much resembled. It is found all through India that this street-preaching does much good.

From there Mr. Prautch took me to the location of one of his schools, where a native teacher gathers for a couple of hours each day forty or more boys and girls, from six to ten years of age, to teach them to read in the native language. It was now getting dark, so I could but dimly see the people who thronged about us. Many of them were the children of the school; mothers also were there with babes resting on their hips, while a good sprinkling of men also came. The place was a narrow alley between low sheds covered with bamboo-leaves and divided into sections a dozen or fifteen feet long, each section making a house for a whole family. It was a strange cluster of homes. We had scarcely arrived when we heard a man calling out loudly, and soon saw a devotee coming near us with a small square lantern, a conch-trumpet, a begging-tray, and a bag into which to put the things given him. A constant coming to him by one and another, mostly women out of the huts, was going on, almost all bringing some food, rice, or flour, which, as his tray was partly filled, he put into the bags hanging from each shoulder. Then, in response to these gifts and attentions, he marked the foreheads of all he could reach with chalk. Mr. Prautch knew of these fellows, but, to enter on a talk, asked him what he marked the people for, and his answer was that he conveyed a blessing with his chalk-mark. A long discussion followed between the two men, quite a crowd gathering round, so that the falseness of such notions uncovered by Mr. Prautch was listened to by fifty or a hundred eager people. It was a wild, weird scene, under the tropical starlight, some palms and other trees growing not far away with their outlines sharp against the sky, the long, low huts swarming with human beings, the listening crowd gathered about us, the two men in eager discussion. The devotee, hard pressed, blew a long blast on his conch, declaring that all who heard it would be saved. Finally, Mr. Prautch struck in and sang, the children whom he is having taught crowding close about him, joining heartily in singing the refrain, which was a sort of doggerel satire on this class of mendicants. The Hindu said that these people would do any thing for him, to prove which claim he said, "Give me a smoke of gongee," when a man brought him a big pipeful of that hateful drug, which he smoked with great apparent satisfaction. Then he called for a bowl of water, which was quickly reached to him. Yet this teacher could not read a word, acknowledging this to Mr. Prautch, and also publicly confessing that he begged to get a living. As he sounded his conch and moved away Mr. Prautch preached Christ to the lingering crowds, sang a hymn with the children about Jesus, and we passed on. Hearing some native music in a yard where Mr. Prautch was acquainted, we turned aside to find half a hundred people gathered about a miniature temple as large as a bushel-basket, in which and before it fire was kept burning. As some attended this fire a man dressed as a woman danced and whirled about among the by-standers, keeping time by cries or hand-clapping with the rude music made by the half dozen players. They were very demonstrative to Mr. Prautch and me, crowding about us to shake hands as we started to go away. From these manifestations of native religiousness we went at half past seven to the ample rooms of Mr. Dyer, where a good-bye meeting was to be held among the English and Americans for Mr. Gladwin, who was about leaving for Ceylon on a mission in the interest of social purity. Mr. Dyer and Mr. Gladwin have both been doing heroic work in this field, and there was need of it, for the Indian government drew a large resource from the licenses granted to brothels, but the revenue has been stopped by the English Parliament since the agitation begun by these two men. Mr. Gladwin was for several years in our mission work; then, leaving that, worked with the Salvation Army, but for three years has labored with Mr. Dyer in this new crusade. About forty gathered in Mr. Dyer's rooms, a psalm was read, songs of Christ were sung, prayers offered, short talks made, all in a free and hearty spirit, being most like simple, intense Methodist social meetings of any thing I have seen since leaving London. Faith, prayers, wide hopes in God's providences and help were urged and well illustrated. Four of our missionaries were present. As we went home through the fragrance of tropical flowers and under the bright moon of an India sky I deemed the Anglo-Saxon race great and strong, partly good, noble, and grand, and partly hard, selfish, and brutal.

LETTER III.

METHODISM IN BOMBAY.

THE city is occupied by quite a net-work of stations. There are three English-speaking churches belonging to us founded by Bishop William Taylor, a Seaman's Rest, two stations of native work, and a brisk station of Woman's Foreign Missionary Society work. Yet in the hundreds of thousands here there are room and call for more work and workers. By location and common acquiescence the Grant Road Church is the center of our missions in this city. It was one of the Taylor foundation. Of this Rev. H. C. Stuntz is pastor, having come to India two years ago, and to this church last Conference. He and his family, consisting of a wife and two-year-old boy, are well and happy in their work. The church building is capable of seating four hundred and fifty hearers, was erected in 1878 by the people of Bombay, and is valued at 35,000 rupees. Last year a parsonage was erected in the rear of the church at a cost of 8,000 rupees, not all paid yet, but borne by the local board. It is commodious and pleasant. There is a membership of sixty-five English-speaking people, with an average attendance of one hundred and fifty, a Sunday-school of seventy-five, and an English-speaking mission at Parel, a railroad suburb five miles out, where they gather every Tuesday evening. In this church are the usual social meetings of a home Methodist church. The ringing personal testimonies to present and full salvation heard here sounded good. Twenty have been converted since Conference. Besides their own support the three churches aid the local native work, contribute between one and two hundred rupees to our Missionary Society, and, including all missionary contributions, give *per capita* about three dollars a member. That is better than some New England churches do.

The Fort Church was the first of the English-speaking churches organized under Bishop William Taylor, and so is sometimes called the cradle of Bombay Methodism. It has a membership of sixty, in charge of Rev. E. F. Frease, who, with his wife and child, came to India last winter. They have worshiped in halls as they could get opportunities, but this year, having decided to build, have leased ground of the Port Trust Company for fifty years, and have the foundations of their church, to the bottom of the lower window, now laid, built out of trap-rock furnished from the quarries close to the city. It is nicely planned, will seat three hundred and fifty people, with an ample parsonage above the church, and is located in an admirable part of the city, on the narrow neck of the island southward. It will cost $12,000, of which sum the Missionary Society will pay $5,000, the remainder to be raised here. They have a membership of seventy, with an average attendance of one hundred and fifty, and a Sunday-school of sixty-five. Mr. Frease does street-preaching by an interpreter; the prayer and class-meetings are well attended, and forty conversions have taken place since Conference. With a church of their own this vigorous society will prosper better than ever, and can then much better push the native work begun by Rev. W. E. Robbins, now carried on by Miss Thompson and others.

The Mazagon Church is located in the south-eastern part of the city. It was organized sixteen years ago, among the English-speaking population, after William Taylor's campaign. It was expected that the population would fill in thickly close about it, but the cotton-mills, soon after erected, being placed in another part of the city, these expectations were not realized; so that it is left in rather a sparsely settled region. Still, there is contiguous to this location a large section of the city in which no missionary work is done save by this church. A debt hung over the pretty church building for some years, which was finally paid by the Missionary Society to make it a chapel for native work. It will seat about one hundred and fifty. Contiguous to it the society has built a fine parsonage, recently finished, and into it the pastor, Rev. W. E. Robbins, has moved. The two buildings make a fine set of property. As members of the church there are only about half a dozen English-speaking people now connected with it, and the same number of natives. The united attendants of both classes number about seventy. There are three day-schools in the vernacular, having together about seventy-five scholars, conducted by the church, and all these are organized as Sunday-schools. One is at the church, the others away from it. There is also another Sunday-school three miles from the church, under its direction, in which there is a large attendance; so that, all told, the church has about one hundred and fifty scholars under instruction on Sunday. Street-preaching is regularly done by native helpers in the vernacular, besides which they sell books, tracts, and gospels. A Bible woman is also kept at work doing the particular work that this class alone can accomplish. About once a month Brother Robbins goes out of the city to a point twenty miles away to preach to a fine gathering.

The native work is in charge of Rev. W. W. Bruere and wife, with their head-quarters in the rented school-building near the Grant Road Church, which latter they use for most of their services. They have a membership, including Prautch's ingatherings, of one hundred, counting probationers. They have quite a regular audience of about one hundred, four Sunday-schools—one in the church and three outside—with over three hundred scholars. They keep up one day-school of sixty boys, with teachers paid by our Missionary Society, besides a boarding-school in which they have thirty boarders with ten day-scholars. They keep up street-preaching in the vernacular at two places, besides much work done in the homes. I visited several of the Christian homes of these people and found little in them that would suit an American housekeeper. This work is very encouraging. Miss Power, a native, does much zenana work. The head teacher in the native school is a promising man from a low caste educated by the Society for the Propagation of the Gospel, and is so eager to work for Christ that he has begged the privilege of Brother Bruere to hold meetings for the natives every night in the school-room ; so from six to eight he is there, talking, selling tracts and gospels, and is thus doing vast good.

To gain a just knowledge of Mr. Prautch's work one needs to know something of the worker. He is only twenty-three years old, having been found in Chicago by Dennis Osborne five years ago, a poor boy of German parents, converted in D. L. Moody's church in that city, surrounded during his years till that time by very disadvantageous conditions, so that he began work for the

Lord but poorly prepared. He had hopes of getting an education by coming out to India, but soon found the Methodist schools here not well adapted to his wants. He began studying by himself, came here, and commenced to work for the Lord. He has now mastered two of the native dialects, so he can do street-preaching, and in the midst of a native locality of sixty thousand people, one of the poorest, worst parts of the city, is doing valuable, heroic work. He is as yet unmarried, but I may not tell what a few months are reputed to have in store for him. He rents a native house and lives right among the people much like the people. If his health is not injured by such a life many things might be said in its favor. He considers his most important work to be the enormous masses of Christian literature he sells to the natives. From February to September this year he and his native helpers sold 60 New Testaments, 5,645 gospels, and 20,130 tracts. They go along the streets, one on each side, crying their books and tracts, which the people often buy with the utmost avidity. Sometimes a woman will send enough money to buy several gospels and tracts, leaving him to send what ones he will. His three most prominent tracts sold are "The Great Physician," "The True Saviour," "The Resurrection." During eight months past he has printed at his own expense, and distributed, 21,000 tracts, and the day I was with him had completed a contract for the printing of 12,000 more. He sells these at such a price that he makes a little on their cost, the margin being used, as also that above his rent and cheap living from the Mission Rooms, in pushing his work among the natives. He has under his direction five schools among the boys and girls, with three teachers, who are paid by the Missionary Society. In these schools are taught the primary things, as reading, arithmetic, writing, geography—then one hour every day the Bible, Catechism, and singing. In these schools are about one hundred and fifty scholars. There are carried on six Sunday-schools, having two hundred and seventy scholars. He keeps two Bible women at work, who visit hospital wards for women, private families, and do what they have opportunities for doing. In the homes they sing hymns, read the Bible, and talk of its truths to the native women as they will listen. By this means from twenty to fifty women are reached every day.

Mr. Prautch has had eight native preachers at work during the year, keeping up street-preaching regularly at several spots; has five places for regular preaching in rooms, for three of which he pays rent, two places lately having been given up because of the inability of himself and assistants to bear the weight of their multiplied duties. An organization consisting of seventeen members is kept up as a sort of adjunct of the native church on Grant Road, twelve having been baptized within a year. He has two or three Europeans whose living he pays for, and who live and labor with him. One of these, with a few rupees only in his pocket, recently went across the harbor, where is a place, ten by fifteen miles, in which live one hundred and thirty thousand people with no missionary work done among them. He has got a home, has begun preaching and teaching, and within two weeks sends word for one of the ordained ministers to come over and baptize two who have professed Christ. Mr. Prautch is responsible for this man's living and the pay of his native helper. One of our pastors, Rev. H. C. Stuntz, will go and baptize these men at once.

The Seaman's Rest was begun only three years ago by Dr. J. S. Stone, then pastor of. Grant Road Church, who first furnished tea to some of the neglected sailors in port; the work so enlarged that a call was made for more space, a small room was rented at forty rupees a month, a revival broke out, and then they had to go to a still larger hall costing one hundred and ten rupees a month. Up to this time the expenses had all been paid by private subscriptions. A. W. Prautch, now in native work, was put in charge of it, and during the first full year nearly three hundred sailors were converted. The city government, seeing the good done by this mission in restoring and keeping order along the extended quays, before unsafe to orderly people from rowdyism and drunkenness, granted two hundred rupees a month to it as long as it should be sustained. At once an American colored man offered to build a commodious house for this amount, and receive his pay for it in monthly installments; so they have just completed on the main street at Prince's Dock a house worth twenty thousand rupees, with chapel, refreshment-room, reading-room, home for the superintendent and assistants, besides several rooms to rent. The present superintendent is Rev. B. Mitchell, a Scotchman, who, four years ago, penniless and almost in despair, was found on the streets of Bombay by Rev. J. S. Stone, and led to Christ. During the present year two hundred and eighty have been converted or reclaimed here, including four captains of ships, besides other officers. Meetings are held every night but Wednesdays and Saturdays. On Thursday nights is free tea, and after that preaching, at which there are often one hundred and fifty present. It is supported by private subscriptions; these are solicited from every ship that comes in as well as from individuals in the city. There is a department for work among native sailors, but not yet made effective. The sailors reached here and helped go all over the world, like those from the East Boston Bethel under Dr. L. B. Bates.

On going to the department of the Woman's Foreign Missionary Society work of Bombay Methodism I found the ladies nicely located in an airy, commodious, garden-embowered home. But these pleasant surroundings must be given up this year, not being owned, but only rented, and circumstances compelling a change. As yet they have not found any new place to suit them, either to rent or buy, for they will do the latter as soon as they can, their choice being to buy and build. Real estate is very high in this city. The Woman's Foreign Missionary Society in America has appropriated the money to buy. The work done here by the women can be roughly divided into two classes, zenana and school. In the zenana work they get chances among all kinds of people, Hindus, Mohammedans, Parsees, Jews, Arabs, Beni-Israelites, and others. The Beni-Israelites are Jews who have partly forsaken the traditions of their race and become mixed in blood and religion with other races. The women usually spend an hour in each home teaching the native women during a part of it to sew, cut garments, read, do fancy work, and the like ; in short, give them something to do ; then the other half hour impress gospel teaching upon them. In this work they now enter about one hundred and fifty homes, so planning it as to visit each one every week. Nearly or quite two hundred women are regularly reached. Miss De Line, in charge of the zenana work here, has five English-speaking helpers, all born in India, besides Miss Thompson, from America. Just now Miss Abrams, in charge of the school, is off on sick leave, and Miss Thompson, who is sister of Mrs. Frease, is successfully doing the work of teacher. These noble women have a wide variety of experiences, passing from the region of utter rejection of their approaches and abuse to the most hearty and eager acceptances of their blessings and help. In their four years of work they have seen quite a number of conversions, some of which are openly confessed; others are obliged from the conditions of their homes and the results threatened to live their Christian faith in secret. Three sisters in one home secretly live their faith in Christ, praying, reading the Bible they keep hidden from their people, and are afraid to ask for baptism, which is here the separating mark and act in their relation to their heathen relatives. A mother with six children, converted to Christ, does not want publicly to be known as a Christian, for then her husband would turn her from her home, from himself and all her children. If thus turned away she would have no home but in the mission. If a man is baptized he can stay at the head of his home though all the rest may remain heathens. In most instances the men are glad to have the women come to their houses with the mission they bring of elevating the tone of their homes and wives, hoping the latter will get the benefits and amenities of Western civilization without accepting the new religion. The women of the mission think much good is being done. "The eyes of India are turning to Christ," says Miss De Line. One native Bible woman, sixty years old, gray, keen, shriveled, but a vast force from her powerful personality, is employed and paid for her work by the Woman's Foreign Missionary Society.

In the schools, of which there are four—three city

schools away from the head-quarters and one there—they have over seventy scholars. In the outside schools the primary branches are taught, with Bible instruction gradually taken in; in the school at head-quarters the purpose is, as it is a boarding-school, to run it up to the matriculation grade, much like a high-school in America. In this was a bright group of girls from six to sixteen years of age. The teachers of this school are paid by the Woman's Foreign Missionary Society, save one Bible woman, who is paid by some American people out of private funds. These schools among girls and boys are raising up cultured, well-prepared native workers for Methodism, whose distinctive Methodistic preparation for work will be of great worth to South India as the years go by. A crying need all through the South India field is for reliable, properly instructed native workers, both men and women.

LETTER IV.

A THOUSAND MILES' RUN THROUGH INDIA.

THE run began at Bombay 7 P. M. Monday, November 26, and ended five days later at Moradabad. The night ride was not good for seeing the country, so that the first two hundred miles must be taken on trust, as I took it, though I could see that we crossed wide rivers, a few inlets from the sea, and a low level reach of country. After a while enough room was attained in the car to stretch out on the seat for a good rest and cover myself in the blankets every one must carry in India for sleeping. Then in what seemed but a short time the fact suddenly came to me that it was past sunrise, that the English engineer on the other side of the compartment was smoking his morning pipe, and that I needed to bestir myself. This I did by looking out of a window to see a tree not a hundred feet from the railway full of monkeys quietly looking at us as we thundered by them. They were so gray as to appear almost white in the bright sunlight, some as large as a big dog, others half that size. All the day groups of similar ones could be seen here and there, sometimes in trees, then on the banks of the railway or in the fields of grain, with the natives letting them get their fill, for these East Indians think monkeys sacred creatures, worshiping them sometimes, so that they are well treated in their roguish pilfering. They looked odd, indeed, with their long tails high over their backs. The natives were bathing as a sacred act in the rivers as we crossed them early in the morning. They seem to think that cleanliness is not only next to godliness, but is a part of it. The foliage, animals, birds—every thing—seemed strange to me. The rice fields, from which the crop had not long been harvested, were sown to wheat for the second crop during the year, and were being irrigated. Most of it was done with water drawn up from wells. Across a couple of upright timbers a roller would be placed on which was a wheel; over the wheel ran a strong rope, on the lower end of which a bullock-skin was hanging, so shaped and tied as to form a great bucket. This being dipped in the water at the bottom of a large well a yoke of bullocks hitched to the rope would speedily draw it up, when it would be caught by a man and emptied where it could run off into a prepared sluice to the fields of grain. One well seemed capable of affording water for three or five acres. The winter crops, there being no rains during this season, can be raised only by irrigation. All the way this method of irrigation was going on.

The trees were familiar-looking, yet wholly unlike those in America. The palm grew rarer and shorter the farther north we went, the cocoanut giving way to the date-palm. The mango-tree, the fruit of which, now out of season, to my great regret, and the boast of all dwellers in India, looks much like a chestnut-tree, the leaves being a little more slender. The "momra" tree, looking not unlike a second growth white oak, yields a fruit out of which a sharp, intoxicating liquor is made, said to be something like rum, on which the people get drunk; so the government has put a tax on it "for revenue only." Acacia or locust-trees of different species abounded, one of them, the "babul," now richly clad with bright yellow blossoms, have persisted from Bombay to Moradabad. Not only are they in bloom, but many other kinds of trees are rich in scarlet or yellow or red blossoms. While ground in New England is frozen hard, and possibly snow-covered, India can furnish along the roads and fields a hundred beautiful blossoms, roses, asters, oleanders, morning-glories, creepers, and others. The yards of the railway stations were many times most profusely planted to flowers. Such masses of them kept driving out of my mind that it was Thanksgiving season, when, in the Northern States, the thermometer usually indicates from five to fifteen degrees below zero. As we came northward there was some change in the trees. To my regret, banyan nearly ceased, as I was wanting to look at it with more leisure than I could have on a passing train. I noticed one peculiarity of this and some other kinds—that the main body, instead of being solid, would be composed sometimes of many sections growing tightly together, but yet distinct. The trees do not cover the country, as in New England, but are loosely scattered over the fields, as in some old pastures with us, seeming, a mile or two away, however, to form complete forests.

From the time I awoke, two hundred miles out of Bombay, the first morning, all the way to Moradabad I was surprised at the vastness of bird life. I kept my eyes now and then steadily glancing ahead toward the engine to see if there was any moment when no birds were to be seen fleeing from the train, and sometimes a mile would be passed without there being any moment when I could not see them. And such birds!—from the tiniest kind of sparrows all the way up to vultures, and adjutants which stood four feet high. These last would stand, a conspicuous sight, on some wheat-field or other, their light gray bodies, white tail and neck giving the impression of a totally white bird. Their head is a brilliant scarlet. Peacocks abound, half domesticated, like the robins in America; and, being considered sacred, the natives make a great row if Europeans kill them or monkeys. The natives never kill any of the birds or animals, so their tameness is a constant astonishment to Western people. Hawks, pigeons, fly-catchers, and other birds would sit on the railway fence-posts and telegraph wires as the train roared along. Birds in brilliant plumage, such as we never see in northern United States, abounded. Paroquets, fly-catchers, hoopoes, and others bore colors from dull gray all along through brown, black, white, blue, red, slate, green, orange, with endless variations in all of these colors. O, how I wanted leisure and opportunity carefully and fully to study this feathered wealth!

If bird life abounded the glimpses obtained of animal life showed that this also was rich, if not so readily seen as the other. The monkeys, with their half-domesticated instincts, were comical and impudent. A jackal or two sneaking away at early morning from the noise of the train, as well as the ground freshly dug up by them overnight in search of moles and other earth-hidden food, suggested how many might be seen and heard under other conditions. Pretty squirrels, striped not unlike the American chipmunk, but with more bushy tail, sought food close by human habitation undisturbed by the Indian boy. They said I should see deer and antelope; and it was true, for the second morning a single one of the latter bounded gracefully away over the plains, while only ten miles out of Delhi a herd of twenty-five deer was seen grazing on the green, succulent wheat three or four inches tall. What a sight for one with hunter instincts! Later still one ran beside the train half a mile pursued by a dog. Then those acquainted with the country told of hares and other small animals in abundance. As we came through the Aravalli Mountains the afternoon of the first day the English engineer told of bears, tigers, cheetahs, panthers, deer, antelope, and smaller game living in them. An English officer last year in a week there killed three tigers, three bears, and one panther, besides other game. In the same mountains are the Bhils—a race of wild men, they call them; rude, unsubdued fellows, whom neither the native rajah nor the English have yet been able to bring under control. They go nearly naked, are warlike, living by the chase and robbery, even attacking the cars in their love of plunder. I was glad we went through the mountains in the day-time.

The people whom I have seen during this run have presented a great variety of conditions, from the well-dressed, inquisitive Parsee to the naked coolie, as poor and thin as a man could be and work. The route has been through several native States which England lets have their own way, customs, and laws, if they regularly pay the demanded tribute. Many of the people went armed with some old sword or dagger, or even with bow and arrows, for England discourages the keeping of fire-arms. It had a comical look to see some half-naked native going about with a long sword tucked under his arm or slung to a strap hanging over his shoulder, while the primitive bow and arrows did not look like very formidable weapons. If they did not have any more deadly weapons they almost invariably carried a long cane like a light club. Some fortifications, as antiquated as their weapons, crowned a hill-top here and there. These natives in Bombay, and for the first day seen out on my trip, wore only cotton goods, but the second day I saw some of the rich ones with woolen garments. Even then, when a thick quilt and my overcoat had failed to keep me warm in the cars through the night, early the next morning, before the sun was up, many of them were lounging about the station bare-legged and bare-armed.

O, the misery and squalor of India's millions! Women toiling in the fields or at hard labor of other kinds, carrying great loads on their heads at building or harvesting or other works, half-naked; men still less clad, slim, poor, and hard-worked, beaten, kicked—who can wonder at their degradation till they worship a thousand things, from a stone set up to peacocks, monkeys, cows, and the sun in the heavens above us? Their methods of work, from splitting wood with an instrument almost as blunt as a sledge-hammer to their wooden plows, were of the crudest kind. Grain was threshed with a crooked stick by people sitting on the ground, and winnowed by the wind. Huts of mud or of leaves and branches, with a fragile thatching, were the only home of some of these people. Others had comfortable-looking houses of brick or stone. But how like the taste of more highly civilized people is theirs! I counted rings on three fingers of a woman, besides bracelets of massive silver two thirds to the elbow. And she, too, seemed proud of her finery.

In much of this country there has been long drought, so the first crops this year were a failure, the rivers have run dry, the pastures are almost worthless, and there is much suffering, actual and threatening. The natives dig up the roots and the few blades of grass attached to them, carrying great bundles for their goats and cattle. I saw two breeds of domesticated cattle—the bullock, mostly white, small, hump-shouldered, big-eared, and then the mouse-colored buffalo, almost hairless, larger, hideous-looking about his crooked lop-horns and projecting muzzles. I saw no sheep, but many goats. The country seems almost a level plain, with ranges of hills or mountains here and there rising abruptly from this dead flatness. Most of the country is highly cultivated, but long tracts through the native States lie untilled, while other stretches seem but poorly adapted to cultivation, having vast quantities of pampa-grass in huge tussocks, the stalks standing from eight to twelve feet high, now ripe and dry. There was more untilled land than I expected. It is certain that this country, so thickly settled, could be made to sustain many more people if all of it were cultivated. The rock noticed was a little coarse granite, much trap, and more of finely laminated sandstone, from the last thousands and thousands of fence-posts being split and used beside the railway. Another kind of fence was cactus-hedges and those grown out of the century-plant. The mud huts of the villagers had no garden or yard of flowers, all about them being dirty, dusty, and cheerless. These people show the abjectest fear of the British, and to most of them every white man is of that dominant race. They cringe, step out of the way, bow low, and studiously deprecate his wrath. In Delhi I had more salutes from policemen and native soldiers in one day than I had received since 1861–65. England treats the people with a disdain that to Americans seems far too harsh even for conquerors of so vast a people as this. My thousand miles were really ten hundred and forty. My exact fare for that distance, intermediate class, was $4.70—cheaper riding than one gets in the United States.

LETTER V.

IN AND ABOUT DELHI.

A CONTINUOUS run of forty-six hours from Bombay has landed me in Delhi. The memories of this renowned city have crowded upon me with peculiar force ever since the cars bringing me were headed this way. To me it has always seemed as though Delhi must be more truly an Indian city than any other of the great ones, for Bombay, Madras, and Calcutta are on the sea-board, and thus must have become much internationalized. To see green trees, bright flowers, fresh-growing wheat, luxuriant gardens and parks in late autumn is very odd, but what we really must have expected. The night air is perceptibly cooler than at Bombay, so that in the native hotel I need all the blankets I secured there. My first experience in a native hotel has been real pleasant, since they understand and speak some English, and I can make my wants known very well. But to furnish one's own bedding when he goes to a hotel is among the curious experiences of a raw traveler. A bedstead, mattress, and one sheet, with a low bolster, made up the part furnished by the hotel, the whole being inclosed in a netting to keep out mosquitoes. Think of these pests troubling one after Thanksgiving!

A guide who could speak tolerable English was engaged to meet me at seven o'clock at the hotel. A "tum-tum," or two-wheeled carriage, was to be there at the same hour to take me to the Khutab Minar, some ten or a dozen miles out of the city. The tum-tum was on hand, but not my guide, so I went off without him, but in the hope that I should meet him on the street near the hotel, to capture whom a clerk went a long distance with me, but in vain. Yet I found the driver a sharp fellow and able to show me around very well. Along we went through the city already stirring, since the Eastern business man is at his shop early. A continuous stream of people met us, bringing cheap country products to the city for the early market; donkeys and bullocks, buffaloes and women, laden with bundles of fagots, dried grass, or dried cow-dung for fuel, a few vegetables for market, masses of reeds for mats, and other things. The road was a good one, such as the British make here, of finely pulverized stone that becomes as hard as a concrete floor. Its sides were lined with trees, now in the richest foliage, acacias, tamarisks, mangoes, and many of which I have not yet learned the name. Birds by the hundreds, of brilliant plumage and odd shapes and habits, were flying hither and thither. I knew the hoopoes, fly-catchers, doves, and some others.

What interested me more than all else was the continuous succession of ruins every-where along this road, something I had heard of but had not fully comprehended. Old buildings, massive walls, towers, mosque-domes, arches, and chimneys extend every way as far as one can see from the road, a very wilderness waste of crumbling brick and decaying sandstone. Ancient Delhi must have extended vastly farther than the present one.

The Khutab Minar was in sight miles of the way, now seen by glimpses through the tree-tops, now hidden, then coming out in fine relief against the brilliant sky. About its base were many ruins, but among them a few huts for villagers, and two or three good buildings for British officers, who are here to keep these noble monuments and ruins intact and to collect taxes in the local district. The Minar is certainly the finest tower I have ever seen, not one built by mediæval or modern purpose equaling it in grace and beauty of finish. It is all the more impressive as it stands among so many ruins, themselves noble relics of an age of great deeds and high civilization. It rises to the height of two hundred and fifty-one feet, slender, of exquisite symmetry, made of richly tinted red sandstone that abounds in a neighboring province and which was brought here for this and other buildings about Delhi—brought all that distance by the cumbersome, slow methods before railways. I think the base is not over forty feet wide, with a gradual taper that is most pleasing to the eye. It is not all of red sandstone, but here and there toward the top are layers of white marble. Four or five balustrades break the column-like surface with pleasing effect, and, as one ascends, afford grateful resting-places for a breathing spell and sight-seeing, for inside this marvelous tower is a spiral passage-way leading, by over three hundred steps, to the top. Up this I climbed, a guide accompanying me furnished by the British authorities — a native speaking good English — who pointed out the sights for me. Beyond us, as well as along the way we had come, the plain was almost a continuous stretch of ruins, attesting the vast populousness at some former time of this rich Jumna valley. A few squalid villages here and there, some patches of cultivated soil, were like spots of life among death and desolation. A dozen miles away I could see the blue Jumna, hardly less sacred than the Ganges, uniting with that river far toward the ocean. Across the plain, a hundred miles or more, could be seen mighty masses of clouds under which I knew the Himalaya Mountains were lying, and with the aid of my field-glass could catch dubious glimpses of their gray shoulders through the rifts and uplifts, thus obtaining my first sight of that gigantic mountain range. I shall soon be among them if fortune favors.

Near the base of the Khutab stands the foundation of another tower, an exact copy of this one, built forty or fifty feet high, when it seems to have been abandoned and now is slowly crumbling into ruins. It is suggested that this problematical Khutab and its twin, started and then not finished, were the two minars of a gigantic mosque, standing at the corners, in the relation to it as is now seen in some Indian mosques on a smaller scale.

Not far from the base of the Khutab stands the famous "Iron Pillar," a huge shaft of solid iron, twenty-four feet above the ground, with a diameter at the surface of the earth of sixteen inches and tapering slightly above. They have dug down twenty-six feet below the surface without finding the foundation on which this pillar rests, so that it is certainly fifty feet long, and probably much more, as it was not loosened by this excavation. Its weight, as it is a solid shaft, is more than seventeen tons. It is not rusted, suggesting to some minds other metals than iron in the composition. Assays by British officials have proven it to be wrought iron, as could be plainly seen by its indented surface. On its sides are inscriptions in Sanskrit, by which it is learned that these at least were made by Rajah Dhava, a worshiper of Vishnu. Its base is said to rest upon the head of the serpent king Vasuki. The origin of this largest piece of forged iron in the world, its object, its age, are all lost in obscurity. Guesses are made with some show of reason that it is three thousand two hundred years old, carrying it back to fourteen hundred years B. C. It was probably an object of worship among the early Aryan races, representing some gross notions that are yet prevalent in the native worship.

On our way back from Delhi the driver took me off the main road to the tomb of Hamousi, one of the noble monuments of Saracenic art. It is surrounded by a high wall and a wide court, stands on a platform twenty feet high and three hundred feet square. The magnificent dome is of white marble, while the building and pavement of the wide platform are of red sandstone. In the wing of the great building are the resting-places of his wives and other prominent people, while his own is under the airy dome. It is all, the towers, platform, dome, graceful fretwork cut from stone, inlaying, and peculiar style, a very imposing structure. Further on were immense forts fast falling into decay; one, the red sandstone walls of which are yet sixty to a hundred feet high, was a mile around. Those old Mohammedan conquerors were giants in their way.

It had been a good forenoon of seeing, and after a one o'clock "tiffin," I went again in the tum-tum, this time with the little old guide who missed me in the morning, to see the points of interest connected with the Sepoy rebellion and the retaking of Delhi. We drove through the wall at the Cashmere Gate to find it still retaining the marks of the sharp cannonade to which the British subjected it and the adjacent walls. Great cannon-ball holes were knocked in the soft brick-work during those dreadful days till in some places it crumbled down. Across the fields, now fine gardens and parks around the homes of the British officials, we went to the location of the batteries situated from three to eight hundred yards from the walls, where the big guns stood which terrified more than they hurt the natives in the city. Then, after days of cannonading, came the spirited assault, the blowing down of the Cashmere Gate with powder, the scaling of the walls and occupancy of this corner of the city when the weak native prince and his numerous army fled from the other side of it. My guide said he was there at that time, a boy of fifteen, and remained in the city with multitudes who were glad to welcome the conqueror.

Two or three miles away is the "Ridge," a rocky rise of ground half a mile long by a quarter wide, where the British residents lived after Delhi was captured by the natives in that dreadful mutiny, and defended themselves with hastily constructed intrenchments, till an army could come from the north to their rescue and to the recapture of the city. A noble monument in commemoration of these events stands on the crest, recounting the deeds of those who fell and those who lived. Not the least interesting was the recorded fact that some of the native regiments were of the faithful ones—the brave Sikhs and Goorkhas, not Aryan Hindus, nor Semitic Mohammedans, but tribes of the aboriginal Turanians, who alone of the Indians were for some time after the mutiny allowed in the British military service. On the same hill stands a granite column about fifty feet high, round, and five feet in diameter, with inscriptions on it, first set up by Asoka, a Hindu prince, a distance from here, in the third century before Christ. It was brought to Delhi about A. D. 1300, and by a magazine explosion thrown down and broken in 1793, then set up and repaired by the British at some recent date. It is a curious kind of Cleopatra's Needle. Odd that those old peoples sought immortality that way.

From there we drove through the city to the "Fort," which now is occupied by a strong garrison of English troops. This is a questionable point in British occupation, so that in the city and in easy reach of it there are strong garrisons. The fort was built by the Mogul conquerors of the Punjab, and is, like so many of them in India, under the old *régime*, a royal establishment as well as a place of defense. Here are palaces, halls of public and private audience, the queen's palace, the king's bath-house, the pearl mosque, and other buildings, all of the most dazzling white marble. The inlaying of precious stones is the first I have seen, and such parts as are intact are beautiful beyond expression. These precious pieces, however, were mostly dug out during the anarchy of previous years, by some rapacious vandals, and where they are gone the English government has had them replaced by colored cements, so that their form is preserved. Figures, flowers, birds, are of exquisite symmetry, while over one archway in the hall of private audience is the renowned sentiment in Arabic: "If there is a paradise on earth it is here, it is here." The pearl mosque, of white marble, is a pearl indeed, the perfection of Saracenic art, and I cannot see how one could enter its spotlessly white corridors and prayer-room and not be devout. Shah Jehan worshiped here, turning his face westward to have it toward Mecca.

Not far away is the Juma Musjid, said to be the largest mosque in the world. It is of brick and the fine red sandstone of this region, and is truly an imposing edifice. Like so many buildings I have seen here, it has first a broad platform, then rising above that the edifice proper. This is not one building but several, arranged around a central paved court, which has an immense well in the center. On the west side is the large prayer mosque, which one enters along corridors of fine columns, to find only bare marble flagging in black and white squares, each black square marking a place for one of the faithful to kneel in prayer. There was not a chair or bit of furniture, save a high desk for the reading of the Koran, almost as small as a step-ladder. Here was more than Puritan simplicity—but among the followers of a *false* prophet! On another side of the court were low rooms for various purposes. In one of them an old priest took me to a cell in which were relics—real ones, to be sure—of Mohammed. First was a section of the Koran written by a grandson of the prophet on parchment in Arabia; a bit of it still older; then a whole one written on paper, several hundred years before paper was invented; one of the prophet's slippers kept safely in a glass case; a hair from his head, stuck with glue to the under side of a glass cover, and last a foot-print of the same wonderful prophet which he made when, some time at Mecca, he stepped on a slab of sparkling quartzite. O, but those priestly fellows, whether at Rome or Delhi, have relics, and then all want backsheesh for showing them. In this vast mosque were gathered forty thousand of the faithful to pray for the success of their arms when the British were to make the assault on the walls at the Cashmere Gate. But Delhi must fall in spite of Mohammedan prayers, and a better faith dominate this city and country.

A hurried run through the bazars, seeing the odd

native products of hand and soil; the purchase of a shawl for the one who could not come along, a retreat to the inviting old dak bungalow hotel, tired and surfeited with marvelous sight-seeing, ended the only day I was in Delhi.

LETTER VI.

A COMMENCEMENT SEASON IN INDIA.

The Methodist Theological School for India is located at Bareilly, and it was my fortune to attend its closing exercises December 6–9, 1888. In company with Rev. E. W. Parker, D.D., and two other missionaries, I had come thirty miles from the camp-meeting ground at Chandusi, because a grand celebration was to be held the following week. I arrived at Bareilly December 6, and listened that night to a sermon in Hindustani by the Rev. C. P. Hard, of the Bengal Conference, on the Master's sending out the seventy. The next day, December 7, was spent in oral examinations and such other duties as fall in the usual routine of a commencement. That evening the students gave an entertainment, literary and musical, that, to my regret, I missed, after which, at the house of the president, Rev. Dr. T. J. Scott, I met the graduating class of seven, finding them a group of men having a noble, willing, devoted spirit and purpose. The commencement proper took place at eleven o'clock Saturday, December 8. Two schools are taught jointly, the theological and a normal school; the latter to prepare teachers for the educational work of our India Mission. In this department four had completed the course, receiving diplomas, but not taking public part in the exercises on commencement day. An audience composed mostly of students, their friends, the teachers and professors, and visiting missionaries, listened.

The young men were on the programme to make speeches, not to deliver orations, but they had selected topics, formally arranged them, and each spoke twelve or fifteen minutes. Here is the list of themes: "The King's Crier," "Times of Refreshing," "Spiritual Food," "The Search for Peace," "The Rainbow an Emblem of Christ," "The Hunt for Souls," "The Time has Arrived," the last being valedictory. This list might stand beside one prepared in a Methodist theological school anywhere in the United States. The names and themes of the graduates do not read well in English, Badshah Ka Naqib being the salutatorian's and Waqt Apahuncha the valedictorian's theme, while their names were, respectively, Chote Lal and Nizam Ali. As the plan and argument of the young men's speeches were interpreted to me I judged they were doing well. The Hindustani speech does not seem to me at all well adapted to oratory, but if I could understand it perhaps my opinions would change. Most of the graduates had done some preaching for several years, and in their gestures I deemed I could detect some indications of bazar service. One or two had features such as an American might covet, good straight, well-cut, Aryan type. Their brown skins, coal-black hair and whiskers, and gleaming eyes were in peculiar contrast to their white-faced, blue-eyed professors.

The programme had on it "Native Music," which, on hearing, made me think its production in any seminary or college in America would create a sensation. The instruments used were three — a long rude guitar, a small keg-shaped drum beaten with the finger-tips, and a little violin of three or four strings, the whole thing not more than eighteen inches long and three inches wide. Two students sang to the accompaniment of these instruments. The key would be pitched high and then run on in a minor monotone, often antiphonal and recitative, rather than the ordinary ways of singing in America. President Scott whispered to me that it was "wild and weird," and at once I added, "rich." Dr. J. W. Waugh, who has been here many years and heard much of it, said to me that he still liked it, the beating of the drum making his heart thump in his breast. The songs were airs and sentiments of the country adapted to Christianity, one being in praise of Christ, another the peace and rest found in him. I enjoyed it greatly, and am promised more of it at the celebration next week. The native Christians especially are adepts in it, and use it to advantage.

Saturday evening a reception was held, at which a fine gathering of English officials, native gentlemen, professors from the Government College, and others were present. Among them was a prince royal from Burma, who escaped King Thebaw's bloody slaughter of his relatives. The English government has brought him here to be educated in their college. His dress was different from that of the natives, and his face decidedly Turanian. Many of the native gentlemen could speak English, with one of whom I discussed American institutions and government, and, later, with another, the proposed Indian Congress. The first one I also plied with questions about the aborigines of India. They were posted on all points.

On Sunday President Scott preached the baccalaureate sermon at eight o'clock in Hindustani; at three the alumni sermon was delivered, and at six I was compelled to preach. I had, by request, spoken a little to the students Saturday at commencement, what I said being translated by President Scott. This theological school has sent out about one hundred and fifty students, all graduates but forty, and with one or two exceptions these men have been true to the teaching received in the school. They are pastors in our own Conferences or for other denominations, and are doing noble work. The two classes now in the school, and the new one to enter, are much larger than the one just graduated, and are considered very promising. Of the seven graduating this year one was a Brahman, two Sikhs, and four had no caste.

In America commencement is associated with warm days, hot sun, a profusion of flowers, and not the bleak winds, frozen ground, and snows of December. Well, let me say that here the sun is so powerful that no one goes out without cork hat or umbrella for fear of sunstroke; not a bit of frost has touched Bareilly, though the nights are chilly, and a profusion of flowers is on trees, vines, bushes, and plants, the yards and gardens producing masses of magnificent roses.

LETTER VII.

INTO THE HIMALAYAS AT NAINI TAL.

At seven o'clock in the morning, December 11, Professor Messmore, of our theological school at Bareilly, and I started horseback from the mission house at Huldwanee, where Rev. Thomas Craven now has charge, to ride to Naini Tal. The course lay along the fine road over the gravel-drift brought down from the mountains, and the first hour's ride, in face of a chill wind blowing down the gorge, was most exhilarating. It gave us a chance to see the mountains during these four miles before getting fully into their recesses. Like all the hills and mountains I have seen in India, they rise abruptly from the plain, broken, jagged, and sharp. As soon as we left the open country the luxuriant vegetation assumed a new aspect; trees not seen on the plains, flowers peculiar to the timber, vines, creepers, and bushes abounded. I had heard much about the creepers on the trees, but was not fully prepared for what I saw. Close beside the road many creepers hung in long straight lines or reaches of thick growth from the ground upward to the tops of the tallest trees. Far off on the hill-sides I could see long stretches of forest, the tops and limbs of the trees so overloaded by the vine-growth that the identity of separate trees was lost under the masses of creepers. The peepul-tree on the plains has a sturdy growth, the trunk sometimes rough and partly divided, in other cases smooth as an American beech. But in the thick forest on the hill-sides I found that it acted as a creeper, throwing itself around the solid trunk of some other tree, inclosing it in its arms as if a sentient thing, making a net-work of formation like lattice clear around the body of the other. It was a wonderful growth. Graceful festoons, suggesting swings for wood-nymphs, often fell close to the ground between two supporting trees. Dense undergrowth of plants new to one from the West in places covered the rich, damp ground. As we rode up the gorge made by the waters of Naini Tal River here and there a little plot was cultivated, wheat, bananas, oranges, lemons, and other products growing on the terraces in great luxuriance, if only water could be obtained for irrigation. When yet five miles from the place Professor Messmore pointed out some of the buildings at Naini Tal, far, far above us. But the good horses carried us up steadily, surely. The trees began to change again, now to more of temperate features, the willow, acacia, pine, and a little short of Naini Tal the oak, appearing. Strange birds flitted among the trees, one much like our robin, another a bluejay whose tail-feathers were full fourteen inches long, and a jungle cock, considered the lineal ancestor of the common fowl, slowly walked across the road ahead of us. He was bronze, red, and black, shaped much like the game-cock, with long curved tail-feathers such as we see often in American roosters.

Three miles short of Naini Tal a big brewery blots the landscape and sends out its liquid curse to blight Anglo-Saxon and Hindu homes alike. Then a steep climb, part of the way on foot, sometimes riding, and being gladly met by Professor Foote, who knew we were coming, we at last, having ridden sixteen miles that morning, crossed the pretty bridge spanning the outlet of Naini Tal, and gazed upon that place of beauty, rest, and health. It is a great basin with the lake in the midst. On every side rise high hills save the way we came, where the water plunges rapidly down the deep gorge toward the plains. The hill-sides, from five to fifteen hundred feet above the lake, are covered with a sparse growth of oak, cedar, pine, and other familiar trees, the level of the lake being about six thousand feet above the sea. Houses of the missionaries, English officials, schools, and churches are scattered on every part of the inclosing hill-sides, helping to make a most charming landscape, as the white stone houses, gardens, yards, and parks cover every part. Under direction of Professor Foote I soon was taken to the home of Rev. John Baume, the pastor of the English-speaking church, and I found in the hospitality of himself and wife most pleasant reminders of American spirit. The mission-grounds, having been bought early in the history of this charming sanitarium along the wise lines of Dr. William Butler's insight, are ample and centrally located, while the church of the English audience is as wisely posted. The boys' school, under the direction of Professor F. W. Foote, is now prospering. He is hoping to purchase a fine property soon, located on the eastern slopes, where it can overlook all the lake and surrounding regions. The girls' school is directly opposite the other, in the more shady groves of the west side, but also in a place giving an entrancing view. Miss Knowles, sister of Dr. D. C. Knowles, has done a noble work in founding this school, both for Indian Methodism and the Woman's Foreign Missionary Society. There is an Anglican church and a Roman Catholic one, as well as a couple of Hindu temples and a Mohammedan mosque, in this quiet mountain nook.

Naturally enough, I wanted to see all I could the two days I had to stay, so the first afternoon Professor Foote came to show me to a spot from which I could obtain a fine view of the great mountains beyond. The twelve-year-old girl of Rev. Dr. J. W. Waugh went pony-back with us to "Snow Seat," a thousand feet above the lake, on the north-east side. From the top of Khutab Minar, near Delhi, I had obtained a tantalizing glimpse of the "Snowy Range;" from Moradabad the white peaks stood out dimly to view one morning, while on the cars in coming to the foot of the mountains I had also caught the white gleam above the lower ranges; but now, as a little behind the sprightly Nora Waugh I reached "Snow Seat," the grandeur of the vast uplift burst fully on my sight. I felt it surely repaid me for much time and trouble. These mountains are not a single range, but a mighty uplift extending more than a hundred miles across their axis. The "Snowy Range" is sixty miles from Naini Tal, and a hundred miles of its extent burst on the vision that moment. All the glory of that sight cannot be put into words. Sharp peaks, snow-clad, for two thousand feet, run up like gigantic saw-teeth, a hundred of them in view at once. Their steep, ragged outline and broken sides showed their formation to be geologically recent, as those close about us did. The declining sun lay a soft pink radiance over the snow that was charming, while the ranges between us and the snow were touched with the lights, shades, colors, and outlines common to such a sight. With the glass I could see great glaciers, the crevasses across two or three of them being plainly discernible by the hollows in the surface of the recent snows. As the sun sank lower it brought out in fine distinctness the profound gorges and spaces in the great range, and at the same time tipped the peaks here and there with a glory all their own. A crag only on some peak would catch the sun, while all the rest would be hidden by a greater peak west of it. Finally, as the sun totally disappeared, a ghostly, ghastly white on the "Snowy Range" took the place of the pink of that luminary, producing an unearthly beauty that to me seemed finer than the sunset. The sky for a few moments held the pink that last was seen on the mountains; above that was a rich green, which in turn melted into orange; then the blue of the untinted sky prevailed. We slowly descended to the dim basin of Naini Tal and the lighted houses.

The next morning Professor Foote, by previous arrangements, was at Mr. Baume's long before daylight for the ascent of a still higher peak, Cheena, to see the sunrise on the mountains. As I waited a few minutes the zodiacal light shot a mighty pyramid of brightness over the eastern mountain-tops, as it is not seen in more northern climes. A ride of an hour and a quarter, first through a stretch of yards and among private houses, then up the ascent by steep, narrow, zigzag paths, our horses puffing heavily as the air grew thinner and thinner, up still around the top of Cheena, through heavy oak forests, till at last, as the daylight had deepened, we reached the crest, more than eight thousand feet above the sea. From this point we could see more of the "Snowy Range" than from "Snow Seat," a stretch of fully two hundred miles. The lights and shadows over the mountains surrounding us and those short of the "Snowy Range" were most exquisite. A slight smoke or mist hung among them in such a way that the tops of the mountains would show the dark green of their wooded slopes, then gradually change below to purple, opalescent, and light smoky blue. The sunrise, brilliant in the gorgeous red, orange, green, and blue of the sky and burnished gold of the cloud-flecks of the east, did not color the snow-covered peaks as richly as I had hoped. We were partly on the wrong side. Still, some rare sights of single peaks being touched with the pink that persisted on the snow the night before were granted us. Then the pure white took the place of the pink as the sunlight increased. Great bars of the sun's rays shot from crests and gorges among the lower mountains, across the valleys and shadows, in a glory that would defy all skill of painter. As we sat on the dry grass that covered the crest I suddenly noticed that masses of edelweiss were growing all about us. I knew it was to be found in the Himalayas as well as in the Alps, but for the time had forgotten it. Some enterprising Swiss should come here and get bushels of it, and, taking it home, sell it as they do in the Alps, at a franc a sprig. A couple of Goorkha soldiers from the garrison below came each with a gun on a hunting trip, and were barefooted, though patches of snow in shady places were on Cheena. These men are aboriginal inhabitants of India, found here by the Aryan Hindus when they entered India. When did these Goorkhas and other Turanian hillmen enter India?

That afternoon, as the shadows began lengthening, in company with Mr. and Mrs. Baume and Professor Messmore, I visited the American Cemetery, where lie the bodies of a number of devoted men and women who counted not their lives dear to themselves, so they might carry the Gospel to suffering India. Mrs. Bishop Thoburn, Mrs. N. G. Cheney, a child of Dr. Butler's, named Washington, are among them. Their resting-place is a retired, quiet nook. Thence we went along shady walks by the west side of the lake to the girls' school, to find its present principal, Miss Easton, frying doughnuts like a Yankee woman, though she declared she was a Knickerbocker. But she could make good doughnuts if not a Yankee. Doughnuts in India! It made one think of his Western home, of his mother, sisters, and wife, all at a time. For five months I had not eaten one. That school there among the trees is a monument to American womanhood that has reared it, and is to be a power to aid Western civilization, with all it means to woman in getting a firm hold in India. From there we went to the famous rock shrine of the Indian goddess Naini, close by the lake-side, where it is said the natives formerly sacrificed a human being each year to the local deity, and they now declare that the goddess will still secure her victim by a person being drowned in the lake every year. For themselves they are now content to kill a goat yearly at this place where I saw the sign of the goddess, some tridents painted on the rock, and a handful of fresh sweet-meats which some devotee had but just offered. A walk by Hangman's Bay, suggestive of the awful days of the mutiny, across the outlet of the lake, up the hill to Professor Foote's, where a substantial dinner was offered us, and also banks of roses grown out-doors, even in those mountains, ended our wanderings for that day among the Himalayas.

LETTER VIII.

AT A CAMP-MEETING IN INDIA.

THEY do not call it a camp-meeting here, but a *mela.* This word means a gathering, and is especially applied to the native religious festivals at certain times and places where tens of thousands gather; and thus the camp-meeting becomes a *Christian* mela. This designation, painted in large characters, is hung upon the trees at the entrance to these grounds, being given in English, Urdu, and Arabic. More than a camp-meeting is taking place. It is both a district Conference and a camp-meeting, hence the aptness of the native name. For several days before the time for opening tents were being put up and preparations similar to those occurring in America at such a time took place. Chandusi, where it is held, is centrally located for the Rohilcund District of the North India Conference. Dr. E. W. Parker, presiding elder of this district, is in charge. It is at a railroad junction, and held, free of any charges, in a fine mango grove.

Let people in New England take a peep at this camp-meeting-ground. It is level, dry, the mango grove covering sixty acres or more, and is divided by the main road running northward from the contiguous city of Chandusi. As I write—December 14, but one would think it early September in America—the leaves above us are all green, the trees full of birds and monkeys, and the sun so strong through the day that one must protect himself from it with a pith hat and an umbrella; yet the nights are thoroughly chilly, but without frost. The mango-tree looks much like a chestnut-tree, low, branching, thick-topped, though the leaves remain on all winter, as is true of the trees in India, though they look like our deciduous ones. The missionaries' tents are all on one side of this road, with the tents and inclosure for the school-girls, while the tents and huts for the native families and the school-boys are on the other side. Centrally, between these two sections, close to the great wagon-road, is an immense awning under which two thousand people can sit—on the ground, and never in chairs, for this is the way the Indians sit. Straw was first spread on the ground under this awning, then native matting and carpeting above that. The American missionaries bring their own chairs, while at the outer edge of the space a few natives may be seen sitting on benches provided.

An audience here presents a unique appearance. Glance at it. The white turbans and jaunty students' caps worn by the men and boys through the services produce, as their wearers all sit on the left of the open space kept as an aisle, a most varied and picturesque effect, in contrast with the dark-brown expressive faces and gleaming black eyes beneath them. At the right sit the women and school-girls, as compactly as people on seats cannot gather, each one having the head and shoulders, morning and evening, covered with a thin, coarse, dark red-and-black calico quilt of native make. In the middle of the day their heads are covered with white chuddars. There are bright faces, full of meaning and hope, as Christianity has come to them bearing its burden of help to woman. A vivid contrast is plainly to be seen between these women and girls and those still in the old beliefs. On the outskirts of these Chandusi audiences are always files of men, usually Hindus or Mohammedans, standing in respectful attention listening to the services; some passing coolie stops, with his load on his head or back, also to listen.

I took a turn among the native cottages under the mango-trees. The sly monkeys are much more afraid of us Western people than of the natives, scampering away as we approach. The people at such a gathering as this set down their tents or huts as each one chooses, little attempt being made at regularity. A few of them have cotton tents more or less commodious, but most of the homes are native-made and peculiar. They are of coarse, native grass, of thatched structure, ten feet long by six wide, their form being like setting a narrow roof down on the ground. Under this primitive covering old mats, carpeting, or straw is spread for sleeping. Their cooking apparatus consists of a small hollow space in the ground, around which, and raised a few inches above the level of the earth, is a horseshoe-shaped ridge of hard, baked mud, six inches across, on which they set their copper kettles or flat iron coverings for baking thin loaves of bread.

The District Conference held a three-days' session December 11–13, which, considering that there are 221 members of it, is quite an affair. Of this number 8 are American missionaries, 19 ordained native preachers in Conference relations, 7 ordained local preachers, and 47 unordained native preachers. The other 140 members are exhorters and teachers, though in some instances one man combines both these duties. This body of workers all had to be taken through the disciplinary course of examinations, reports, and appointments, so that their duties were hardly less than those of an Annual Conference. One specialty in the reports was the amount of collections, looking to self-support. After the work, character, and progress in studies had been ascertained, seven were recommended for ordination and four to admittance on trial to the Annual Conference. It has become a rule here to keep a man in the work four years as a local preacher, having him take the course of study prescribed for local preachers before he can be recommended to the Annual Conference on trial. At this District Conference nineteen were granted local preachers' license, and all given work but two, who hold some government office. Sixteen young men were recommended to the theological school at Bareilly. It will be seen from these things that Dr. Parker's duties are not light.

The real camp-meeting was opened by a sermon from our native pastor at Moradabad, Hiram L. Cutting. It seemed earnest and practical as its outline and sentiment were given to me. Miss Leonard, the holiness evangelist, was present and spoke a few moments on her specialty. The noon hour was given to the young people from the five school stations, Bijnour, Moradabad, Budaon, Bareilly, and Shahjehanpore. Their literary programme consisted of recitations, songs, Bible paraphrases, a debate, essays, and the like, and was deemed fine in its merit and delivery. "Sweet Home," sung in English by Miss Doherty, Mrs. Parker's assistant, and Miss Jeffreys, assisted by six native girls, was inspiring. One of the marvels of that hour was to see two young women enter the debate with two young men—and, as it would be likely to happen in America, beat them—the young women standing there, modest and bashful, to be sure, yet before two thousand people, and that in India, where woman has been taught for scores of generations that she is only a beast of burden, a thing of use, man's slave, to be kept veiled, a prisoner in her own house. Christianity is teaching some of the daughters of India a few of their privileges. At four o'clock in the afternoon was a grand parade of the Anti-Tobacco League, in which more than eight hundred walked, the banner for the largest number at one place being awarded to Moradabad. The tobacco habit here is even a greater burden than in America, and this movement among the native Christians, the preachers, teachers, and young people, having been inaugurated and carried out by Drs. Scott, Parker, and others, is full of worth and promise.

The preaching was done partly by native preachers, partly by Americans. Rev. Mr. Lucas, from the Presbyterian Mission, was present and preached once. As all the sermons were in the vernacular I could get them only by their being translated to me as they were going on. One of the districts of the North India Conference is in charge of a native, Zahur ul Haqq, who preached Saturday morning. See him as he stands there addressing the great audience of eager listeners! He is elderly, has gray whiskers and hair, the former heavy and long, the latter scant and curling a bit on his neck, the top of his head bald. Such a head and face are worth looking at! If there is any thing in the shape of heads his is metaphysical, logical, a high pointed one, while the face, the heavy brows, Roman nose, and the large strong mouth show a man of firmness and energy. Such he is. His height is slightly more than medium, his build firm, somewhat inclined to corpulency. How is he dressed? In a long loosely-fitting coat of quilted calico, such as many of the men wear, combining the cut of a dressing-gown and overcoat, and reaching nearly to his ankles, his feet inclosed in good shoes and stockings. His manner of preaching is direct, forcible, animated, and his points on the theme that Christ came to seek and save are well put. Mr. Haqq was formerly a Mohammedan. Being present at a love-feast, and listening to the testimonies, he believed, was soundly converted, and, having been previously educated, was set at work with most pleasing results.

Sunday, as in America, was the great day of the feast. It opened with a love-feast at eight o'clock. Dr. E. W. Parker, presiding elder, was in charge, with a dozen or twenty other missionaries present. The singing of our familiar church tunes to words that one does not understand conveys a strange impression, but I could sing the English words in the loud volume that swelled in the vernacular from two thousand natives. Those two thousand under the broad awning in the midst of green groves of wide-spreading mango-trees are an inspiration to a Western man. The dark, earnest, happy faces of the men and women, of the boys and girls, as they show so pleasantly in contrast with white turbans and caps, and the dark red, green, and brown chuddars, speak volumes for the Christianity that has set them right with God and man. As they begin to speak, the men, who are all seated on one side of an open aisle, and then, after a while, the women on the other side, it can be seen, if not understood, that they have an experience to tell. O blessed gospel power that sets free the tongue to tell of its victories!

Here are wise men grown gray during twenty-five

years of labor in our mission work in India, and working beside them men who once were Mohammedans, Jews, Hindus—and even Turanians, that old race inhabiting this country before the Hindus. Of the missionaries some were from Europe, most from America. A Kentucky Presbyterian mingled his joy with an Ohio Methodist. Said one native worker: "A year ago this meeting prayed for my work, and God has been blessing me in it; and now I would like you to pray for it the year to come just four minutes." An old man like Abraham, leaning on his staff, said that he was the Lord's; living he was the Lord's, dying he was the Lord's. Another: "I want my heart to be a fountain of grace, to drink myself and offer to others." Many said they loved the Lord with all their heart. One from the Bareilly Normal School said he had been to the camp-meeting six years before, and never received any light, but that at his own town a Salvation Army girl had enabled him to enter the light. Another said the time was when he could not speak in meeting; now he could not keep still for the love of Christ in his heart. A high-caste Brahman who was put into jail at Bareilly for helping to mob one of our native preachers in the bazar, and who had said he should become a Christian when he got out, spoke, saying that once he was not saved, but was now. Another, "Once I was blind, now I see." Many recited Scripture, others hymns. The witnessing lasted two solid hours, and in that time those who kept count say that nearly three hundred spoke, and then when Dr. Parker asked all to rise who wanted to witness but had not done so the mass who stood up was so great that it seemed as though no one had spoken. It was a scene certain to assure any who may question if missionary work in India pays that at least in the Rohilcund District it pays a thousand-fold.

Probably sixteen hundred or more native Christians sat under the awning at that love-feast. After witnessing a call was made for the unconverted to come forward for prayers, and thirty-three soon responded, mostly young men and women, and numbers of them later witnessed to salvation. At noon, in connection with Miss Leonard, the evangelist, I was set at work by Dr. Parker with the native preachers and teachers. A hundred or more of these were present under the awning at the same time that other meetings were going on elsewhere. The woman's meeting-tent was full to overflowing, while the boys' meeting and the girls' were also full. At the awning I spoke of the baptism and power of the Holy Spirit, Rev. Dr. Robert Hoskins of our mission translating. It seemed slow, difficult work, yet I hope good was done. Miss Leonard spoke after me, and almost all of those present came forward seeking the fullness of the Spirit, and many deep, full consecrations were made. It was a time of power and of freedom obtained from all sin. Following this came a service at which four men and nine children were baptized.

At three o'clock the great meeting of the day took place. Rev. Dr. Johnson, of the Lucknow District, preached to an immense audience, including Hindus, Mohammedans, nominal Christians, and those active in the work. The awning space was crammed and at least a thousand stood up outside those sitting. It was a time to inspire a man. Dr. Johnson, using the text, "If ye love me, keep my commandments," and standing centrally under the awning, powerfully impressed the respectful listeners. Following him came two rousing exhortations, first by Rev. Dr. Hoskins, then Rev. Dr. Parker, the whole crowd nearly all staying to the end. It was one of the opportunities of a man's life to speak to so many who were generally regarded as heathen.

In the evening another interesting service took place. Hardly any save native Christians were present, but about two thousand of them were seated under the awning. Rev. Dr. B. H. Badley spoke on Tit. ii, 14—on holiness as a condition for successful work in God's vineyard. It was a strong sermon, its main features being translated to me, as were those of Dr. Johnson's. I spoke afterward on the theme of the sermon. Immediately following that a sacramental service was held under the conduct of Rev. Dr. P. T. Wilson, assisted by three American missionaries and three native preachers. It was a most interesting time. It was estimated that eight hundred persons partook of the sacrament. Lines, sometimes double ones, reaching across the awning were formed on the carpeting, and the hearty acceptance by the people was most pleasant. Those who had been of diverse races and far distinct castes knelt side by side. As the service was closing Dr. Parker knelt, as it happened, by the side of a Hindu boy for the sacrament, and one native preacher brought him the bread and another the wine. The whole scene was affecting; the still moonlight night, the broad awning lighted by lamps hung on the supporting poles, the dark faces of the listeners, the varied costumes, the issues discussed, the close attention paid by the people, all combined to make it a scene never to be forgotten.

So mightily was I impressed with the day and all its promise that I sent Chaplain McCabe this note, which he flung out to the American public:

"CHANDUSI, INDIA, *December* 16, 1888.

"DEAR CHAPLAIN: I wish you could have attended the love-feast of the mela here this morning. At least 1,600 Christians were present, and in two hours' time almost 300 spoke in true Methodist, Christian spirit. They were all the way from the old man leaning on his staff to the sprightly boys and girls ten and twelve years old from the day and Sunday-schools. The singing was uplifting, though I could understand the tunes better than the words. The glory of God was present. It was about as hard to stop their testifying when the time came to stop as it is sometimes in America. These people wanted to tell about the Christ whose death had redeemed them. It was almost worth coming clear to India to see and hear. After all had spoken who could have the time a great host stood up together to testify by that. Then, as Dr. Parker invited them forward for prayer, thirty-three came, sixteen men and seventeen women, most of whom afterward professed conversion. If the work of getting money lags in America the conversion of souls here does not. This district, the Moradabad, reports this year 1,475 baptisms. The cause goes on; the missionaries are shouting happy. Every-where the demand is for more workers. Push for the money and send on the workers. It is God's time and man's opportunity. The day all through has been a glorious one. Thousands have waited on the word. Thirteen were baptized this afternoon."

Monday morning a song and prayer service was held, after which the appointments of native local preachers, helpers, exhorters, and teachers, made by the District Conferences, to the number of about two hundred, for both Presiding Elders Haqq and Parker's districts, were read. It seemed like the close of an Annual Conference. Then the mela ended, and every one set out to his home and work. Who can weigh the good done for time and eternity?

LETTER IX.

EDUCATION WORK IN NORTH INDIA CONFERENCE.

VERY soon after landing among the Methodist missionaries here I became convinced that the schools sustained in the cities and villages were among the most successful agencies used to build up our work broadly and safely. Subsequent information and inquiries have confirmed and strengthened that opinion. One of the problems that has always confronted the Church, from the earliest centuries, has been how to make pure, real, and intelligent Christian character in the converts from heathenism. Think of Paul's letters, along these lines, to the Corinthians, Galatians, and others. The Roman monks who led our Anglo-Saxon ancestors to the truth, as can be seen by reading the history of the early Church in England, wrestled with the same problem. One just converted from the worship of idols, the spell of superstitions, the force of heathen customs, and from the long list of mighty influences which in paganism combine to dwarf and enslave the spirit, cannot in a day or year pass from those things to a broad-minded, firm, free Christian character. Many of the old roots will remain. How to build up character, then, is a mighty problem here as every-where. During nearly a generation of experience the missionaries have found that the work which can be done in the evangelical school is one of the most potent means to this end. They are wise who put large sums of money into the schools.

Take, for instance, the system of schools set in motion by the munificent gift of Dr. J. F. Goucher, the head-quarters of which are at Moradabad, under the direction of Dr. and Mrs. E. W. Parker. There is the Goucher High School for advanced pupils in that city; then a hundred schools are scattered over the old province of Rohilcund for both boys and girls. Of boys' schools of the primary grade Dr. Goucher's endowment supports sixty, in which there are being taught more than two thousand pupils. The conditions upon which his endowment is used make it obligatory that the teachers hired shall be Christians and members of the Methodist Episcopal Church, that each school shall be opened every day with reading of the Bible, singing a Christian hymn, and prayer, all in the vernacular. In addition to this the teachers are urged by the missionaries to visit the parents and friends of these boys at their homes after teaching hours, to talk with them and interest them in Christianity. These schools, according to Dr. Goucher's conditions, must be in villages and communities that are inquirers after Christianity, and be regarded as evangelical forces seeking to lead the children and people to Christ. Out of these primary schools the brightest and most promising of the boys are being passed, after examination, to the high school at Moradabad, where they can have the benefit of one of the hundred Goucher scholarships awaiting them. Dr. Goucher sustains forty girls' schools of primary grade also, located and conditioned like the others, from which there is going a constant stream of the most promising of the girls to Mrs. Parker's school at Moradabad, where Dr. Goucher has a few scholarships, but which he is said to purpose increasing to forty. All through the North India Conference similar schools of primary grade are sustained by mission funds, or otherwise, feeders of the various graded schools established at the great centers. In the two high schools at Moradabad, and at other places, the young men and women are prepared for matriculation in the government universities at Calcutta, Allahabad, and elsewhere.

Through the one hundred schools sustained by the Goucher Fund about three thousand families are directly reached; and over three hundred thousand people, those in the four castes — Mazbi Sikhs, Leather-workers, Sweepers, and Thakurs—that are most fully patronizing the schools, are more or less positively reached by that agency. During the five years this fund has been operative, between one and two thousand souls have been converted through the means thus put at the disposal of the missionaries. Here is a field so promising that its success should lead other rich Christians of the United States to put their money at work for Christ in it. This is done by some. Mr. J. H. Frey, of Baltimore, before his death had seventeen scholarships in use at the Bareilly Theological School, and in his will secured to the Oudh District enough to support about thirty primary schools. Mr. W. E. Blackstone, of Chicago, has put $3,000 into the new training-school and deaconess home at Muttra. Let the good work go on. In all the North India Conference this year reports 488 schools, with over 1,600 pupils. O, but the cry there is on every hand here for workers! Not less than a thousand openings for work in the North India Conference alone, with magnificent promise of success, must be refused this year for lack of means and workers. The sum of forty or fifty dollars will sustain a primary school a year like those found already to produce such rich harvests.

A remarkable paper on early marriage, prepared by Mrs. Dr. Mansell, and read at a district conference, had so much of worth that it has been printed and widely scattered. It claims, among other things, that the physical deterioration of the Indians is owing more to marrying too young than to the climate. It is a startling statement, and if it can be sustained by facts and figures opens up new demands on Christian care and philanthropy. Our missionaries seek delay in marriage among the young people under their direction, and in this effort commendable success is being reached. Already later marriage, better food and clothing, and other things are giving a sturdier physique, and with that a better brain-power; so that the young people sent up from our schools to government examinations for the universities and other fields succeed better than non-Christians, for they are found to be mentally and physically better able to stand the excessive strain of great intellectual efforts.

It is the policy of our missionaries to build up graded schools at each of the larger stations, so besides those at Moradabad they are at Cawnpore, Lucknow, Bareilly, Budaon, and elsewhere, for boys or girls. Like those at Moradabad, they are fed from the lower schools, though some of the young people come directly from the Christian families. In these schools have been prepared most of the native workers used by the missionaries. They get culture here that both in degree and kind they would otherwise lack. Along with the regular studies pursued the great principles of Christianity are taught, and thus they become rooted and grounded in the faith, and at the same time get almost wholly freed from the baneful effects of the heathenism which must always act on their parents, who have failed of similar advantages. Preachers, exhorters, teachers, both men and women, zenana workers, helpers, and others are sent out from these schools by the scores, so that our widening fields are partly supplied. But the demand is greater than the supply. Hundreds of native men and women could be judiciously set at work at once in the three India Conferences if they could be obtained.

When a young man shows special aptitude as a prospective preacher, he is, on finishing his course at some one of these schools, sent to the theological school at Bareilly, where he can have a three-years' course to fit him better for the ministry. His schooling then does not cease, for he is usually required to take the course of study for local preachers, and serve in that office for four years; and then, if promising enough, is recommended to the Annual Conference, where he takes the regular Conference course during the four years as we do at home; and this year they have presented to the Conference a post-graduate course which the preachers can elect to carry on after their regular course is ended. By these means there is being obtained a fine body of native ministers who are doing good work for God and Methodism. These men are from different nationalities—Jews, Hindus, Mohammedans, Turanians—and from all castes—Brahmans, Rajputs, Sikhs, Chamars, Sweepers—and of no caste. That God is no respecter of persons has illustration here. High caste, low caste, outcasts, sit together, study together, eat and work together, sing and pray together, lifted to the high estate of children of God. Cultivated women, without whose elevation India cannot be elevated, sit as wives or sisters with these men, having the many-phased enfranchisement that Christianity gives to all.

Methodism in India feels that the time has come for yet higher education of its youth, the same as early Methodism felt in the United States. It must have full colleges. It justly dreads to send the young men and women carefully taught Christian truth in the high schools to mingle, in a great university, with the Hindu and Mohammedan young people to be found in government colleges, lest in some instances they become drawn away. A growing number are prepared every year for matriculation, so that a college for young men and one for young women are imperatively demanded. This need is so pressing that last year the Conference voted that Dr. Badley, in charge of the Centennial High School at Lucknow, should go ahead a year with his class beyond matriculation; and this he did. In the same city the Girls' High School, Miss De Vine in charge, had had its classes carried into a college department two years under the efficient teaching of Miss Kyle. Here, then, is an embryo college for young men and one for young women. They are demanded by the advanced needs of the young people, to save them fully to us, to prepare still more highly cultured workers in our mission, and to give among the people due prominence to the exalted place we occupy in the field of education.

Indeed, Dr. Badley has taken steps already toward building a college. A board of trustees has been organized several years. At Lucknow, directly opposite the mission compound and the Centennial High School, is an open plot of five acres, formerly belonging to government, which has been presented to our missionaries for the purpose of erecting a college. It is worth four thousand dollars. It is most opportune, and comes in answer to needs and prayers. It comes when government is favorably disposed to mission work and schools. It comes, on the other hand, when the missionary treasury is so depleted that it cannot devote any thing this year to building. The conditions of the gift are that it must have a building erected on it, which the government will approve, within two years. Plans have been submitted which the government has approved, a contract for building, most advantageous in price and payments, has been concluded, and our missionaries feel that some way, by some means, the project must go ahead. Here is a chance for some rich man in America to build himself a lasting monument and make a name fragrant with blessings to humanity. What chances India offers for money to go on perpetuating its rich blessings and multiplying its living forces coined into Christian character in the young people it can send out to help in redeeming those masses!

LETTER X.

IN AND ABOUT MUTTRA.

THE railroad run from the Chandusi mela with Professor Foote and Dr. J. E. Scott and wife, though tedious in slowness, was most pleasant in associations, and the awaiting ghari at the station at nine o'clock at night was gladly welcome to take us to the mission house. An early *chota hazari* next morning prepared us for a drive of four hours about the city and mission property. Our mission at Muttra is a recent venture, and already has fine promise. Nine acres of land from which our folks were kept for some time were finally secured at advantageous conditions on perpetual lease, and on this land already five mission buildings are going up for both the parent board and the Woman's Foreign Missionary Society. The location is airy, sightly, commodious, while the buildings seem to be fine adaptations to the needs of the hot India climate. Several points for mission work had been opened near Muttra; in the heart of the city a school at which a hundred boys already are in attendance. Here and at two places where mission work is begun more than a hundred thousand people live. O, but the swarming masses of people to be seen in such a city as this! In driving through the streets the utmost care must be taken not to run over them, and the native driver is constantly shouting the idiom, "Save yourselves!" Where the boys' school is kept Dr. Scott has Sunday services, and meets every Sunday evening a packed house of the educated natives and others, who eagerly listen to the Gospel. What a chance for a missionary! A block is for sale cheap, fronting on the main street of the city, and reaching back to the Jumna River, that I hope can be secured, and which could be used for school and church purposes. Under the shadow of some Mohammedan minarets rising above a fine mosque a location could be secured by perpetual lease, with ample room for a hospital, training-school for women, and a dispensary. If only the money could be had for these purposes this holy city of the Hindus could be so entered at this beginning time as to give grand promise of victories for Christ.

Muttra is one of the most sacred cities of India. It is a center, here and at Brindaban, only six miles away, of Krishna's worship, as one of his incarnations is located at this place in the myths regarding him. Here, on the banks of the Jumna, he is said to have rested, the place now being marked by a stone, after his victory over Kansa, an uncle who tried to usurp the government. An ancient stone fort, said to be two thousand years old, was Kansa's stronghold. From the railroad bridge we could see half a mile of the bathing "ghats," where hundreds of natives were going down into the river in the sharp cold of the early morning to bathe as a religious rite; but you are glad on sanitary grounds that they do so. The Jumna is only less a sacred river than the Ganges, and where they unite their waters near Allahabad the location is considered peculiarly holy. After seeing this interesting view for a while we wandered along these "ghats," seeing in one place near the river-bank a tall sandstone tower raised to mark the spot where, two hundred years ago, a noble Hindu lady performed suttee with her dead husband's body.

Holy monkeys ran about in the temples along the river-bank, thievish, dirty, disgusting, while sacred turtles lifted their sluggish heads above the waters of the Jumna to eat the sweets thrown as offerings into it. In another place, where there was a swarm of bathers going into the water and coming from it, two or three stone arches stood, grown old in the passage of years, under each of which some rich rajah had years before been weighed over against his weight in money, and then the coins scattered among the crowds of waiting people. As we were there a new one, farther up the court from the river, was being built, under which a certain rich man was to be weighed at the great mela which was coming off in March, and then his weight in money to be scattered among the expectant masses. All this is done to gain merit for this world and the world after this one. Get these devotees converted to Christianity, and what missionaries they would make to unconverted peoples!

Not far away was the pretentious house of a man who is said to be so rich that he stands in the relation to the banks of India that the Bank of England does to the money matters of Great Britain. He is worth, it is reported, fully a hundred millions of dollars, the accumulations of several generations, to which he has added that of his own shrewd dealings in the banking business.

Many of the houses in this city are very fine, according to the notions and needs of Eastern architecture; much beautiful carving in wood and casting in bronze adorn the doors and fronts of the costly mansions. The temples here are also very rich, one almost opposite the banker's house being especially so, as it is the peculiar care of this man of rupees.

A city of such wealth and pilgrimage offers to its people special advantages, so that in their physique they show good living, being the tallest, plumpest lot of Hindus I have yet seen, their food seeming to have given them better growth. They eat no meat at all. The worship of Mahadeo, a most foul, disgusting superstition, and of grossest impulses, is the prominent idolatry here. One cannot tell of the emblems and practices. If Paul saw at Athens as gross worship as one can see in such a sacred city of India as this it is no wonder his spirit was stirred within him. Dr. Scott and his vigorous wife are deeply moved at the situation, and the Church will expect to learn grand results from their hard work here. He is popular among these same sleek, fat Hindus, but the victories of Christ will be likely to chill their regard for him.

In the afternoon we drove six miles from Muttra to Brindaban, another holy city, not now so lively as the former one, but to be especially a center of interest at the March mela. Then pilgrims by the ten thousands from all parts of India will be here, so religious are this people. A railroad spur by that time is to reach from Muttra to Brindaban, and crowds will avail themselves of this mode of transit, even though it is offered them by their Anglo-Saxon conquerors. The way the people of India ride on the cars since their pundits have found that the principles of steam locomotion were foreshadowed in the Vedas is most surprising. Every train is crowded, and you seldom see a train of less than a dozen or fifteen cars. In these the high castes, middle castes, low castes, and even outcasts and women ride. The cars in India are a leveler and civilizer as well as a convenience.

All along the drive from Muttra to Brindaban were temples, shrines, and the palaces of the rich, who come here a part of the year for religious purposes, as Americans go to the mountains and sea-shore for recreation. The grounds and gardens about some of them were elegant, but in most cases showed neglect and that touch of indolence and decay which is so indicative of tropical places. A jungle lay off from one side of the way that is a kind of boar-park in which the British officers enjoy the classical sport of "pig-sticking."

Brindaban is named from a sacred plant which grows about here, the "brinda," an obscure weed, I found, when they showed it to me, of the *labiatæ* group. Odd, is it not, that human beings, of the noble Aryan race, too, can be found to worship a little plant like that? Man, when he is started wrong, can go that way very far.

In the outskirts of this city we came to a new temple in course of construction. It is a thing of wonder to all observers, owing to its costliness and its proof of the activity of Brahmanism. If changes are going on in India looking toward the decay of idolatry this and other things show that it yet has much aggressive vitality. This temple, like most of them in the East, consists of a great court, at one side of which is the real fane, with many accessory buildings adjacent. The principal stone used is red sandstone, or rather pinkish, of which vast quarries are found in this part of India. The temples, forts, and palaces, in all the great cities about here, are built of this beautiful stone. Even as far north as Delhi the same stone is used, the wonderful Khutab Minar being made of it. It is fine-grained, firm, enduring, yet easily worked from its evenly stratified structure. Much white marble was also used, and it is costly, a block two by four feet from Guzerat costing five hundred rupees. Out of such a block they were fashioning the form of Krishna, which they were to set up as the god of their worship. Was I a heretic, that I could not see the reasonableness of their making a god themselves out of stone, and then worshiping it? Krishna was to be set up in this temple in three shapes: first, when he was a child; second, when grown to manhood; and third, in another form. Nearest to these images was being made a court or room for persons of rank and women, while further away the less choice public must be satisfied with a remoter distance from the god. The marble-work of columns, screens, panels, and the like, was being inlaid with precious stones, these being found to be, as they showed them to us, carnelians, agates, lapis lazuli, green flint, malachite, and the really costly turquois. They also were using shells, the tints made by these being most delicate in the white marble. This inlaying was much more coarsely done than some I saw at Delhi, the art seeming to have been at its height at the time of the Mogul emperors. The pieces set into the marble are stuck fast by a fine kind of cement. One favorite mode of inlaying for coarser work is to put black marble into white. I have seen this in many other places as well as here.

This temple is designed for a kind of eleemosynary institution as well as for worship. Back of the main temple are long corridors of rooms and spaces in which food offered at the shrines will be given out to beggars. This provision, where there is so much poverty and extreme want as in India, would be most valuable if those needing it could get its benefit, but such as mostly profit by it are the lazy priests, fakirs, and devotees, who might better be at work to support themselves. There were rooms for women to live in on one side of the court. A busy mass of workmen were toiling here and there, some squaring the big blocks of sandstone, others deftly fashioning the marble-work, others inlaying, and a few, the sculptors, at work on the images. All were eager to show us about and answer the questions put to them. The chief architect showed and explained the plan to us, and could speak good English, having been educated in one of the government colleges. They do not build lofty structures in the East, like our churches and cathedrals, but like this one of two stories or platforms, with an uplift above those two. The cost of this magnificent pile is to be about thirty lacs of rupees, or a million dollars, and is borne by the rajah of the native State of Jeypore. He taxes his subjects mercilessly to raise the money for such a purpose.

From the temple yet building we went to the "Seth" temple, with vaster court area than the new one, and were permitted to go into only one part, the holiest place being inaccessible to such as we were. Fat priests sat reading Hindu books, with a pupil or two in front of them, or they lay under the perches stretched on mats to doze away existence. In this temple it is reported that eight thousand widows and other women live, compelled, those with me said, to pander to the vices of the throngs of priests and fakirs in the temple and about it. Most of these women were in the parts of the temple that we were not permitted to visit, though we saw a few of them, and these were veritable hags. We stopped to talk with a group of priests and pupils, to find that one of the young men could speak English, as he had been a student in one of the government colleges, and was purposing to return. The gates leading to this temple were huge and finely carved with figures of Vishnu, and also the Hindu triad.

Not far away was the well-known Govind Deva, a temple shaped like the cathedrals of Europe, built of the splendid red sandstone, and now falling into decay. How it came to be thus built is not known, but the surmise is that some European architect a century or two ago was commissioned to put up a temple, and so gave it the architectural cast of a Christian church. The nave, transepts, corridors, choir, and all the traditional parts of a cathedral are here. After seeing the temples built in Eastern style this one seemed very strange. During a Mohammedan conquest it was partly destroyed and then restored. Some most elaborate stone-carving is done, both inside and outside. Dr. Scott is calculating on using it some time as a Methodist church, and even had us suggest the place in its vast nave where the pulpit ought to be set! After all, stranger things than this have occurred in the conquest of the cross. Among the other temples visited in this holy city of the Hindus was that of Behari Lull, all lined inside with costly marble. This man now lives at Lucknow, but his temple is kept in tolerable condition. On its top are almost as many figures cut in marble as on the roof of the Milan cathedral. About it are also huge lions carved in stone, and twisted columns of exquisite symmetry. The richness of some Indian stonework is very great, if the taste is not along the approved lines of Western art.

The past season, when at the mela the multiplied thousands were here, our missionaries, both men and women, were on hand also, preaching Christ and his gifts to those religious devotees. The good done by such a course at such a time cannot be known, and is not always apparent, though in some instances men who have heard the missionaries at those places have come to them later to learn more or to receive baptism, while in other cases many have professed conversion and been baptized at the mela itself. Little opposition is made to such procedure by the Brahmans, though the strong arm of British law no doubt compels a salutary respect. Dr. Scott was preparing for a much more pretentious time at the coming season, and visited a rich native who had some buildings to rent, to secure them for himself and helpers against the ingathering in March. What a sight for a raw American to see, and how I should like to be that man!

LETTER XI.

AT AGRA.

I KNEW that three fine things awaited me at Agra: the promising mission work, the fort, and the wonderful Taj. The last was one of the few sights that out of the many I was to view going around the world I had greatly longed to see. Getting into the city at midnight from Muttra, Professor Foote and I went to the dak bungalow, not calling at Rev. Mr. Clancy's till after our *chota hazari*. It was too late for the delightful rides frequently offered me in the fresh, cool morning, but we were able to look over the mission property, which, as at Muttra, has made most commendable advance in the short time the place has been occupied by us. I think our mission has been established but a year and a half at this point. A broad plot of ground has been secured, on which was already a fine large building put up by some European, that affords ample room for both the missionary and the representatives of the Woman's Foreign Missionary Society. On one part Mr. Clancy has a church that will seat about five hundred people, nearly done, built of brick taken from the old city wall, where they were put by Akbar, and are doubtless three hundred years old. In another part a building for the use of the native girls who come to the city for attendance on the large government medical college is going up. Our mission schools are sending many finely educated young women here for a medical course, that after that they may do noble service for God, the Church, and their afflicted sisters of India. Among the workmen at both the church and women's building were many women, carrying mortar and bricks high up the ladders to the walls. I saw the same thing at Vienna. Christian Austria is thus, in the work of women, not a whit ahead of heathen India. But here, at least, it is a mercy to these poverty-smitten people to give the women a chance to earn a few pice a week to keep soul and body together. At the other building children as well as women were at work, boys not more than seven or eight years of age carrying baskets of dirt away like the older ones. In the East, when excavations are made, no carts or wheelbarrows are used, but workmen —women and boys and girls as well as men—carry the dirt away in baskets on their heads. I saw this done at road-building in Palestine and Egypt, as well as at all excavations in India; but in this, again, Christian Europe is not ahead of heathen India, for the same kind of work was done in the same way at the excavations in Pompeii. At the dirt-carrying in Agra the overseer stood with a bag of cowry shells, a hundred of them worth about an American cent, being used there as currency among the poor people and shop-keepers, and as each woman or child had carried off a basket of dirt and returned for another he gave to him a shell or two, making in this way a constant incentive to rapid transit. They said as much work could be obtained from the gang in half a day through this device as in a whole day without it. I noticed that each child would carry about three or four quarts of dirt at a time, while the women would bear away about a peck. There being a large number at work, they looked like a row of ants coming and going.

The fort is an immense thing and a fitting monumental relic of the Mohammedan occupation. They say it is a mile and a half around it, and in the times of poor artillery and less scientific modes of military attack it must have been well-nigh impregnable. It was one of the few places away from the sea-coast that during the terrible Sepoy rebellion was successfully held by the British. We entered a huge gate-way across a deep moat to find red sandstone walls sixty feet or so in height, here and there mounted with some antiquated cannon, and used only to be preserved. The British soldiery occupy it now as a kind of arsenal, and into some parts of the spacious inclosure they do not allow visitors to go. In Akbar's time it was more than a fort, since it inclosed his palace, judgment-hall, mosque, and other royal needs, as well as the barracks and fortress for his armies. The judgment-hall is now walled up where formerly it was open, the roof having been sustained by strong columns. The portico, which the emperor occupied to execute judgment, is yet open; and they showed us the wide black marble slab on which he used to sit during those fatal hours. Two immense wooden doors, composed of the sweet-smelling sandal-wood, are carefully preserved, having been captured at Somnath by Lord Ellenborough in his Afghan campaign, and brought here for preservation. They are wonderful specimens of the work that Eastern despots used to have done, as they had at their command almost limitless resources of wealth and work. They are richly carved and inlaid, while on one panel are three metal bosses, said once to have been on the shield of an Afghan emperor.

The palace proper is quadrangular, like most of those Eastern buildings, inclosing a court laid out in fine gardens, walks, groves, and shady nooks. Much of it all is dilapidated, yet enough remaining to attest the magnificence of this once royal residence. Here were separate sections for the different kinds of wives, one for the Hindu wives, one for the Mohammedan, one for the Persian, and so on. It is claimed that he also had one European wife. Near by is the deep well, now mostly walled in, where he used to drown his bad-tempered or faithless spouses. What tales all this old palace could tell! A parchesi board lies in a small court that is forty feet across, composed of party-colored marbles, on which the game was played, with beautiful girls to run hither and thither in place of the ivory pieces when the game was played by hand. It is now damp and moss-grown from disuse. Below were wide spaces among arches, columns, and corners, where the royal wives were said to have played hide and seek with merry laughter and shout, clad only in Eve's habiliments before the fall. Far down we entered the beginnings of a passage that was said to lead under the river to the Taj, and a second one to Secundra, five miles away, where is the mausoleum of the renowned Akbar. Doubtless these are mere rumors that have no truth in them, but there is little knowing what those old despots would take a notion to have done when they had so much wealth and labor at their disposal. Among the most artistic things seen was the canopy over one of the royal seats, a single piece of marble eight feet in diameter, most exquisitely carved and inlaid. The Palace of Glass is a bath of fine proportions, about the walls of which are thousands of little mirrors set at all angles, each mirror being about as large as a silver dollar. Nothing made me think of the *Arabian Nights* as much as this room. The fountains in it, the bubbling water, the little cascade, all suggested the wondrous stories of that marvelous collection.

For the emperor's worship there was the Pearl Mosque, and a pearl it is. Like the one in the old fort in Delhi, it is small, but the perfection of Saracenic art. It stands on a platform of red sandstone, and within has none of the tawdry show of worship to be found in some of the Christian sanctuaries, but a marble tesselated floor marking a spot where the devotee can kneel for prayer with his face turned toward Mecca. Pity it is that those Moslems in the East have so divorced worship and morality. The terrible climate of India is touching every thing in and about this old fort; worn sandstone and marble, broken columns and doorways, moss-covered walls and crumbling brick-work, all show the sure and swift decay.

The Taj is a mile out of the city and immediately on the banks of the Jumna. About it lie scattered other tombs and mausoleums, for the Taj is a tomb itself, built by the great Shah Jehan over the remains of his dearly loved wife. If it is barren and suggestive of desolation and death about the Taj, one enters a true Eastern paradise when he approaches the building, for a large space is walled off for fine gardens, walks, and fountains, through which wall you enter the gardens by a magnificent gate-way of sandstone and of black and white marble, in some instances inlaid in quaint, beautiful designs and texts from the Koran. The government protects all this elegance of gate-way, walls, gardens, and tombs, so that they shall not fall into decay nor be despoiled by vandal hands.

As you stand at the gate looking in, the Taj is seen three or four hundred yards away, white and still, through a perspective of trees that reach out their green leaves and branches over the walks and fountains. The gardens and groves cover many acres inside the walls, and serve actually as a botanical place, the well-posted Scotchman in general charge being eager to get some American ferns to add to the fine lot of Asiatic ones he already possessed. Trees and ferns I could see in other countries and in other parts of India, but there is only one Taj in the world, so I urged forward to that. As we came near I saw the building stood fronting us as we approached from the south, and was on a white marble platform three or four hundred yards long and two hundred wide, with a height of about twenty feet. In the center of this platform stands the Taj. At each end, on a slightly lower plane than the Taj, is a mosque where the sad emperor could worship as he came to the tomb of his departed love, the one at the west end being used for this purpose, while that at the east end was put up, they said, as a companion-piece to complete the artistic effect. The tall minarets, that are indescribably graceful in their slim, straight beauty, rise at proper distances from the Taj and the two mosques. They are almost always a copy of the great Khutab Minar near Delhi.

As we came upon the platform a genteel guide approached offering to show us about, but that was not necessary for Professor Foote and me as long as we had in Mr. Clancy one who had been there so many times. My first impressions of this building were to be overwhelming, I supposed, and when I was not so overwhelmed I was disappointed. Who would not expect to be profoundly moved at its presence after reading Dr. William Butler's fine description and that of Bayard Taylor? But there I was in the presence of the charmer, and it seemed only a fine structure of white marble,

Oriental in outline and make, but not marvelous at all. Was it that I was sated by the vast sight-seeing of the months since I had left home, or was I too tired that day, or was the Taj a thing too highly extolled? We went into it, about it, down into the crypt, off to the ends of the platform, entered the mosques, and came out of them to look again, so as to give the building all the chances possible to captivate; yet even under the enthusiasm of Mr. Clancy added to all the rest I did not become enthusiastic. A similar lack affected Professor Foote.

Inside, on a level with the platform, is the large open space under the dome, which rises a hundred feet or more above you. Here, within a railed space, is a duplicate of the tombs of the beautiful Noor Jehan and her royal husband side by side, as they really are in the crypt below. Every word or noise under the great dome is sent back in an echo that is far the finest I have ever heard, even after the famous ones of Naples and the Yosemite. A second story forms passages with the elegant fret-work that is the delight of all travelers, yet which is more substantial by far than I had supposed, the marble from which the tracery is cut being two or three inches thick and far too substantial to suggest floating away. Much of it is inlaid with precious stones, carnelians and agates seeming to predominate. Every-where the white marble is also inlaid in black marble with texts from the Koran, until it is claimed that the whole book is thus preserved. The real tombs of the empress and of Akbar below were very richly inlaid; the rose at the head of the former was said to have had in its center a fine diamond, and one could see where it had been picked out by some thief. In several places the inlaying was most beautiful and costly. After two or three hours we went away, still not greatly charmed, but with a plan to come in the evening after the moon was up and see it by that witching light.

We waited until the moon, just at the full, most fortunately, was an hour high, and then found our way again to the grounds of the Taj. It was smoky, so that a weird dimness partially hid it as we approached, but as we passed through the gate-way along the avenues of trees I saw it was with a different effect from the morning. Little sound save the distant howl of a few jackals and dogs disturbed the quiet; the men and boys at work about the gardens in the day were all gone, and no one, save the sleepy guards, the silent guides, and a visitor or two like us, was to be seen. Mr. Clancy said the impression of a bubble ready to float in the air was created in his mind by the rounded dome, but I could not catch such a feeling. The moon was at just the height to throw a shadow most richly on the west side of the white Taj the same time that the east side glittered with a soft, pearly radiance in the full light of that orb. We never know the light of the sun or moon in America as they do in India. The nearest the moon's light comes in America to look as it did that night is when its full rays glow upon the winter snow. The light and shade about minarets, the dome, the corners, and recesses, added greatly to our ability to comprehend the structure and to take its effects into our minds. Again we went inside to listen to the echo. The space seems to have a certain key-note, so that words spoken at a particular tone and some of the strains of singing filled it and prolonged the echo as other words and tones did not. The echo—such is the shape and size of the dome—is sweet and soft and exceedingly musical. It floats about the space, at first almost as loud as the originating sound, and gradually grows less and less, but so slowly as to linger much longer than you would expect it to do. The later refrains become so distant and sweet that they seem to be not of the earth, but of the far-away heaven. We wondered if Akbar did not come there at night, and, as we did, seem to hold converse with heavenly visitants, his visitant, of course, the one for whom his passion was so great. We sang familiar hymns, to listen to the strains of Christian song come back from the dome where the Moslem Akbar would have counted it most despicable to have such Christian sounds occur or such Christian infidels stand.

By this time the Taj began to get me into its power. I was perfectly willing to be captivated if it had the power to do so, and thus did not struggle against it, nor would I seek captivation by straining after it. Then we went out and around the platform, getting views from every side. It was quiet, rich, solemn, and so unearthly as to seem almost ghostly; no one wanted to talk loudly, and even the heavy footsteps of our thick shoes seemed out of place. A man and woman, Western people of some nation, were wandering about the same as we were doing. Mr. Clancy said he had an impression, as he walked from it, that it would all vanish as the airy structure of a dream, but I did not feel so. He says that he is more and more impressed with its unique beauty every time he visits it. The cry of some water-birds a few hundred yards down the river was a pleasant break to the impressions that came to me, for I was getting under the spell more and more. The glitter of the golden star and crescent above the dome was in fine contrast with the subdued pearly gleam of the spotless marble below.

Then we went off the platform among the trees of the garden to get views from that vantage ground. We would so stand that the upper part only could be seen, the dome and towers and minarets, while all below was hidden by the trees, but still it did not seem to float, though it greatly enhanced the beauty, for the white above flooded with moonlight was in charming contrast with the vivid green below. The white seemed more pearly than before, the dim distance heightening that effect. The minarets, that had seemed taller in the moonlight than in the day-time, when seen from among the trees seemed even more graceful than before, and disconnected through the green leaves they at least appeared to me as though they might float away. We tried the view from twenty points of outlook, now with the whole dome in sight and the minarets hidden; then with the dome hidden and the minarets in sight; then only small sections of each dome and minarets seen through a space as a green-encircled perspective. The thick mango-trees and others thus aided us in an endless series of views, each different from the others, and each new one presenting new phases of beauty and enchantment. Finally, seeking the flagged walk leading back to the great gate-way, we walked slowly backward to see the changing aspects thus offered. Once the pointed graceful tamarisks shot up into the white walls of the Taj like great inlaid columns of green marble; then as we receded the dome and towers and minarets seemed indeed to rise gradually, more and more the farther we went back, till at last the dome and all did seem to float out on the light air, and the full impression of that enchantment came to me. I gave one long gaze to photograph it on my memory, and turned away saying that should be my last look, and hurried toward the gate-way. I went thirty feet, it may be, clinging to my purpose, when the wonderful thing overcame that purpose to get away—I could but turn and take one more look, as the departing lover might turn and take one more look on the one he is leaving; but once turned I gazed again and again, now with my face directly toward the Taj, now over my shoulder, till I stood on the raised platform leading out of the gate. Then I knew I must take a last look. In the haze and distance it had grown dimmer and dimmer, yet it was able to be distinguished, the dome, walls, minarets; and all these were also distinctly shadowed in the still water in the tanks down the wide avenue leading from the gate-way to the Taj. Gazing hard so as never to forget its vision, I finally turned, passed through the gateway to the carriage, and rode away with a little feeling that it was all a dream. O, the beautiful, wonderful Taj!

LETTER XII.

NANAK, THE PUNJAB REFORMER.

INDIA is a hot-bed of religions. Hinduism supplanted an extensive system of early practices among the Turanian aborigines, fragments of which remain to this time in tree-worship, devil-worship, and the like. Then the elaborate Hindu religion, after holding sway here for two thousand years, was compelled to meet in life-and-death struggle with Mohammedanism, the latter being propagated, not only by the sword, but by preachers, missionaries, and by all those influences so likely to be urged by conquerors. Last of all has come Christianity, for the first time meeting these great systems fairly, as it has met and overcome other great religious systems. It follows that such religious ferment as must have always been going on here would produce religious fanatics, teachers, and leaders. Buddha, one of the greatest figures in the world's history, arose as a reformer. Another, less known, and whose influence, not so great as that of Buddha, has yet been very important in modern times, was Nanak. He was born near Lahore, in the Punjab, in 1469, and died in 1539. His effort along humanitarian lines was to combine the best from the Hindu and Mohammedan religions, reconcile these two antagonistic races, and form out of their worthy beliefs a wholesome system that should be better for both. To attain this he accepted the mission and claims of the Arabian prophet, and at the same time the reputed incarnations of Vishnu. In the very age when Luther and Calvin and Zwinglius were seeking to change the trend of the Christian Church from bad to better the Indian reformer was struggling with a similar problem in India. The Indian reformer's problem met with poorer success than that of his contemporaries in Europe, and after some variations of fortune through the generations the project degenerated into a warlike movement.

Nanak seems to have begun his public life by becoming an ascetic, like all religious teachers among the Indians, but, gradually becoming dissatisfied with the life and teachings of those about him, he struck out a new path. In the Indian speech an exalted teacher is a guru, and such he became, and is so called by his followers. His teachings during his life-time, while forming a large share of the sacred books of the Sikhs, called Granth, have had much added to them by later gurus, of whom, including Nanak, they reckon ten. After four of these gurus' time, whose teachings, calculated to lead to purer lives and more nearly correct beliefs, had attracted a large following, the sect became troublesome to the rulers of the Punjab as partisans and even as rebels. The city of Amritsar was selected by the fifth guru as the sacred one of the Sikhs, and it is still considered such by them, though representatives and teachers of this religion are to be found over all the country.

The Granth, now accessible to English readers through a good translation, is the best witness to the tenets of the reformer and the system since grown from them. It is probable that his teachings were not committed to writing at first, though how they were preserved is uncertain; but after three or four generations they and the additions were written out, and are now treated with more than reverence, being actually worshiped systematically at Amritsar. At that city, in the middle of a wide tank of water, stands a beautiful white marble temple, under the golden dome of which is the Granth spread out on a silver stand richly adorned, where a continuous stream of worshipers is coming and going. Musicians chant the praises of this worshiped book, priests wait on its altar as on the altar of a god. At the close of a day's services the tired book is carried to a house near by, where on a rich soft bed it is supposed to sleep and recuperate for another day of toil. The book became thus sacred owing to the course of the tenth and last guru, Govind, who, instead of nominating his successor, as the gurus did before him, declared the Granth as the form of the guru, and that any Sikh wanting to confer with the guru would find him embodied in the book. The Sikhs consider the guru their incarnated mediator between Hari, the Great God, and themselves, in this being like the adherents of almost every great religion, dimly reaching out into the darkness after the Desire of all nations.

Of course the purpose of Nanak to combine the two faiths failed. There are so many things in them which are utterly antagonistic that it could be supposed it might have been seen from the beginning. Indeed, Govind, the last guru, repudiated both Hindu and Mohammedan teachings in many respects, and himself taught that God is not to be found save in humility and sincerity. The One God was to be served, superstitions were to be abandoned, pure morals kept. Still, in many respects the reformers, from Nanak to Govind, were not wholly able to emancipate themselves from the philosophy and tenets surrounding them. Starting at first as a peaceful, reforming faith, it became by the teachings of the last guru a faith of the sword, to be propagated by that the same as Islam. The caste system so dreadful in the Hindu cult, while declaimed against by Nanak, continued to be tolerated, and finally has as rigid lines dividing its two classes now, householders and mendicants, as the Hindu beliefs. If in the start Nanak, as claimed, urged the brotherhood of man, there came need in the early history of the Sikhs that the reformation itself, in this respect, should be reformed. While having a wife and two sons, he favored ascetic practices by his own life and teachings, though he put a nobler construction on the family life than many other Indian reformers. He placed great stress upon another Hindu religious custom, that of repeating the name of a god, or muttering. The name of the Great God, Hari, is thus to be uttered continuously, by which course many and important blessings would come to the devotee.

Nor was Nanak more fortunate in his dealings with the theory of transmigration, that awful shadow hanging over all Hindu life and practice. The old belief that many hundred thousands of these changes must take place before man was perfected for heaven was accepted by the Sikhs. Nanak's scheme, while remotely teaching theism, can also easily be accused of being pantheistic, since mankind and all material things are but the forms of Hari. The whole creation, according to some of his teachings, is but a self-evolving of God. Still, in this faith, as in many of the Indian books, glaring contradictions are easily to be found. In Nanak's system it would naturally follow that contradictions in respect to this question should occur, since Mohammedanism teaches a pure theism and Hinduism extreme pantheism.

The outcome of Nanak's proposed reform is doubtless much different from what the reformer hoped. There has been no fusion of the two old faiths. Instead of peaceful, contemplative religious practices the Sikhs became vindictive warriors. After Govind's death, who, by his teachings and by the military organization of the Sikhs, had prepared them for their new destiny, they sought independent existence, fought with one and another of the rulers of the Punjab, till, on the decay of the Mogul Empire, they so succeeded in their purpose of autonomy that by 1764 their organization was perfected, their commonwealth, consisting of twelve States, made up. Most of these Sikhs were of the Jat race, supposed to be distinct from Hindus and Mohammedans, a strong, tall, brave people. They issued at this time their own coin, and took other steps as a free State. At the close of the last century, and the first forty years of this, they had an able, ambitious leader in the famous Runjeet Singh, who, appealing to arms, gradually subdued neighboring chiefs with his "Lions of the Punjab," and, pushing his successful armies, drilled by European officers to great efficiency, into Afghanistan, conquered Cashmere and Peshawur. He obtained from an Afghan king the famous diamond Kohinoor, which later came into possession of the British crown. At his death the Sikh power, the military product of the peaceful Nanak's teachings, controlled twenty millions of people. In ten years from that time it had been utterly shattered by bloody contact with the British power in two wars, and all the Punjab was annexed to the English dominion. Every good Sikh hopes for the time when they shall return to power in greater splendor than ever before. But England made good use of the brave Sikhs, for many of them were soon incorporated into the native contingent, and when the mutiny arose in 1857 they generally remained loyal to the British, doing some noble fighting before Delhi and elsewhere, by which they greatly aided in establishing British supremacy in India. They could the more readily remain true in such a struggle when Hindu and Mohammedan were united against the British, since their own existence as a nation began by repudiating the faith of both those peoples.

Nanak's religious followers are now variously estimated to number from half a million to three times that number. While holding many Hindu and Mohammedan beliefs and customs, they still appear to come nearer to Christianity, in the doctrine of God, if not in personal purity, than either. Their teachers are earnestly listened to by many people, as at melas and other gatherings they appear as public instructors. In our mission at Moradabad and about there our missionaries have come in contact with many Sikhs, one of whom, an old teacher, earnestly and diligently seeking more light, finally, in hearing of Christ and Christianity, heartily accepted the truth. Many of the same sect, nominally, at least, accepted our faith, when, in 1868, a deep spiritual work passed over them, since which time numbers from among them have become preachers, exhorters, teachers, and successful members of our native churches. Nanak himself, were he now living, might become a grand preacher in the Methodist Church.

LETTER XIII.

A DAY AMONG INDIA'S PAUPERS.

It was the 21st of December at Cawnpore. For fifteen years it has been the custom at this place to raise a sum of money in the English-speaking Methodist church to buy presents for a crowd of mendicants, the things given being clothing, flour, salt, and the like. It is done for the holiday season as a Christmas gift. This year about seventy-five dollars had been raised. Every Sunday during the year a couple of Englishmen, members of this church, the Foy Brothers, in important business here, have such native poor as will do so come to their bungalow, where they preach to them, both these men being local preachers. To each of these natives they give a pice, half a cent, every Sunday. The people who listen to that Sunday teaching and preaching are the ones to whom the Christmas presents are given. The distribution took place under wide-spreading trees in front of the home or bungalow of the Foy Brothers. There were assembled when I reached the place two hundred or more natives, with some American missionaries and other Western people, besides several employees and police of the bungalow. A Bible and hymn-books were brought out, one of the Foys read from the first chapter of Matthew of Christ's birth, a hymn or two were sung, and prayer offered by the native pastor. Two or three of the visitors spoke to the motley crowd in the vernacular, to whom they listened well for heathen beggars.

During this time I had a chance to look at them. They were the most miserable mass of humanity I have ever seen. Seated on the ground, each one only partially covered with ragged, dirty cotton cloth, they had evidences of many kinds of disease. Such evidences could the more easily be seen for their arms, legs, heads, and brown bodies were mostly naked, though it was winter season. Many were lepers, whom they permit to associate with every body in India, their fingers and toes gone, their noses or ears eaten off, while others had great white blotches where on their skin the awful disease had begun its work. The sores of leprosy are dryer than I had supposed, so dry that they usually do not have to be bandaged. Others not touched with the fatal leprosy were blind, or lame, or broken in health, or old; some with skin diseases, or warped out of shape by rheumatism, or cripples from their birth. Possibly an American city like New York could furnish such a revolting mass of beggars, but I doubt it. One of the blind men had been taught to read with raised letters, and had his book with him, though it possibly was owned by the Christian mission.

Not all the mass that sat there in the tropical sun that day belonged to the hundred or so that gathered to hear Sunday preaching, and as these were all certain to get some present the others constantly sought to cross the dividing-line between the two classes and mingle with the elect ones. It was interesting to watch them hitch along the ground or suddenly try to dart across the space when the backs of the Foy watchmen were turned. As the religious services closed the beggars were conducted by these attendants and police in twos and threes to the place where the piles of clothing and food were awaiting distribution. During this movement I was able to see better than while they were sitting the dreadful suffering of some of these people ; and as I had just come from the scene of the bloody Cawnpore massacre during the Sepoy rebellion the two combined to break my heart. These little groups were so pathetic! An old couple, gray and shriveled, tottered along side by side, each sustaining the other; one would go hanging heavily on another's shoulder; a blind woman was led away by her old husband; two blind young men were directed by an old woman, presumably their mother, while another blind one, a stalwart young man, was directed by a ten-year-old girl holding one end of a stick while he clung to the other end. Men with their fingers eaten off by the leprosy would come holding up the stumps to awaken pity ; others hobble along with their toes gone. A woman whose lips and mouth were covered with a huge cancerous growth came and stood mutely waiting for her dole, her great black eyes being the most beautiful I ever saw, soft, lustrous, and gentle as a deer's. One woman could not walk, her limbs being so drawn out of shape, but sitting on the ground she went along hitch by hitch, a few inches at a time. Soon after her came a man moving in the same way, whose fingers were gone, and his feet to the instep, with leprosy. The photographs on my memory of that hour will never fade.

The garments given out were jackets made of cotton puff, thick and warm, some skirts for the women, a few coarse chuddars, the enveloping garment for women, covering the body and head, and also a few thick goat's-hair blankets. About a hundred and fifty garments were given away, only one to each person. Farther on they had some bags of coarse flour which they gave out in doles of a quart or two to each, and a handful of coarse salt. Many of those not included in the Sunday attendants received some of these things. Here they vociferated, crowded, and almost fought to get at the distributers, for the native attendants and police could not make them mind like the English at the clothing-pile. They took the flour and salt in their dirty old chuddars, or garments, and reluctantly went away. I was anxious to see how the man whose fingers and feet were eaten off by leprosy, and who was hitching along on his haunches, would carry off his flour and salt. They had given the poor thing a cotton jacket, which he had flung over his shoulders; in the bend made by hitching up his legs he had an old rag that he spread out on the ground, into which he received the flour and salt. The latter he carefully gathered into a brass can slung under one arm, then he rolled up the flour in the rag and put it in its place in front of his body and went hitching off. Even one old fakir was there, a saintly old Brahman, whose six-corded string, tied over his bare brown shoulder, was as precious to him as the witness of the Spirit is to a Methodist. The old women were the most veritable hags I have ever seen, there being nothing beautiful in aged heathenism. A few Christian women, some of them gray, were helping take care of the crowd, and their looks were noticeably different from those of their pagan sisters. I was glad that the Foy brothers, after twenty or thirty years of contact with these people, had warm hearts toward them, for after all they were men and women. But O, what men and women! Heathenism's fruit!

LETTER XIV.

ANNUAL SUNDAY-SCHOOL GALA AT LUCKNOW.

It is always held at the Christmas season. This year the English-speaking school had its picnic December 27, the native schools theirs on December 28. Ever after my purpose to travel through India this winter I had planned to be here at these gatherings. The note of preparation had been heard for a long time, as they began to collect money in November, getting four hundred rupees, which were used in presents and prizes. The prizes were given for regular attendance, committing Scripture verses, and other excellencies and attainments. The *fêtes* are held in Wingfield Park, which has ample grounds, good swards, delightful drives and walks, where all can fully enjoy themselves. The park and its trees and flowers do not hint of winter as Americans think of that season. None of the trees are leafless, but those like our deciduous ones have massive tops of heavy green leaves. Besides these are some palms, the date, fan, sago, and others, with their long columnar trunks if fully grown, or those just starting from new settings. Along the walks are early beds of pansies set out but two or three days, but already blooming, while near by are groups of rose-bushes, with enough blossoms to show what varieties they are and how great will be their magnificence when, a month later, they will be in full bloom. The closely clipped grass is kept green by irrigation, the same as all the plants are watered. Gigantic growth of bignonias climb over trellises or to the top of some old tree, the orange-colored blossoms just beginning to adorn their leafy columns with great clusters of pleasing forms. Morning-glories, creepers, poinsettas, and other climbers are trained in picturesque places, and send out visions of color and beauty that tell little of icy Christmas seasons. Birds twitter through the trees and shrubs; among them the classic bulbul, with its self-assertive top-knot, pretty scarlet and black markings, is an attractive figure. The hum of the cricket, the lazy flight of a butterfly, the sun beating down so strong that I dare not stand in its glare save when covered with an umbrella, so combine to deceive my time-calculations that I am not having a real Christmas, but a summer picnic season.

At eleven o'clock, the 27th, the children and grown folks were all gathered under a wide awning, where singing, prayer, and some words from a Wesleyan missionary and myself were spoken; then the prizes were awarded, presents distributed, and a good time generally enjoyed. Ample tables were spread at which the children first were served, then the grown people. In the meantime three elephants, with huge wooden saddles, had been brought to the grounds for our use, and many a boy and girl, both small and large, was quite willing to lose the dainty cakes, sweet-meats, and fruit in order to secure the coveted ride on the elephant. As a part of my riding around the world I ought, of course, to ride on an elephant, so here was my chance. Behold, then, Dr. B. H. Badley and myself sitting on the wide wooden *howdah*, facing one way, while an American and an English lady sit facing the other way, having climbed to our places by means of a short ladder.

The elephant has crouched down at the command of his driver, who, sitting astride its neck, uses to enforce his commands a sharp, murderous-looking iron prod, and, as the load is completed, at a cluck from the driver, the huge animal begins to get on its feet. The first part of the rise is to its forefeet, which causes a lurch of every body to the rear, then getting on its hind feet causes another lurch forward. Once risen, the great beast moves off with four or six persons on his back as though they were feathers. The motion of elephant-riding is apt to cause nausea, like the motion of a ship at sea. They allowed the "Sahib" from America the chance of three rides, none of which was very lengthy. A merry-go-round, a revolving swing, some athletic exercises, etc., were able to keep the children interested till late in the afternoon.

The really great day of the gala was the 28th, when the thirteen native boys' schools, represented by about sixteen hundred pupils, had their good time. Early in the morning a note from Dr. Badley to me informed me that I was expected to meet them at the native church and head the procession through Lucknow on the back of a big elephant. Of course I hurried there, and was soon, with himself and others, on the foremost of six elephants leading such a procession as this world seldom sees. Five government elephants were loaded with the prize boys of the schools, then following was a line full half a mile long of boys with their teachers, each school designated by an appropriate banner; and Mr. Maxwell's printing-office was also represented by a hundred of its workmen and a fine banner. Those on the elephants carried flags of England and the United States. Each school had its native band also, the music being of various grades of merit and many varieties of kinds. Flutes, fifes, drums, bugles, and others made at least a noisy demonstration. The people of the city flocked to the street sides to see us, and many came on their house-tops. By special favor our elephant, once a wild one in the jungles, but now fully obedient to the driver's word, was stopped that we might see the great procession as it slowly passed us. The boys enjoyed it, and every face was beaming with excitement and interest.

In Wingfield Park the boys were seated on carpets under the same awning used the day before, with the teachers, friends, and visitors outside. A hymn, prayer, then singing by a chosen lot from six of the schools for a prize that was awarded to a group of four boys whose performance was highly creditable. Four much smaller boys stood in that great gathering, not one of them ten years old, and sang most sweetly, forming a picture, as they stood in front of their banner, such as is full of hope and promise to India. The prizes given out by Dr. Badley were silver rupees and Dr. Kidder's centennial medal. They were awarded those who had committed the Golden Texts, the selected verses, the topics, and the outlines of the year's lessons. Twelve pupils were also honored who had been present every Sunday. Three or four of us talked a little to the boys, who were enthusiastic, and, by a sweeping vote, sent their *salaam* by me to President Harrison in the United States. That gathering was a strange one to a new visitor. Such bright black eyes, such expressive brown faces, such endless variety of costumes! These boys were mostly Hindu and Mohammedan boys, but, being taught in the day-schools in different parts of the city, and every Sunday in the Sunday-school, their lessons for all days are in the vernacular. Many of them are being led to Christ, and a great number believe, but owing to home surroundings delay in publicly confessing him. Dr. Badley says he has a mortgage on them all. The Centennial High School, Dr. Badley's immediate charge, has many Christian boys going through a course of study about equal to American college preparation, but beyond this the doctor is taking a fine class through freshman studies this year as the starting out of the Lucknow College that will carry students to the B. A. degree. Land to build such a college has been donated by the government, and work will soon begin on the building. I think such a college is demanded to conserve our church interests and to hold to us the young men educated by us to matriculation.

As these Hindu, Mohammedan, and Christian boys crowd close to each other under the awning at Wingfield Park you can see in them one of the most hopeful promises for our work in India. Look at them. Their jaunty student caps by no means cover their fine-shaped heads, but sit lightly on the top, and are of as many colors as we can think of. Mostly white, but red, brown, green, blue, some like open lace, others elaborately worked with needle-work and gold or silver threads, they present a variety far beyond an American gathering of women at the season of changing millinery. Then the coats, vests, pants, slippers, and other parts of clothing almost defy description. One nawab's son, not in a Sunday-school, was shown us. He had a gold-trimmed cap with a silver tassel of large size, massive gold chains and a locket about his neck, a coat of bright colors also gold-wrought, a green silk skirt, white stockings, and leather shoes. A young man wore a purple needle-worked cap, a brilliantly yellow coat of silk lined with red and edged with the same, while his pants were a tobacco-brown. These people seem to catch their colors from the brilliant plumage of the birds, the bright tint of their flowers, and the burning light of the sun as it floods the rich landscape, and then put it all into their adornments. This taste would appear gaudy under the gray skies of America, but I have not felt pained by it here. Natives put into English suits do not look well. Their native costumes fit them much better. In the mass under the awning a few of the pupils had their foreheads painted to show their special native deity, but not more than half a dozen in all the large numbers. It was a great thing for them to enter such a procession, to sit with others, and to remove their forehead paint. Christianity is working its way into Indian life.

If they were willing to mingle in a Christian procession, sing Christian songs, and carry Christian banners, they could not overstep caste lines enough to eat together. So, on the dismissal of the crowd from the awning, each school divided into two or three groups, the Hindus by themselves, the Mohammedans the same, thus compelling a third group, the Christians. Each group gathered under some wide-spreading tree, where in the shade they ate their sweets. In the case of the Hindus men of their own caste came along to see that none was defiled or any mistakes made in the observances. I wandered out among these strange groups to find at every place a separate lot of candy, or sweets, as they call it here, having besides candy variously made sweetmeats, at making which the Indians excel. Two or three men would be dividing out these confections with funny little plates or basins made of leaves. So thick and tough are many of these native leaves that they can be pinned by twigs into such cups and perfectly serve their purposes. Each pupil received from a quarter to a half pound of these sweets, and was made as glad by them as the boys would be in America. But here was an odd thing. Almost every boy did up his sweets in a handkerchief, or otherwise, to carry them home to his parents and other members of the family. His respect for them would not permit him to monopolize his rich dainties. When I approached one group of Hindus and began closely to look at the confections the head-master of that school warned me, in tone not to be mistaken, not to touch any of the food. It is impossible for us, with our ideas, to comprehend the restrictions of caste in this and other ways. At another place they gave me in the leaf-basket a pupil's allowance of the refreshments.

The meaning to our mission of such a day is very great. Such displays attract attention in various ways, serve to lead other children to the day and Sunday schools, carry conviction to those who see them of the grand success of our Church, and have been blessed in many ways. Then the Hindus and Mohammedans have so many holidays, melas, and other gatherings that to give the Christian children a similar festival once in a while does much good. A similar gala was observed this year by our mission at Cawnpore. Our missionaries have learned much wisdom in pushing our work, and in some ways they are having such success as no other missionaries are having. I am glad to see this success and to be at Lucknow at the Christian *fête*.

LETTER XV.

CASTE.

No one at all familiar with India but has heard about caste. From its use here it has become a word hateful to all reasonable people. Still, to some, even in our own home-land, others must be of their own grade or clique to receive much recognition or encouragement. Christianity intends to do away with all this kind of thing, but evidently has not wholly done it in the home churches, though more nearly there than anywhere else in the world. Here, instead of being a mere nominal thing, it is a most elaborate, far-reaching power, with results and practices that in their minutiæ are of the most exacting nature. Knowing our aversion as Westerners and Christians to such things, a transient and casual observer like me does not see very much of it, though enough still to show some of the horrible things that can be done in its name.

They say here that the word is the Anglicized form of the Portuguese word *casta*, meaning race, and from that people came into use by the English to denote the different classes into which the Hindus are divided. Some one has suggested that probably the system of caste had its origin, not in religious sentiments and practices, but in those of a division of labor and duties inhering in the natural condition of conquerors and conquered people. Indication can be found of this in the Hindu *jati*, race, applied to the system, and *varna*, color, since the conquering Aryans greatly prided themselves on their color being lighter than that of the aboriginal tribes they found in India. Far back in their sacred books, the Vedas, it is found that only two castes were recognized, the Aryans and the Dasyus. The first were the lordly Hindus, the Aryans, who in those times came down from Central Asia into the plains and valleys of India, and, wresting this country from the aboriginal tribes, the Turanians, called them the Dasyus, the second caste. This dispossessed race was driven before the more civilized Hindus into the hills, jungles, and mountains, or else were partly incorporated with the conquerors as servants and slaves. From these conditions seem to have arisen the Hindu terms of the system, for the two races were much different in many ways, perpetuating, no doubt, all the usual race antipathies likely to arise under conquest and contrast. The long residence of the Turanian tribes in the tropical climate had no doubt made them brown or black before the Aryan conquest.

Manu, the great Indian lawgiver, has as fanciful an origin of caste as even the most wonderfully imaginative Indian could wish. He makes the number of castes four. To begin with, Brahma was born in a golden egg, and then, that the world might be peopled, this god caused the Brahman to issue from his mouth, the Kshatriya from his arms, the Vaisya from his thighs, and the Sudra from his feet. The Brahmans were the priests, the Kshatriyas the warriors, kings, and rajahs, the Vaisyas the householders or farmers, while the Sudras, those native tribes that embraced the Brahman religion, were given menial duties. Those of the native tribes that did not yield to the claims of the hierarchy were the Dasyus, or outcasts, and to them,

8

such as were in subjection to the Hindus, were assigned the most degrading duties, and despised accordingly.

Bearing in mind that the real origin of caste must have been from the different races and general division of duties as a more civilized community developed, the increase of those castes from two or four to the multitudes that are now to be seen about one is to be traced, no doubt, to the division of duties and employments that would naturally be demanded as a vast increase in population and industries took place. But the fanciful Indian accounts for the increase of them according to his own tropical imagination the same as he does for their origin. Manu is again authority for saying that the four original castes intermarried various ways, and so gave rise to sixteen different castes, and these again by intermarrying produced the multitudinous ones of later times. But beyond their real multiplication through the division of employment no doubt other causes were operative, as the division of castes already established into clans that in time grew to be independent, the separations that would naturally occur among the people through jealousies and quarrels who were not firmly held together by national coherency, and also by the differences of thought and practices that would be likely to arise through the adoption of new gods, dogmas, and religious rites. In all these things the ferment, which must have been even greater in past ages than that now seen in India, might most easily and naturally have produced caste as now found.

The lordly Brahman during those ages was not modest in the assumptions for himself or light in the punishments inflicted on the lowly Sudras. They say that when the Brahman came into the world he was born above the world; was the chief of all creatures, with the idea that whatever exists in the universe is all his property. Poor fellow! If I should judge by some of the naked, dirty beggars I have seen belonging to this caste they must be dreadfully defrauded out of their rights. Even if a Brahman should be occupied in crimes of any sort, the king, they taught, should not slay him, but might put him out of the kingdom in possession of all his property and uninjured in body; and since no greater wrong is found on earth than killing a Brahman the king should not even mentally consider his death. The lowly caste of Sudras, however, could not claim such amenities. If one killed a Sudra only such observances should be practiced as those practiced for killing a cat, an ichneumon, a daw, or a frog, a lizard, an owl, or a crow. The Sudras, the books teach, were created merely for the service of the Brahmans, and the latter may take possession of the goods of the former with perfect peace of mind, for nothing at all belongs to the Sudras. Not less strange was the punishment decreed upon a luckless Sudra who should fall into evil-speaking of a Brahman. For violent words toward a Brahman a Sudra ought to have his tongue cut out; for insulting his name and caste, a red-hot iron, ten fingers long, should be thrust into his mouth; if, through insolence, he should presume to give instruction to the priests the king should cause boiling oil to be poured into his ear and mouth. No religious instruction should be given a Sudra, but if any one did it both he and the Sudra taught would sink into the darkness of the hell called the unbounded.

Think of such a system with hundreds of gradations and thousands of observances, and even then one only gets glimpses in his mind of the absurdities and sufferings of the caste system. Possibly no people in the world has ever been so priest-ridden as the Hindus. The aboriginal tribes before them had no castes; the Mohammedans who later conquered the Hindus have had little or none of such notions. It is no wonder that in the Buddhist revolt against such a system the masses of the people would fly to a faith that had in it no place for caste. Nor is it any wonder that the Brahmans made a persistent, deadly struggle against Buddhism, and finally, for their own preservation, drove it entirely out of India. It is interesting to conjecture what would have been the condition of the Indian people had Buddhism prevailed through all the generations to the present. It is certain that those races that have accepted Buddhism, the Burmese and the Chinese, are better off many ways than the Hindus.

To us of independent customs and spirit it is hard to comprehend the thousand ways it attempts to touch every thing connected with one's existence. Having its origin in the blood, so that one born a Brahman, or to one of the lower castes, it proposes to regulate for the babe the ways of nursing, for the boy and grown man the ways of eating and drinking. Be it said to the honor of Brahmanism that there is little drunkenness among the Hindus, and they despise the one addicted to strong drinks. Caste regulates the way a man shall wash, anoint his body, be clothed, ornamented, sit, rise, recline. A Brahman insists that the people believing his system shall travel, visit, speak, read, listen, in a certain way; one shall meditate by rule, and by rule do his working, singing, fighting. By the prescribed way only shall social and religious rites be performed; a law exists for all occupations, education, errors, sins, transgressions, for associating with others, for avoiding them, and for casting one out of his caste or fellowship, for defilement and purification, for fines and other punishments. By its laws property is inherited, possessed, conveyed; while it regulates bargains, losses, gains. In death, burial, and burning, caste laws shape all things, and even propose to go beyond death in its assistance and commemorations. Is it any wonder that under such a system India is moribund? A race that under it has done as well as the Hindu can be expected to do wonderful things when living under so broad and catholic a system as Christianity.

Already Christian civilization is doing much to weaken the hold that caste has on Indian character and custom. Many a young man and young woman educated in mission or government schools has thereby been elevated above all caste, though in the beginning having come from one of the lowest grades. It happens sometimes that children from the different castes coming to the mission schools are troubled about associating in class-rooms and in eating with one another, but the judicious missionary after a while shows that in a Christian school there can be no caste. A certain missionary gets over it by telling them that Christianity lifts its believers above all the castes. The natives themselves are coming to recognize this. They have told me of one of low caste who, on being educated in the schools, and becoming a successful physician, was honored, when he returned to his native village, by all castes, Brahmans as well as others being hearty and officious in their welcome to him.

The improved modes of transit throughout all India, the good wagon-roads kept in finest shape by the government, the railways and lines of steamers along the coasts, are all of them actual earthquake rumblings of the coming shock that will overthrow the whole thing.

When the railways were put through the valleys and plains of India against the protests of the Brahmans, they appealed to the government to furnish them with separate cars to ride in; but the government would do no such thing. It seemed odd to me even to see the way the different castes would rush together into one of the fourth-class cars of a great through train. Thus there was little of the exclusiveness possible, and the subterfuge of the fakirs that their sacred books predicted the railways, and so they are at liberty to use them without contaminating themselves, is a funny somersault. Riding in an intermediate railway carriage one day, I had for companions only a Brahman and a British soldier. In his lunch the soldier had some beef, which the Brahman, finding out, kept far away from the package. To plague him the soldier offered him a piece, but the disgust and horror on the good Hindu's face were most interesting. Yet he was bound to be as polite as the soldier, so he offered us some of his parched rice pressed into thin cakes, which on eating we found very palatable. I wondered if he felt in any degree rebuked by our catholicity.

Doubtless to such a community as India possesses caste offers a few good points. It makes a minute division of labor possible, and that is always a gain to populous, advancing countries. It is bound to protect and cherish those of its own caste even if it treats the needy of other castes like dogs. In matters of cleanliness, needed greatly in a country so populous as India, and in a climate so hot, it impels to great care. But these are what could be reached, and should be without the evils that caste brings. Some of the Indian people are awakening to the fact that the racial deterioration so marked in the slender men and women of the

Hindus must be largely owing to the early marriages demanded without recourse by the caste system. Poverty must be intensified by the compulsion of each man to continue in the specific calling of his father. The whole tendency is to make labor degrading. Caste causes intellectual blight as well as physical, stands in the way of progress, of reform, of personal liberty, of any thing like national growth or patriotism. Its pride, arrogancy, depressing force on the aspirations natural to man, point to it as something that should not stand. It cannot perpetuate much longer the tyranny of its past and present. The projection of Western ideas and of Christianity into India, the opening of all offices by the government to any of the people, the initial awakening of some of the educated Hindus to the absurdities and enormities of the system, are all joining with many other influences not so apparent in forecasting the eternal doom of the horrible incubus.

LETTER XVI.

RELIGIOUSNESS OF THE INDIAN PEOPLE.

FROM the first I have been surprised at the multitudinous indications of worship. Temples, mosques, shrines, idols, are to be seen on every hand. It seems like what Paul saw at Athens. The three great native races, Mohammedans or Semites, the Aryan Hindus, and aboriginal tribes, all appear to have had a deep religious purpose, well carried out here in this country. Hinduism is a gigantic system, with its many gods, temples, priests, ritual, traditions, customs, caste, sacrifices, and interminable books, while Mohammedanism is but little behind it in many of its visible signs of worship, the mosques even rivaling the temples of the Hindus; the aboriginal tribes have much of the ancient nature-worship still in active operation in many parts of the country. Possibly the Hindu surpasses all others in the elaborate phases of his worship, for to him all things must subserve his religion. He has his sacred cities, rivers, places, days, gatherings. His eating, washing, work, marrying, traveling—every thing—is regulated by this thought. To us who put less stress upon outward appearances all this show is not wholly in taste. It suggests, however, a deep religiosity. Perhaps they are not more exclusively so than Christians, only one is constantly meeting cases that seem strange to us matter-of-fact Westerners. If morals were not so separated from these pious practices we could hope so much of the latter would make a people upright and happy; but, unfortunately, there is a complete separation of religion and morals in the East. The Mohammedan Bedouin east of the Jordan will rise from his prayers toward Mecca, and proceed to rob you at once, and coolly kill you if you resist. Hardly less safe are you here in India, save under the all-powerful protection of British law. Some devout Hindu may be a thief, a libertine, or a beater of his wife.

India abounds in holy cities and sacred spots. Benares is so holy that he who dies there is sure to go to heaven, and having been there and bathed in the sacred Ganges at its ghats is to have a passport to bliss. Muttra and its adjacent city of Brindaban are considered in some respects equal or superior to Benares. Legends of their gods are usually connected with these holy cities. At Muttra Krishna did some of his most remarkable deeds of valor. At the junction of the Ganges and the Jumna is a very holy spot where tens of thousands at the annual mela gather in the search for salvation. Where the Ganges issues from the Himalaya Mountains at Hurdwar is another holy region, and a continuous throng of pilgrims come here to worship, bathe, pray, and carry away the holy water for future use. At Amritsar, near Delhi, is a shrine-temple that calls devotees hardly less than Hurdwar and Benares. Not alone the Hindus, but the Mohammedans and aboriginal tribes, have their places of special sanctity. In the devotion of Mohammedans Mecca holds the highest place, but the great mosques here fall only a little behind that in sacredness. The Turanians are quite given to sacred spots and towns. Beside the beautiful mountain-enclasped Naini Tal is a hole reaching down among the rocks, where flowers, sweets, fruit, and grain are constantly offered, and where once a year a goat is now sacrificed in place of the human sacrifice formerly offered. The whole genius of these religions seems to be that man is to be saved by his works, his acts of devotion and penance.

One is surprised here at the number of pilgrimages he sees taking place. Those on such journeys are usually marked by some part of their apparel, but more often can be distinguished by their baggage. Slung at the two ends of a bamboo stick will be two rude baskets of bamboo slits, in each of which is carefully carried a jar containing the holy water from some sacred place on the Ganges or other river. Besides the jars the pilgrim will have a bit of food and a few other things necessary for his journey. These pilgrims can be seen coming and going in little knots or alone on almost every great thoroughfare of India. In some instances there is no distinguishing mark by which these devotees, who have been to some sacred place or shrine, can be identified. At the season of their melas the tide of pilgrimage is very great. Benares, Muttra, Brindaban, Allahabad, and other places are thronged by the gathered multitudes, all in search of rest, happiness, money, and many other objects. The missionaries seize upon these occasions to preach Christ to the masses, and frequently much truth is accepted by the people.

But the local shrines as well as the sacred places afar are well patronized. In Bombay I saw niches in the sides of houses where some image, often but two or six inches high, was set up, and devout people offering it flowers, sweets, nuts, and the like. Red ochre is a favorite thing with which to smear these precious divinities. Oil is also used. A young priest stood in front of one image there, that seemed to be specially prominent, dipping up the oil that had run down from the form of the god into a little tank, and selling it out the second and doubtless the hundredth time to those crowding around. When a little was obtained the devotee had the priest pour it over the idol, to drip down and be sold again. At the crossing of a large bridge at Lucknow I noticed a woman and boy burning a bit of incense and placing some flowers, sweets, and a pice, a coin worth half an American cent, in a shrine only as large as a man's hat. Interested in such peculiar devotions, I asked our missionary, Mr. Maxwell, if I could not take the coin away to keep it as a memento. He said I could, as some one else would soon take it if I did not. Waiting till the devotees were through their devotions, and then a moment for them to get away, I approached the shrine, but a native was before me, who quietly appropriated the money. He evidently held no notions of its being sacred, for on Mr. Maxwell's offering him another pice for it he readily made the exchange, and I secured the choice coin. In Benares, in the very streets and far back from the water of the Ganges River, would be stones to mark a sacred spot, and on it little bits of food or bunches of flowers would be offered.

Many of the Turanians worship objects of nature by such means that one can see the proofs. Under the sacred peepul-tree would often be found little shrines or platforms of brick and mortar for worshipers. On the branches and twigs of this and many other trees one would frequently see bits of cloth hung as an offering, while in the Himalayas, and among the hill tribes generally, cocks and other birds are thus devoted. There is one section of the Himalayan tribes that makes the plant euphorbia its supreme god, and has also its god of cholera, small-pox, and fevers. With them the mountain streams are deities, as well as many more trivial things. I could not help wondering if much of the worship and superstition of the common people of India was not part of the Turanian cult preserved in spite of Hindu faith, through Buddhism and Mohammedanism. So much of it is puerile superstition and gross sensualism that from the better teachings of the old Vedas there must have been some dreadful trend downward. Possibly the natural trend of a system so imperfect as the Vedic will account for all the degradation, but I doubt it in this case.

Sun-worship is still practiced by some of the Indian people, both among the old tribes and the Hindus. Many a time I saw at Benares and elsewhere the upturned face and outstretched hands toward that luminary. Doubtless this would be less degrading to human life and morals than much else of their systems. Birds and animals of one kind and another are also objects of worship. The peacock is so sacred that if one is shot by a Westerner, near a village, the villagers raise a great outcry, fearing famine, disease, death, and other calamities to themselves for the sacrilege. It was strange to see these birds, only half wild, and know their immunity from harm. The monkeys are held in much the same reverence, and have by this protection not only increased to great numbers in some localities, but have become destructive pests to the farmers. As an indication of the decay of certain native superstitions it is interesting to learn that in some districts they are seriously considering the necessity of exterminating these pestiferous simians. All life is differently regarded in India from what it is with us. Birds and animals are never killed. Even the deadly cobra is regarded with such veneration that the natives do not kill it. Hence animal life of all kinds swarms throughout the country. One from the West is astounded at it. So strong is the native reverence for life that even the missionaries do not kill the wild animals and birds for meat that they otherwise would do but for this sentiment. One of the missionaries was sent to a locality abounding in deer. Having a gun, he used to shoot one now and then for food. An old Brahman with whom he talked about the Christian religion said: "You claim to be a good man, yet you kill these innocent creatures God has made. I cannot believe you will do that if you are a servant of so good a God as you tell about." It compelled the missionary to lay aside his rifle and shoot no more deer. In spite of such reverence for animal life more than one part of their cult enjoins animal sacrifice, that of the worship of Rama, the monkey-god, and of Kali, the tutelary goddess of Calcutta, being prominent. I was too late by an hour to see the daily sacrifice of a goat at the shrine of the former god at the monkey temple of Benares, but the clotted blood was yet on the stones and posts. On the contrary, at Calcutta I did see the entire act of sacrifice. It was so out of consonance with the usual spirit of the Hindus toward animals that it appeared the more shocking. To place this along-side of other things I saw, the patience with thieving monkeys, the immunity offered to crows, kites, vultures, and other rapacious birds, created a powerful contrast. In Bombay I saw a man smear the sides of a tree with melted sugar, to which the ants crowded in myriads to get the daily food there regularly given them.

I have not seen as much of the fakirs' methods as I expected, yet enough to get practical insight into their ways of doing things. These methods, like many of the grosser forms of idolatry, are gradually disappearing. In Bombay I saw one fakir measuring his length along the dirty street, walking at each time of rising only as far as his head reached from the point where he set his feet before. No one paid any attention to him, and he was too much absorbed in his practical mode of sanctity to pay any attention to the passing crowds about him. In Huldwanee, at the foot of the Himalayas, one sat on his haunches backed up in a little recess in a stone wall built under a sacred peepul-tree, and there with the chill air blowing down from the mountains was nearly naked, as a disciple built a bit of fire from grass and twigs in front of him in the bazar. Mr. Craven suggested to him that such abnegations could not win him salvation, and that instead he should come to Christ for what he was seeking. He boldly declared that he was worshiping Christ, but Mr. Craven assured him he could not in that way. The abjectest sight of this kind I saw was in the streets of Moradabad. A fakir under some vow was lying on his back and making what progress he could toward the spot or shrine of his vow by hitching along sideways, a most slow and painful mode of locomotion indeed. His underside was protected from the lacerating wear that must take place by a matting of straw fastened to his otherwise almost naked body. One could not see such efforts to win salvation as these without knowing that behind it all was a religious sentiment, which was the sublimation of centuries of intense religiousness, and which, directed into ways of truth, would make these idolatrous Indian people, as we know those converted do become, self-sacrificing, devoted, and persistent Christians.

I was greatly interested in learning about some of their methods of prayer. A string of beads from a sacred kind of wood, or those composed of the seed of a certain kind of fruit, affords means of continuous praying. One will see a man going along the street with such a string of beads dangling loosely in his hands, muttering in an undertone, as he slips the beads along the string, the name of his god—"Ram, Ram, Ram." If he wants his prayer to be three or four times as efficacious he will put the right hand, holding the string of beads, into a little bag with the thumb out, having texts from his sacred books inscribed on the bag, and, counting them over, pray in that way to the god Ram. I tried to buy a string of beads hanging about the neck of a dirty Brahman, but he would not sell them short of a ruinous price, though in a bazar I did secure a new string, which perhaps was safer for me to handle. These Brahmans are sometimes contemptuous to us Western people. In their cult such lazy fellows are superior to princes and kings, though they may be the veriest beggars, and in nakedness. I think their contempt for Western people must be diminishing, as almost always they were respectful, and often eager to please. To them many things are lawful that are wicked for others to do; hence till British laws rudely shook them up their course was often high-handed and peculiar. India people, from Brahman to Sudra, need the Gospel most of all things.

LETTER XVII.

AMONG THE MISSIONARIES AT SHAHJEHANPORE.

THEY promised me three or four days of seeing hand-to-hand missionary work among the non-Christian villagers out from Shahjehanpore, and for this I gave up a week of hunting among the tigers, elephants, leopards, deer, and other large game in the "Tarai" near the foot of the Himalayas, but finally lost both. On my getting here Dr. Hoskins said it was a poor time for his outside work, as it was New Year's week, my arrival being December 31. If I lost both my coveted hunting with Mr. Craven's native Christians in the jungle and the outside mission work, I have still had rich compensation. There is a double mission here, that of the city and outlying regions one way, while the orphanage at East Shahjehanpore, in charge of Rev. C. L. Bare and wife, is the head-quarters for another important mission station. As almost every-where through these regions, our work is very promising, with many most pressing opportunities which, for lack of men and means to enter upon them, must be allowed to remain unused for the present.

A Yankee abroad becomes hungry for several things—the loved ones left behind, the dear old flag, the congenial associations, and even for the food on which he grew and thrived. Is it a wonder, then, that I was delighted, in this typical household, to sit down to a surprise of real Yankee dishes—salt codfish, buckwheat griddle-cakes, mince-pie and apple-pie? Then the next day, added to these were baked beans and brown bread, hot and luscious. They had received a box containing possibilities for these things all the way from their son at college in Boston.

I found this diligent missionary, who is burdened with the care of multitudinous duties and claims, indulging at odd hours his high literary tastes in translating into English a large and important portion of the Vedas that has not yet seen the light in our tongue. In doing this he is first compelled to make his own lexicon of Sanskrit terms. When this great work is done it will add not only another valuable classic translated from other tongues into the English, but it will bring deserved praise upon this scholar, as well as lengthen the long list of those missionaries who have added to our philological knowledge and treasures.

The school work done here is of the most promising kind. Not alone is it organized for the boys, but also for the girls. The latter are attending the central school to the number of forty, and the steady increase will soon demand much larger quarters than now, while through the city and near by two more primary schools are going on with about two hundred girls in them. It is due the girls, as well as the boys, that they have these advantages of Christianity. Then, too, India, as all other countries, can rise no higher than her women are elevated, and here, as every-where in Christianity, woman has vast duties to perform in winning souls to Christ and teaching the better way. The boys' schools are also most prosperous. The central or high school for them has about one hundred and fifty boys, in buildings owned by the mission, while other schools are filled with those of primary grades.

Of the high school nearly half the pupils are Christians, so that the influence for the truth is deep and good. I have told in another letter of the Sunday-school I visited in this city which is held in the place and among the pupils of one of the primary schools. The work is all charming and the prospect most promising. A good-sized native church meets in the mission compound, to which I had the pleasure of preaching, the translation being made by Dr. Hoskins; while at a small English church near the railway depot I also had the same pleasure.

Dr. Hoskins wanted me to attend street-preaching with him one week-day, which I was most glad to do. A great wagon was filled with native Christians from the mission, some of whom had instruments, so a brass band was pretty well represented. Another wagon carried Dr. Hoskins and me. On a corner opposite a market-shed they placed a box that Dr. Hoskins mounted, the band played, and then for ten minutes the preacher spoke to the crowd of two hundred or more that had collected. After him one of the native preachers spoke a while; then I did, Dr. Hoskins translating. The band put in the interludes. By this time occurred what usually takes place there—a Mohammedan moulvie or priest came near, and mounting a piece of timber also began speaking, but in antagonism to Christianity. Some of the people on the street had run to a mosque and told him of the work of the Christians, so he had hurried to offset their teachings. Their stock-in-trade argument against Christianity is that it is not monotheism, and that Jesus was of impure human origin. The whole scene was strange. The light dust of the street and moving crowds filled the air, the noisy babel of tongues was continuous, the marketing did not cease, the rumble of carts and tramp of passers made a din, the Mohammedan preacher attracted as much of an audience as we had, the two crowds partly coalescing. Boys stood with cages of partridges on their heads, which they teach to fight, while others carried bulbuls on perches for the same purpose. Passing teams were stopped that their drivers might listen to the preaching; men with great loads on their heads paused to hear the truth. The missionaries like this hand-to-hand work, and I do not wonder at it.

At East Shahjehanpore is the orphanage for boys, and this demands American missionaries for its directors. Rev. C. L. Bare and wife have about two hundred boys here, some of them doing little besides regular school work, being considered promising ones for teachers, preachers, and the like; others are taught the trade of making shoes and carpentry much as they would do in America, while some poor blind ones were busy making ropes from native grass. These ropes and cords, while not as strong as cotton and hemp, are still very serviceable. Their rope-walk across the yard of their shop, their funny way of twisting the ropes, the facility of the blind boys in laying the grass into the first strands were all most interesting to me. These orphanages, like this and at Cawnpore, and that for girls at Bareilly, are among the richest gifts of Christ to India.

An incident will illustrate this claim. On a winter day years ago one of our missionaries, Mrs. Humphrey, of Budaon, sat warming her feet at the cozy grate, when she heard a feeble call at the door, "Mem Sahib," and going there found two boys, the one carried on the back of the other. The older one said, "We are starving, and we heard you kept children here." So she took them in, fed, clothed, and educated them. One grew to be a successful physician, and though from the low caste of farmers was honored, as he visited his native village, by having a chair brought for him to sit in, as is done only for those whom they desire to honor most highly. That simple fact led a young fellow who saw the matter to look into Christianity, who in turn became educated and was set at preaching. This preacher heard of a "guru," or teacher, in a native state who had obtained a copy of the New Testament which he had set up as an idol and was worshiping it. To this teacher the native preacher went, taught him the better way of using the book, brought him and his son to our mission, where they are now workers in the ministry, and teaching. Such wonderful things are constantly being done.

The grounds of the East Shahjehanpore Orphanage, formerly the residence of an English official, comprise about twenty-five acres, with a good home for the missionary, ample buildings for the shops and school, and houses for the pastor, the teachers, and servants, while in another part is a home for widows, in which about a dozen find refuge, and which is mostly self-supporting. Here is also a dispensary in charge of a native physician, where he gave last year more than ten thousand prescriptions. Such piteous facts as come to the knowledge of these physicians! The baleful effects of heathenism smite the body as well as the soul of those in it. The government gives five hundred rupees a year in medicines to this dispensary.

The orphanage owns some fields that are too large to be carried on by the boys, so they are let out to regular farmers at about nine rupees an acre. The gardens into which they took me afforded, in the dead of winter, strange things in that season to a Yankee. There were green peas and beans, new potatoes, turnips, tomatoes, radishes, lettuce, and the like, kept fresh and growing by water drawn from a deep well. The gardener, pleased with my visit, plucked for me a big bouquet of flowers—roses, heliotropes, peas, beans, two kinds of jasmine, myrtle, and other flowers, the fifth day of January!

Not the least interesting thing was a day of hunting in the jungle and another day of going to the native Christian village of Panapur. This is a place where the land bought by the missionaries has had a number of the native Christians settled, in which they are mostly saved from the sharp persecutions of their non-Christian neighbors. It is ten miles from East Shahjehanpore, most of the way on one of those superb roads of India that are as smooth and level as a floor, laid down of the peculiar lime concretions filling the soil, which they all call "kunker." From that road it is three miles into the jungle, or timber, most of the way scrubby growth of Indian trees covering the ground. No other native villages are very near, and while this experiment is not wholly a success it is not nearly a failure. Two or three hundred native Christians have comfortable homes, with a church and a school-house. Their fields, only in part a success, because of the alkaline soil, are yet productive, while they are creating a good influence for Christianity on the villages about them. Word had been sent ahead a day or two of our coming, and an hour set when I should preach to them. The Christians had scattered the news to the contiguous villages, so that through the jungle from several of these numbers had come to listen, who, together with the inhabitants of Panapur, made the church full, and more. An American who could meet and preach to such an audience and not be deeply moved would have cold blood indeed. There were old men and women whose hair was sprinkled with white, lithe, agile young men and women, while in front, squatting on the mats, were dozens of boys, and all through the audience children of smaller size. I urged that they should do just as Jesus would want them to do if he were present among them. I was introduced, as usual, by our missionaries, as "Padre Dr. Knox, Sahib," the padre being the general designation of preacher in India, from the expression taught by the Roman Catholics of different nations long before Protestant missions were introduced. The sahib is the native term of respect. In this motley gathering were Brahmans, Rajputs, Christians, low-caste villagers, men and women, so that the old caste exclusiveness was dreadfully shaken up in the Christian church. A young Brahman, who only a year ago had stealthily approached Mr. Bare with a club from behind to kill him, and was seized by some of our native Christians, was there, an attentive listener, and, having been a seeker of the truth for some months, told our missionaries that now he was ready to be baptized. The leaven is working all through Indian society. Grim old Rajputs, the remnants of the warrior caste, are sitting in meek tractableness at the feet of our missionaries.

We wandered through the village to see some of the industries of the people. Women sat under the porches busy at rude spinning and mat-making; others were cooking, all were glad to see the Americans. When leaving the village we were attracted by some native music, and going to it with Dr. Hoskins I found a wedding was being prepared for. In one of the mud huts half a dozen women were seated on the mats in a circle, chanting to the rhythm and movement of their instruments the virtues and beauties of the bridegroom. It was in the house of the bride, and behind some curtains, or blankets, she was supposed to be hidden. Dr. Hoskins told me the burden of their chanting was the brightness of the groom's eyes, the strength of person, the prettiness of his lips, the sleekness of his hair, the amount of his possessions, and the like. The instruments were a native drum or two beaten with the finger-tips, a kind of tambourine, a violin of two or three strings, and others as rude. It was at once a strange and interesting sight. On our first approach they ceased, but were persuaded to go on after a little such coy reserve as is usual with good singers. The young Brahman and a young local preacher of the village went with us a long way on the road as we finally left, a custom often observed as a native village is visited by some one whom they wish to honor. I noticed this custom several times.

Being just at night as we came out through the timber, the monkeys that had kept out of sight during the glare of the sun were now up the trees by the dozens, scampering down to run off if we went toward them. Some exquisitely beautiful sparrows, the males rich red, black, and yellow, the females brown and dun, were gathered in large flocks among the tall grass and reeds. They were not more than half as large as the smallest American sparrows. At the junction of the jungle road with the main one, in an open yard, or khan, was a group of pilgrims returning from the Ganges, each with two jars of the sacred water slung to each end of a bamboo stick. They were preparing their frugal supper over a fire made of grass and leaves, and were not at all averse to talking about the Christian religion and life. They seemed ashamed to claim sin-washing power in the water they had, and declared they were only hired by a rich man to go and bring it to him.

LETTER XVIII.

A DAY OF HUNTING IN INDIA.

WE planned the day before to steal out at half past three in the morning; so at three the faithful cook tapped at my door, saying, "Chota hazari, sahib," which meant an early lunch for me. The vehicle for going the thirteen miles to good hunting-grounds was a two-wheeled bullock-cart, with a small box-rack filled with dried grass and a seat for me, upon which I did not sit much of the time, finding it easier to lie on the dried grass. The hours until daylight were enlivened by chimes of howls and barkings from a chorus composed of jackals, foxes, and dogs. The zodiacal radiance in the East is much greater than in the United States, so that we were not without light; then through the thin clouds the morning dawn gradually broke, and soon I was peering into the dim light for game. With me were the head-master of the orphanage school at Shahjehanpore, and the manager of its industrial department, both of whom could speak English well; then a man to drive the bullock-cart, one to care for the master's horse, and one to carry my gun. It is easy to have a lot of servants in India. Some herons, plovers, and ducks were gathered about the muddy pond-holes, and my second attempt to secure a shot at some ducks succeeded better than one at a flock of plovers, for I killed a green-winged teal, almost exactly like those we have in America. A shot by Frank, the master, placed another in the bag. A flock of another kind that we failed to get a shot at were very large and fine. Pigeons were common, and during the day we bagged quite a number of them, though they were so small we usually tried to get two in range before firing. They were much smaller than the blue pigeon in America, being more like the turtle-dove. There is difficulty in stalking birds of the water habit here, as there are hardly ever any bushes about the pond-holes, but open ground. There are vast numbers at this season of the year; they congregate about the larger ponds, till in one place you can see hundreds of them, and, as the plains are level, they can be seen from a long distance. The largest of these water-birds is the adjutant, a tall wader, standing more than four feet high, dull lead-color, with a bright scarlet head. Some are brown, black, or black and white. Herons, ibises, cranes, pelicans, and others gather into one flock. Strange, but true, that three or four of these herons are fine to eat.

At ten o'clock we came to a village where the manager and the master were known and where the Methodist mission has a native preacher stationed. His house was open to us and his stable to our tired beasts. From there we pushed for the jungle after getting a second lunch or breakfast. The walk of two miles through fields green with wheat, dal, sugar-cane, potatoes, and other grains was a novel sensation for me the fourth day of January, at which date I have been used to going hunting or fishing with a sleigh or snow-shoes. The jungle, toward which we toiled through a sun so hot that I was compelled besides wearing a pith hat to carry an umbrella, was like a second growth of scrub oaks in Virginia, with the addition of sharp thorns and hooked prickles on at least half the vines and shrubs. Making our way far into this to a tall tree, one of the men climbed it to look out for deer, but could not descry any. So we went beating about to see if we could find one. They said there were boars, foxes, and peacocks, besides other game, in there. But we toiled our devious way for a long time without seeing more than one lone rabbit that suddenly hid in the thicket, and many small birds, when, not more than twenty yards in front of me, there was a quick rush from a dense mass of bushes and vines; but the big game, whatever it was, kept out of sight till it had run some distance, and then, turning a short corner toward my left, a beautiful deer bounded into sight; but so thick were the bushes that I got only a snap shot at it with buckshot, missing it, and then trying again at long range with triple B shot. At that shot I thought it fell, but if it did it was quickly on its feet, and, bounding away, ran in sight for two or three hundred yards. It did not run in even jumps, but would make two or three low short ones and then bound high in the air with a leap that must have been twenty or thirty feet long. Well, there were two shots at one deer with no results save to show us, after being nearly discouraged, that deer were in there. Again we scattered out in the jungle, the manager and master each having a gun, when, after a few minutes, I heard a shot from the manager at my left and a loud cry which I knew meant that the deer was coming my way. In an instant I saw it a hundred yards or more away, making flying leaps, and, though knowing it was practically useless to try buckshot at such long range, I fired in hope —a useless one, for the shot struck into the ground short of the game, when that one, and two others which came out of the thicket near by, went leaping off together. Try to imagine the feelings of one with the hunter's instincts strong in him making such work shooting deer in an Indian jungle! An hour's following after them through the thorns, prickles, and stiff brush, under a sun that beat on me a hundred and thirty degrees of heat, did not serve to improve my feeling of disappointment. Turning then to make my way toward the village, as I had agreed with the others, and coming out of the brush into some spots of tall grass, to help at improving my feelings a rabbit scooted away from under my feet and a couple of partridges flew in good shooting range, but all the time my gun in both barrels was loaded with buckshot. I drew one charge, replacing it with fine shot, but after that did not see a partridge or quail. Tired, heated, and footsore, I joined the others, to hear that a glimpse of a boar had been obtained by the manager's servant, and that was all.

As we were going across the fields the farmers at work told us of a herd of ten or twelve deer having been seen in a great sugar-cane field that day. Toward that we went half a mile out of our way to find that another farmer close by the cane had seen them go off toward the jungle an hour before. The master brought in another duck from a pond to which I was too tired to go. Again a deep dip into the lunch-basket sent by the missionary's wife, an hour's rest, and we were ready to go back home. It was then four o'clock and the game was out on the fields, so that we had a better chance than going into the village. Plover and pigeons were too far away for me. I let the others go after them. Then the master, horseback, saw a couple of young adjutants, and, calling two of his men, he chased the birds over the wheat-fields till he ran them down, and his men picked them up, bringing them to the orphanage alive to tame. In the meantime the manager and I, with our guns, went to a pond at which we could see a vast flock of waders gathering, and, creeping within about a hundred and fifty yards, I fired with a barrel loaded with triple B shot, and one of the immense herons was my reward. If one was left two or three thousand flew away. Just at dusk I shot another from the top of a tree whose stretch of wings was eighty-two inches, while the first one's wings stretched just one hundred inches. I had determined to shoot only those birds that were edible, and, strange as it may seem to American gastronomists, both these herons were fine birds to eat, being assured so by the men with me and by the missionaries before going out. I can bear witness to the fine flavor of the smaller one, for I ate heartily of it for dinner before writing this letter. With a good bag of small birds, two immense herons dead, and two live adjutants, we had a fine lot of game as we made our way slowly back to Shahjehanpore. But not so slowly, if we were on a bullock-cart. The white, hump-backed bullocks here are trained to rapid going compared to American oxen, so that we made the last ten miles in three hours. But in order to do so our quondam driver was obliged to work his passage. He was the master, who, giving his horse to the manager, came and took the regular driver's seat. That seat was on the tongue of the cart, far ahead between the bullocks. With a short, tough stick in his right hand to use in striking or punching the beasts as he wished, he would do with his left hand what all bullock-drivers here do, curl the tail of the near ox, sometimes giving it a sharp twist, then push the hips of first one bullock, then the other, to one side, all of which things, and various native cries and shouts, are intended to hurry up the team. Yet all of these means did not produce speed enough to suit him, so he spread my umbrella and used that first one side and then the other to frighten the bullocks to greater speed. They could not run away with us, for there is always a rope passing through a hole between the nostrils to guide and hold them. In a chorus, similar to that of the morning, of jackals and dogs, we pushed ahead, so that nine o'clock found us at home, tired, but a jolly set, such as hunters are apt to be.

LETTER XIX.

THE BIRDS OF INDIA.

No sooner had I landed at Bombay than I found myself in the land of birds. Crows, whose cawing was coarse and rasping, were tame as sparrows in America, perching on the fences, porches, in the windows, and even entering houses to steal food and trinkets. They are smaller than American crows, with gray about the neck and shoulders. One species, not common, is black all over and larger than these. The kites were also numerous in Bombay, great brown fellows, acting as scavengers about the streets and houses, and, like the crows, half-domesticated.

The crows, hawks, kites, and vultures constitute a most valuable force of scavengers. Refuse of every kind about the great cities is picked up by them. In this they are also aided by the pariah dogs and the hardly less tame jackals. The latter skulk out of sight in the bushes, hedges, and jungles near the great cities in the day-time, and do valuable service at night in cleaning yards and streets. It seemed a sad degradation, however, for the beautiful hawks and kites to leave their normal habits of capturing live game to pick bits of decaying meat, broken bread, and dirty scraps. So numerous are these birds that they gather sometimes about the cities in great flocks.

The Indian people never kill birds nor animals, so they not only increase to great numbers, but become familiar to mankind. I was told that the kites would sometimes snatch a piece of bread or meat from one's hand, and I saw one trying to get some meat from a small dog by swooping savagely down upon him. On the Towers of Silence, where the Parsees of Bombay lay the bodies of their dead friends instead of burying them, huge, fat, lazy vultures sat gloomily waiting for new victims to eat.

A ride of a thousand miles to Delhi and Moradabad showed me a glimpse of India's wealth in birds. The cars would start up almost a continuous flock of one kind or another. All of them are new to one from America, yet most of them can be located at sight in their classified families. Every pool or pond-hole of water had some representatives of the waders—great, tall, scarlet-headed adjutants slowly walking away from the rumble of the cars; pelicans, cranes, ibises, and other tall ones were also common. The mud-hens, rails, grebes, plovers, ducks, and others could be seen flying, diving, running away, or standing in silent fear as the train thundered past them. A peculiarity I noticed at Shahjehanpore was a flock of herons flying in a waltzing movement, keeping a general course, indeed, but sailing around and around each other.

In this country the peacocks are considered sacred, so they are quite common, and though not domesticated, are hardly wild. One sees them about the fields, hedges, and gardens, with little fear of the natives. If an Englishman shoots one a great uproar is apt to follow among the superstitious people. There is another sacred bird, the Indian roller, as large as a blue jay, and allied to the fly-catcher. It has most beautiful plumage of blue, green, black, or buff, the wing bars of deep and light blue, making it very attractive as it flies.

I saw it many times sitting on the telegraph-wires, watching for insects along the railroad. I hardly wonder that these two birds of such brilliantly beautiful plumage are held sacred by the Hindus. A kind of bird the name of which I have not learned other than that of "hang-nests" has the peculiarity of building its nests attached to limbs of trees over pools of water. I first noticed these on the way from Bombay to Delhi as they hung over pond-holes made by grading the railway. The nests, bottle-shaped, eight or ten inches long, are a veritable pocket. They are made of tough grasses, hair, and the like, so that they endure long after serving the purpose for which they are built. In this place, and hung on slender limbs, they are secure from the snakes and other vermin that so often rob nests. Sometimes several of these nests would be hanging from one tree.

The fly-catchers are a fine family of birds here. One, a large, black, forked-tailed bird, is called the "king crow," from its ability to drive those thievish fellows from their nests. It has the habit of the shrike in catching small birds. It also selects the telegraph-wire for a perch. The same place is chosen by a smaller, pale-green fly-catcher, that often sat still, like the king crow, as the train rushed by. This family of birds is also represented by several bright-colored species, which follow their valuable work, giving most pleasing sights.

The number of the starling family I have seen is very great. Two of them have become as domestic about the streets and native bazars as the English sparrow in the United States. Their name here is mynah. They are dark, about the size of a robin, go in flocks, and when flying the common mynah shows broad white bars on its wings, reminding me of the

10

mocking-bird at home. This family has also some bright-colored species that I have not seen. The natives occasionally tame the common mynah, teaching it to say "Krishna," the name of one of their gods. One species has acquired a fanciful name among the English people, that of the "Seven Brothers." It is claimed that seven of them always go together, but on counting a number of these groups I have found that the rule does not always hold good. Several times seven were present, to be sure, but at other times there was a lack, owing, they assured me, to the fact that one or two were out of sight for the moment. I presume this regular number may be a whole family, two parents and five chicks of the present year's brood.

The most charming kinds of sparrows are to be found here. Possibly the season was not the best for finding a large number of species, but those I did see interested me greatly. Not that I was pleased to see the troublesome English sparrow, that in America we so much regret having introduced, and which I saw every-where the Englishman stays, but the native species were beautiful. A few species were as gray and unobtrusive as our home ones, but others were much more brilliant. One kind that I first saw in a great cage at the Bombay market, and afterward in the country, was much smaller than our smallest species, and of a brilliant black, red, and buff. Others had some yellow, in that approaching the canary-bird. As is common with such birds in the winter season, they went in flocks; their loading the tufts of tall grasses, searching for seeds, was most interesting.

Of the robins I have seen three species, though they tell me there are several more. The coloration of one was a black head and back, with under parts buff, much like our orchard oriole. Their high colors, as compared with our brown matter-of-fact robins, are most interesting. The scarlet tanager is very like ours, being possibly a bit more slim, its back and head black, breast light, the body a brilliant scarlet. The nut-hatch was as saucy when I saw him as he is in America, running up and down the body and limbs of trees. Woodpeckers found ample chance for their peculiar mode of getting a living among the luxuriant growth of mango and other kinds of tropical trees. They are mostly black and white, as with us, the males having the usual red head. One species has a bright golden back, mottled breast, and red head, being in size like the yellow-bellied woodpeckers of America.

A bit of a bird, slim, graceful, white below, gray above, well deserved its name of wagtail. Immediately on alighting, or when walking away from one's approach, its tail was most nervously jerked up and down.

I was surprised at the number and antics of the kingfishers. Used to but one species at home, I was hardly prepared to see half a dozen here. None of them is as large, I think, as the belted kingfisher in the United States, while some are as small as our bluebirds. Every pond, river, and brook in this warm country teems with fish, so that there is ample food for them. Often I saw them hovering and hanging over the water, curiously peering down into it, and then like an arrow shooting downward after their prey. Their plumage, in some instances, is most brilliant, one especially being almost as green as a paroquet.

Ah, what is that loud, sharp screeching? Look, it is the paroquet's nervous scolding. Such noisy fellows as they are! They never seem at rest, but always to be moving and screeching. I think they fly the most swiftly of any bird I have ever seen. They shoot like a bolt from tree to tree. I have noticed three species, one very small, green, and a great pet; another like him, but larger; the third larger still, green, but with scarlet about his head and bill. I have seen two or three great flocks of paroquets, at which times their screaming was almost enough to deafen one. From the cars I saw a grain-stack literally green with them, but the roar of the train hindered my hearing their noise. Frequently a native gentleman going on the cars will have two or three white parrots taken along with his luggage, kept in charge of a servant, and chained to their perches.

Of the pigeons I have noticed three species. One, of which I have seen but a few specimens, is almost as large as our common wood-pigeon of the United States; the others are both smaller. The most common of these is a small one, much like the Carolina dove of the southern and central United States. This one is somewhat lighter, with more delicate tints in the color, a part of them pinkish and soft as the shading of a sea-shell. They afford delicious bits of eating, as I can attest by those I shot during my stay at Bareilly.

I cannot tell much of the quails and partridges, though I have seen many different ones, for the sight has been but a hurried one from the cars while passing. A kind noticed several times has a bronze or old gold colored back, a wide, long tail, the two combined making it an elegant object as it would sedately walk away from the railway. But I especially want to tell of one. It was among the foot-hills of the Himalayas toward Naini Tal, in the road, as three of us were riding horseback. They had told me of the jungle fowl, generally considered the wild progenitor of our common barn-yard fowl, and there one of the cocks stood in the road, looking almost exactly like our American game-cock, slim, bronze and black, and rusty red, with four long arching blue-black tail-feathers. I could easily have thought him belonging to some of the villagers not far away.

Up among the same hills I saw a blue jay that was a magnificent fellow, shaped and colored much like our own, but with two variegated tail-feathers full fourteen inches long. Such a bird hopping through the branches of the trees was a thing of beauty. A treepie, related to the magpie, seen on the plains here, is hardly less a brilliant sight, being of similar size to the jay, with long tail, and with colors of black, white, nankeen, and gray. The magpies are an attractive group from their number and striking party-colored plumage.

Every one reading Eastern books or stories of travels hears of the bulbul. I did not get a sight of these till I had been a month in India. Then at Lucknow, among the beautiful trees in the Residency Park, where the British during the Sepoy rebellion held out so successfully, I saw the common bulbul and the red-whiskered one the same morning. The note of this so-called Indian nightingale is by no means as fine as that of several American birds—say the bobolink, mocking-bird, and the thrush. But he is a pretty fellow. He is of the size and shape of the bluebird, has a black head with a pretty tuft on it, a brown back, a gray-mottled belly, tail white-tipped, the under tail-coverts being a bright scarlet. The red-whiskered bulbul is larger, like the other in shape and top-knot, but has more scarlet below and a large blotch of it on each side of his head.

It seemed to me a great change from the fighting and struggle going on in 1857 at the Residency to the hundreds of pretty songsters all over the grounds and among the trees, shrubs, flowers, and old ruins. I saw the same morning for the first time a honey-bird, a most iridescent fellow, hanging about the flowers somewhat like the humming-birds, with which it is closely connected. Its bill, which it wiped on one side and the other of a limb on which it was sitting, was long and slender.

The hoopoe is another of the fine-looking birds of India. It frequents the ground, probing holes with its long, curved bill in search of insects and worms for food. The tall tuft on its head, the variegated color of its plumage—brown, white, mottled, and copper-colored—serve to make it an attractive bird. It is quite tame, so I could approach close to it in the gardens.

The vast number, the strange species, the tame habits of the Indian birds fascinate one used to collecting in America.

LETTER XX.

AT THE NORTH INDIA CONFERENCE.

Through the kindness of Dr. and Mrs. E. W. Parker it was my privilege to stay quietly at the historic city of Bareilly during the session of 1888 as an interested observer. Bishop Thoburn was present after his long and eventful stay in America, entering here upon old territory, but on new duties. It was his first Conference as bishop, but the work of presiding was not new, since he had several times been president of the India Conferences.

They gave him a reception Tuesday night, at which a church full of eager listeners waited to hear what he would say. Dr. Waugh and other missionaries spoke hearty words of welcome; so did one of the native preachers, Hiram L. Cutting. The last said his heart was filled to overflowing with thankfulness that they now had a bishop of their own in India, and that this was Thoburn. He was a good representative of the native sentiment.

In response to these unanimous words of welcome from natives and Americans the bishop spoke most wisely. He recounted the peculiar providences that had led to his present onerous responsibilities, and urged that he would use his new office in serving the brethren and the Church. If the new missionary bishop is always so much in the spirit of the Master's teachings, and if the suggestions of his course are always thus carried out, the Church, whose eyes are earnestly directed upon this new venture, can well congratulate itself upon its election of this man to the episcopacy. His presiding has been as gentle and unassuming as his reception speech.

When the fraternal delegate from the Presbyterian Mission to the Conference wished that the churches of India might become one even in name, the bishop responded that "as denominations we get closer together, not by discussing differences, but on our knees."

At the "after-tea" prayer-meetings the clear, simple manner in which the bishop presented the ways and needs of high attainments in the religious life was most pleasing. There is a necessity at home, of course, to be filled with the Holy Spirit, his joy, power, and wisdom; but when missionaries stand confronting such gigantic systems as they do here, and think that it is their work to supplant these with the teachings of the Bible, they are in fullest need of all those things that come alone through God's indwelling.

The recruits for the India work and the former missionaries returning made quite an array, seventeen together; but of these only two were men. These two men, as Bishop Thoburn showed some time ago in the *Western Christian Advocate*, were all he could secure out of about a hundred who, on his issuing a public call, offered to go. Many were rejected by the physicians, either on their own account or that of their wives; others were not prepared in their education; family complications hindered others; a few backed out, and so on, till *two*—think of it, ye men of American Methodism!—*two men* and *fifteen women* were here at Conference as a fresh offering freely laid upon the altar to do God's work for Methodism in India!

I have been declaring to my parishioners at home that Methodism, from the number of young men and women standing ready to go, could, in a year or two, send a thousand new missionaries into the foreign work, if only the money could be had. But I was wrong. I humbly confess it to those who heard me. The men in all the millions of Methodism cannot be found! But the women can be found, it seems. Fifteen to two! God bless the Methodist women! It is reported that the Woman's Foreign Missionary Society never lacks those ready and prepared to go. I hope this ratio is not a fair per cent.; it cannot be. There are certainly many young men in America who have for India the spirit which thirty years ago sent out Parker, Baume, Thoburn, Waugh, and others. Of the eleven who came to India in 1859 six have gone home to heaven, and all of the other five—Dr. Parker and wife, Thoburn, Waugh, and Baume—were here at the Conference this year. What a record!

And these older missionaries are now pleading for men to come here and stay. One remaining only three or five years barely gets efficient in that time, so that his valuable services are lost if he goes home. The climate drives a few home in a hurry, and some that return do not come to stay, but simply remain a while and then go back. If the mission authorities can possibly find men who will devote themselves for life to mission work they will do most wisely. In a few years the present Nestors of India Methodism must lay down the burden, and while a few others of wide experience and tried usefulness are here aiding them not enough of younger men are staying to meet the prospective enlargement of the work some years ahead. So the cry goes up to the

Mission Rooms, "Send us men who will stay their lifetime!"

It was a first-class inspiration to hear the presiding elders' reports. Up among the foot-hills of the mighty Himalayas, and among the aboriginal Turanians in the dense jungles, where only these very men can live in the summer heat, on the rich broad plains of the North-west Provinces, in the mud villages, in the great cities, along both banks of the sacred Jumna and more sacred Ganges, the work is pushing, growing, succeeding. Like a conquering general's order for an advance to be made all along the line, it seems the great Captain has given orders to the missionaries of India, and the shout of victory goes up every-where.

I wonder if Dr. Parker's Rohilcund District is not the banner district in all Methodism this year in the number of baptisms? Look at the returns—1,457. One man alone, Dr. Wilson, baptized 450. Dr. Parker says: "Such is the success that on my district three times as many could have been baptized had not the missionaries made it a rule to teach the seekers the great truths of Christianity thoroughly before baptizing them." On every district and station are success and enlargement. Indeed, every American missionary in charge of a station is really a presiding elder, for he has from a dozen to forty native preachers and teachers carrying on the work in all parts of the cities and among the scattered villages.

It transpired in the report on self-support and the important discussion which followed that only a small amount *per capita* can be secured from the people. This is not to be wondered at when it is recalled that our work is largely among the poor people; and in India this means volumes. It means families of three or five who live on four or six rupees a month—that is, one dollar and a half or two dollars. They told of a man with three children who entered into contract to receive for his work five rupees for three months, whose wife by spinning could earn seven eighths of one rupee a month, and was permitted to catch the dripping from some sugar-barrels and also pull some edible weeds from a grain field. That family lives on less than one dollar a month. Of course the living is much cheaper here than in America, but this sum furnishes only the barest necessities of life. Little from such a family can be expected. This question is a great one, and our missionaries are wrestling hard with it. Still, in both native and European work there was raised during the year for all purposes the very fine sum of 109,697 rupees.

A feature at Bareilly unique to me was the Woman's Conference. It was my privilege to attend one day, and the reports rendered by these earnest women of the work done in schools, hospitals, zenanas, orphanages, and in other places was most fascinating. Defeats mingled with victories, but the latter predominated. They have here regular sessions, receiving reports, laying out plans of work, examining classes both of American and native women—of the former even the wives of the missionaries that are not under direction of the Woman's Foreign Missionary Society. Their reports are printed in the Conference Minutes. The new scheme of deaconesses is to be tried, with much hope embodied in it for India, such homes having already been started at Calcutta, Muttra, and Lucknow.

The school results are among the most promising in the mission field. There are 408 in the North India Conference, including those for boys and girls, native and European, with over 16,000 pupils. These are all the way from letter-learning to college classes. Each school is a center for direct or indirect evangelistic activity. In all of them the great truths of Christianity are taught, and as many of the children are from non-Christian families they are constantly influenced toward the truth. Not all of them will be led to Christ, of course, but good is done in giving them the beginnings of an education; they become acquainted with Western thought and spirit that is opposed to idolatry, while many of them become Christians. Connected with almost every day-school is a Sunday-school, where nearly all these children are taught the truth an hour or two every Sunday. The missionaries feel they have some claim on all these pupils, and the good seed is certain to produce fruit. The recent purchase of a splendid new building in a beautiful location at Naini Tal for the boys' school at a cost of 52,000 rupees and raising it to the grade of a high school; the decision to proceed to the erection of the new college buildings at Lucknow, as well as other positive advances in this field, show rapid growth and independent spirit.

The Sunday-school report also showed magnificent advance. During the year there has been organized an increase of 109 schools, making the whole number 703, with 26,585 pupils—a gain of 2,672 during the year. Of this increase 1,544 were rated as Christian children. Many of the converts were gathered from these schools. If a year's report shows a tendency, the trend toward schools in which both sexes are present is strong, as of the 109 new schools 57 are mixed; while another pointer is that 1,032 non-Christian girls, but only 96 non-Christian boys, were among the gain. I saw some of these native Sunday-schools—not the ones alone in chapels and school-rooms—but those under trees or in mud huts, and I do confess that they were a wonder and an inspiration to me. Such eagerness to learn, such swarms of them as came, such unique appearance in face, dress, and customs, would have created a sensation at Plainfield, N. J.

The statistical reports, like those of the Sunday-school, were enough to cause joy and shouting. The whole number of communicants is 7,974—a gain during the year of 1,924, with 1,952 baptisms, 520 more than last year. They say that such a per cent. of gain all around the earthwide Methodism would have added 200,000 to our Church last year. Missions pay.

A characteristic incident occurred one day. In a village about twelve miles out of Bareilly some of the Hindus beat one of our teachers—not an uncommon occurrence. These men were caught at it by the police, so that the government had a case against the offenders. But it was optional with our people whether the prosecution should proceed to a fine and six months in jail. It having occurred on Dr. Parker's district, he advised, as they all came to him, the culprits begging mercy and promising to treat the teachers well hereafter, that they should be brought before the Conference, allowed to make their confession, and let go.

So, for the moral and prudential effect of the thing, they came before the bishop, five stalwart, fine-looking natives, made their confession, and the kind-hearted bishop said gentle, forgiving words, shaking hands with each one. By a quick motion one kissed his hand, and another said, "You are our father and mother"—one of the highest native compliments. All showed complete gratitude. It was a time and place for manifesting Christian feeling.

It was not strange that these missionaries in the love-feast Sunday morning, and at other times, should exult at the growth of this mission. Just thirty years ago eleven people gathered at Lucknow, constituting the working corps; now, of natives and Americans, there were more than a hundred. Then there was not a native convert, now thousands. Then they had two native helpers—Joel, and another given them by the Presbyterians; now there are hundreds. In that Conference, as in this, Baume, Thoburn, Waugh, Dr. Parker, and Mrs. Parker took part. Their exultation was, "What hath God wrought!"

At the two services Sunday nineteen men were ordained, twelve to the office of deacon and seven to that of elder, all natives. It was profoundly impressive. God is raising up a great body of workers here. These men have been tried for several years, according to the purpose of our missionaries, who are very eager to test well those they put into orders before granting ordination. It is worthy of note, and may be an assurance to people at home, that men raised up through our schools here from the lowest castes are grand workers. Indeed, many of the Americans claim that caste has not vitiated the intellect of these people, but that the lowest caste men are the equal of the high caste men. As the bishop laid his hands on these men, his first duty of this kind, he says his vision reached out till he saw millions instead of thousands coming to Christ in India.

I hear from missionaries, from government officials here a life-time, and others, that the abject, senseless spirit of idolatry is departing, that a return to the older purity of Hindu worship is apparent, and that the power of mission work is greater and grander than ever before.

The Conference is held in midwinter. When New England people in furs are taking sleigh-rides, here from the gardens and yards they cut great banks of roses, bignonia, bale, and other flowers to enliven the Conference rooms. It looks strange to a Yankee.

LETTER XXI.

THE NATIVE RACES OF INDIA.

INDIA presents in its races a complete world. The Bible tells us of three great divisions of Noah's sons, Shem, Ham, Japheth. Modern science confirms the book at this point, as at many others, giving us the same three great races, the Semitic, Turanian, Aryan. All these three races are well represented among the natives of this country, not to speak of the modern influx of Europeans since the conquest of India by the British. There is the lordly Briton, who is much inclined savagely to despise the effeminate natives, and I learned, as never before, the meaning of "the iron heel of the proud oppressor." The natives fear the power and the personal presence of the Westerners, regarding all white-faced strangers, until they learn otherwise, as belonging to this dreaded nation. While among the crowd at the bathing ghats on the banks of the Ganges at Benares I heard the Mohammedan guide tell the people I was an American, and from that time I could plainly see that they regarded me with less servility and fear than before. Still, educated Hindus told me that under British rule their people are the best off they have been since the Mohammedan conquest, and I could believe it.

These three great races have each at different epochs had more or less complete domination of India. The Semitic race is represented by forty or fifty millions of Mohammedans, the Arabs, Persians, Afghans, and the like, who in the tenth, eleventh, and twelfth centuries pushed the conquests of Islam beyond the desert regions of Afghanistan into the vastly rich valleys of the Indus and Ganges, and to the Deccan. Their conquests were strenuously opposed by the native Hindu kingdoms, but the superior strength and energy of this new race, the force given their advance by their great religious fanaticism, the deterioration of their opposers and factions among them, conspired with other things to enable them to extend their dominions to the Himalayas and the Indian Ocean. They generally became wise administrators of affairs, did not exterminate the conquered peoples, nor did they attempt to convert by the sword, relying rather on peaceful modes of propagating their faith. The result was that the Aryan Hindus changed in but small numbers from Brahmanism to Islam. This Semitic race is easily seen by a traveler in India to be taller in form, with thinner features, more aquiline noses, less obsequious, and more restless under the British yoke. Several of the native States remaining are the kingdoms established by this race, and left practically intact by the British.

Going back in history, possibly to fifteen hundred years before the Christian era, beyond any authentic data, indeed, regarding it, we find the second of these great races, the Aryans coming into India, doubtless through the northwestern passes by which the Mohammedans entered. This race, the Hindus, is a section of that race represented to Western history by the Greeks, Romans, Celts, Teutons, and Slavs. Philology and other evidences prove conclusively that the brown Hindus of India are of the same race as their recent conquerors, the Anglo-Saxons. Long separation of each section from the parent stem has caused great differences in complexion, physiognomy, habits, and speech, but once their ancestors were the same people in the central highlands of Asia, from whence part emigrated north-westward, the other south-eastward. It seems as though it must be impossible that these slender, effeminate, brown people had the same ancestors as the white-skinned, large, strong-limbed, progressive races of the West, but it is settled beyond all cavil to be the fact. The Hindus have had a wonderful history in this country. The account preserved by their own and histories of other peoples show this fact. Persian and Macedonian conquerors had reached them before the Mohammedan came. Their literature, the Vedas, the Mahabarata, Ramayana, and other books, show their mental force and fertility. The kingdoms they set up were many of them of imposing proportions, their laws most extensive, their religion, rites, and systems most elaborate, their industrial attainments among the very foremost in the world in their epoch.

But the Hindus were not the first inhabitants of India. Before them the Turanians were here. As the former came in they found the latter already thronging the rich valleys of the great rivers and the extended plains. Their civilization was inferior to that of the Aryans, and their power also, hence they could not stand before the invaders. The subsequent history of these people shows that many were reduced to a low condition of servile labor; others were driven to the hills and jungles where they still subsist, and still others retained throughout all the changes of India a certain autonomous condition, and can be found to-day as nations or peoples. Such is the kingdom of Nepaul; the nations of Tamils, Telugus, Kanarese, and others. History also gives glimpses of considerable kingdoms of this race that arose long after the Hindu conquest. Bema, a native hero of the King Arthur type, has many monuments of his greatness about Bijnour and Moradabad, mounds, tanks, and the like. The low-caste people retain many of these traditions and legends, though the Hindus have always tried to blacken his character as one neglecting Brahman rites and despising caste. On his conquering large sections of the country he proclaimed that no worship should be performed, no oblations offered to, and no gifts bestowed on, the Brahmans. A Sudra monarch was reigning in the seventh century when the Chinese traveler Hwen Thsang visited Mandawar. About the same epoch a lot of herdsmen rose to eminence about Bareilly, whose reservoirs for caring for their cattle still remain. They are said to have had a city extending seven miles along the Ramgunga. Three or four hundred years later, in the eleventh century, the aboriginal tribes of the same locality asserted their independence, and for four or five centuries maintained by their bravery and their strongholds their claim to be a distinct people.

Special interest attaches itself to these people among missionary circles, for the most successful work done in Christianizing the natives is among them. This is recognized not only by the earnest missionaries in the field, but by as high an historical and ethnological authority as Sir W. W. Hunter.

In the older writings of the Hindus these people are rated as dogs, slaves, outcasts. They are the Sudras—the Dasyus, whom the lordly race that has conquered them is to domineer and despise. To them is remanded the most menial kinds of toil; they are to be scavengers, sweepers, farmers, flayers of dead animals, leather-workers, and the like, the kinds of toil that would most deeply degrade an Aryan-Hindu. These thus degraded have been counted in the lowest caste in the Brahman system. Their relation to the higher castes, and to the Hindu gods, even on their conversion to that faith, was hopeless and impossible of improvement.

Of those that fled to the mountains the Bhils of West India furnish a good example. They live in the Aravalli Mountains, and are often spoken of still as wild men. They are born robbers, and only a few days before I passed from Bombay to Delhi on the cars they made a partially successful attempt to wreck and rob a train on the road over which I passed. They live mostly by the chase and robbery, and of late British law is reaching them, causing them in some instances better to recognize the claims of others. Even yet some of them will not meet the tax-collector, but when he comes near their jungle-retreats, on his letting them know by beating a drum that the time has come for them to pay their dues, they wait till he has gone away, then bring their tribute in the rude products of their gardens and jungles, laying it where the collector has been, and, retiring again within their fastnesses, let him come in peace to carry it away. Some of them are skillful archers, shooting with great force by lying on their backs and bending the bow by the aid of their two feet. Most of them now have fire-arms, though others have their primitive weapons. I saw in the native State of Rajputana some armed with bows instead of guns. Others carried a rude sword in a scabbard hung over their shoulders.

But all are not so wild as the Bhils. In the great jungles skirting the Himalayas, which are so malarious that no European can live in them, save during a few weeks of the winter, and where even the Hindu cannot endure the climate, these old tribes live in perfect immunity from fevers. They were doubtless driven there by the Aryan invaders, and are now quiet villagers. They build their huts ten or a dozen feet from the ground on posts to protect themselves from the tigers and leopards that infest those awful jungles. I saw some of these huts beside the railroad from Bareilly to Huldwanee. In the Himalayas they are also quiet villagers, tilling the soil, making rude cloth, doing some mining of copper and iron, and in the malarious valleys, which sometimes rival the jungles, are free from the fevers that attack all others. They seem to have lived so long in such a deadly atmosphere as not to be affected by it.

The most compacted and unchanged of this Turanian race persist in considerable nations in South India, the Tamils, Telugus, and Kanarese. It is estimated by the British authorities that there are nine millions of the Kanarese, twelve millions of the Telugus, and sixteen millions of the Tamils. Being pressed back into the hills and mountains, they have been influenced less than others by their conquering neighbors and enabled to retain more of their race characteristics. These and some kindred tribes represent the family of languages that philologists call the Dravidian. It shows only remote relationship to the other two Indian groups of the Turanian speech, which some students have called the Kalarian and Thibeto-Burman. The people speaking these last two dialects doubtless entered India by the north-eastern passes of the Himalayas, while those speaking the Dravidian by the north-western passes of the Hindu-Kush.

Not only are they found in the jungles, spurs of the Himalayas, and in compact peoples, but multitudes are found in just the condition to which the Sanskrit writers assigned them long before the Christian era. They are the Sudras—the men of work, considered so vile and low as not to have any caste. As sweepers, farmers, and the like they have lived through long generations in the condition given them by the inexorable laws of conquest, religion, custom, and lawgivers; patient, hopeful, enduring, but now with a future opening to them through Christianity.

Many of these people have accepted the Hindu religion, and in turn have doubtless engrafted some points of their earlier cult upon the Brahman system. The efforts made by the Brahmans to convert them to their own faith seem to have been thus far only moderately successful. In a state of partial neglect those who have been considered worshipers of the Brahman gods have kept much of their ancient faith, hence do not present a pure phase of the Hindu cult. In other instances, while in contact with their conquerors all these long generations, living with them as their servants, doing their hard drudgery, and subject to all the allurements to change to the faith of their conquerors, these strange people have not become Hinduized, but, retaining the worship of their own race-gods, are now counted as "devil-worshipers." It is the custom, history shows us, for conquering peoples of another faith to denominate the gods of their vassals as mere devils. So the Roman missionaries who evangelized our Anglo-Saxon ancestors called the Teutonic gods, Woden, Thor, Freya, and others. The Spanish conquerors of Mexico in the same way regarded the gods of the Aztecs and Toltecs. Here in India it is only the old story of the dominant race and religion.

I was half inclined to think that if I were compelled to worship the deities of either the Hindu or the Turanian tribes of India I should choose the latter cult in preference to the former, for in a broad sense the Turanians are nature-worshipers. The forces of nature, the rain and rivers, the flowers and trees, the birds and beasts, are surely less degrading to the nobility in human character than many of the teachings of the Brahman faith, with their infamous emblems, their spirit and practice in the field of human sympathy and morals. These aboriginal tribes are very religious in their way. Vast varieties of charms, amulets, magic, are used by them. With the bodies of the dead they bury implements, utensils, and weapons for use in the world beyond, showing by this a vivid hope of immortality, and they make offerings to the spirits of departed ones, with many strange and intricate rites. Most of these tribes, especially those of the jungles and hills, down to modern times, offered human sacrifices. It is a notion of some, doubtless a memory of their migration from that direction, and with a hope of returning, to bury their dead with the feet northward. They seem less bigoted than the Hindus, and for this, and not being so intrenched in caste and rigid exclusiveness, are found to be more accessible to the teachings of Christianity than any other race in India. The wonderful work done among the Telugus by the Baptists can be better understood when it is known that they are one of those almost autonomous nations. So of the Karens of Burma, an allied tribe. The surprising influx to our Church from the low castes of the North India Conference, especially on the Moradabad District, can be explained in the same way. The missionaries are finding that these people will listen to and accept the Gospel; hence they turn to them.

The physical aspects of this race vary from those of

some Mongolian characteristics among the Indian slopes of the Himalayas to those of many negroloid characteristics of the plains. Still some of the mountaineers, as the Paharis above Almorah, are much less brown than the Hindus of the lowlands. They are a sturdier race physically than the Hindus, possibly owing to their having done more manual labor than those through the passing centuries. Some of them, especially of the Mongolian type, have a remarkable development of the calves of the legs, in this making a curious contrast to the thin legs of the Hindus. Often they develop great strength as porters, wharfmen, and at other kinds of labor requiring muscular power. Their disposition is usually kind and gentle, and they make most faithful followers. In war they have proved themselves of brave and spirited disposition. They have been much used by the British as soldiers, the Sepoys of Clive and Coote being mostly of these people. Long after the dreadful Sepoy rebellion none but these aboriginal people, who remained true to the British during that fateful time, were permitted to enter the military service of the government, though of late any of the natives may enlist. The native regiments that did not mutiny in that struggle were Turanian, the Goorkhas, Sikhs, and others justly renowned for their bravery. When Disraeli startled Europe by bringing a contingent of Indian troops to the English stations of the Mediterranean to enforce his demand that the matters about Constantinople be settled as British diplomacy saw best, those troops were not Aryan-Hindus, nor Semitic Mohammedans, but Turanian soldiers, the aboriginal tribes of India.

LETTER XXII.

BENARES, THE HOLY CITY OF THE HINDUS.

A RUN of three hundred and fifty miles from Bareilly to Benares has brought two of us, Ernest Badley, son of the Rev. Dr. Badley, and myself, to this city of the saints. Of course one who visits India at all must see this place. Ernest, being familiar with the vernacular, is a valuable companion, as well as a pleasant one on his own account. A guide who could speak English was engaged and consulted as to the sight-seeing, a ghari was hired, and an hour or two after our arrival we were off for the banks of the sacred Ganges. The hotel is in the English quarter or cantonment, so that we secured a charming ride of nearly four miles through the native streets and bazars, seeing in them the ceaselessly interesting sights of an Indian city. A short distance from the river's edge we left the carriage, making our way to the water down a steep bank among piles of rocks, wood, and other obstructions, to find boats and queer craft of one kind and another moored to the shore in crowded confusion, among platforms for bathing, stone steps, cells of fakirs, drying clothes, nearly nude men and only a little less uncovered women, all of them worshiping by their peculiar methods, or vociferously begging backsheesh of us Americans.

Securing a boat for us two large enough to carry at least two yoke of oxen, with an upper deck where the guide sat with us, to point out the sights, with the rowers below, we pushed out into the stream, and then were able to look back on the banks. Up and down for nearly a mile there were the most unique, most strange and lively religious scenes I have ever witnessed. It was one of the fifty feast-days of the year, and the sight presented at eleven o'clock was not lacking the activity and vividness that usually characterizes it only at early morning. These banks, up which the water must rise thirty or fifty feet at the rainy season, are mostly paved with a succession of stone steps, coming down from the foundation of temples, palaces, and buildings above to the water's edge and continuing even below that. On these steps hundreds were bathing, only high caste people here, while those of low caste could bathe along the sandy shores which could be seen farther down the river. Priests, sleek, fat, their heads mostly shaven, were every-where among the bathers, directing their ablutions, reading from their sacred books, selling flowers and sweets for offerings to the river, in their way doing faithfully the offices of their order.

Soon the boat came to the burning ghat, and as this was the first time I had seen bodies thus being disposed of I had the steersman fasten up so we could see the affair to our heart's content. One dead body, wrapped in white cloth, smeared with red paint or ochre, lay with its feet bathed in the water of the river, awaiting its time for burning. The priests tramped over it while at their duties as though it was only a log. Close beside this one was another body that had just been laid on the pyre, the wood piled up cob-house fashion three feet high and about six feet long and wide. As we came one was touching the body with the sacred paint, then a white cloth was spread over it, which was also smeared with the red paint. Then other sticks of wood were laid on the body, one way and other, until enough was put upon the pile to consume it. When all was ready the priest in charge, taking a brand on a handful of dried grass from the fire burning at another pyre, ran twice around this pile with the flaming bundle, and as he dropped it another priest, with a handful of dried grass, lighting it at this fire, stuffed it into the funeral pyre, which was quickly ablaze. To hurry the burning the priest poured some kind of oil, possibly clarified butter, on it. Just above this one was another in full blaze as we came up. Through the flame and smoke I could see the partly consumed body, arms, skull, ribs, and other parts. Still another was nearly burned up, at which one of the priests was working, crowding the brands and the disjointed members together with a long bamboo pole. When the fire got so low that it could not burn the fragments any more he pulled the crisped bent trunk out of the coals and roughly pushed it with the bamboo stick into the water of the sacred Ganges, where, food for fishes and alligators, it sank out of sight.

Several other bodies in different stages of consumption were burning here and there on the steep banks; on one side, overlooking it all, an old priest, sitting on his haunches, evidently had charge of the proceedings, for he gave directions every now and then in a loud voice. A few idle spectators, possibly the friends of the dead, also sat on their haunches near by, but there was no sign of mourning. I noticed, as an attendant brought earthen jars of water to quench the dying embers of those fires from which the charred remains had been removed, that he approached the fires by backing toward them; then one of the priests, coming in front of the water-carrier, would, by a sudden push, throw the jar and water from his head upon the fire, breaking the jar and spilling the water at the same time. I judged it must be some symbolic act, though why they did so the guide could not tell.

The scenes at the bathing ghats were exceedingly interesting. We watched them for hours. Little platforms just above the water, built of bamboo, were here and there thrust out over the river, the two planks composing the floor being a little space apart, between which the bathers could wash themselves or their clothing. For these people seem to believe Wesley's saying, that cleanliness is next to godliness, though never having heard of it; more, their cleanliness is a part of godliness, since to wash and dry their clothing at the sacred river is a part of their worship. So on that day rich Hindus, men of rank and office, and gentlewomen in rich clothing, would wash their garments and hang them in the light breeze to dry. The grown people took the whole proceedings in a grave enough way, but some of the boys made it a gala time by jumping in, diving, swimming, and pushing one another off into the water. Occasionally a man standing to his middle in water would quickly dip himself three times fully under the muddy tide. Many had baskets and bundles of flowers, sweets, leaves, twigs, grasses, and the like, and were casting them one by one upon the water, so that the slow current was carrying away a continuous lot of these things spread upon its surface. At one place a woman, squatting beside a large pile of yellow marigolds, was casting them in, one by one, as a priest stood there evidently reciting from some of the sacred books. Another woman, who stood in the water above her knees, having bathed her face, joined her hands in adoration toward the sun. Several times I saw the people thus pray to the sun. They would dip up some of the water in their hands, and by a peculiar process squirt it out through their fingers; while others would take the filthy stuff in their mouths, either to drink it or squirt it away.

Along the very brink of the water little stone and brick shrines or cells would have sitting in them a fakir or priest, though many were vacant. In the great temple far up the bank some kind of worship was going on, as we could hear rude music and strange sounds from them. These temples and palaces were usually built, the guide said, by some rich rajah or prince, making a place for him to occupy for the time being, as he came here for worship. Above one built by the king of Nepaul were immense brazen glistening fixtures of some import or other that I could not learn. Bells here and there were hung up that would be tapped from the outer edge, not swung to and fro as we ring them. Very few of these temples or palaces are of architectural beauty. Among them was a Mohammedan mosque built by Araunzebe, as though these people meant to force their belief upon their former subjects, its minaret tall and graceful. Many of these buildings are in partial decay, others have their foundations undermined by the river, so they are leaning or tumbling down. Are they, like their system, touched with final decay and collapse?

Here and there along the banks were platforms built of brick and mortar six or ten feet wide, and as high, on which a fakir would sit reading from his sacred books to such as would care to listen, his place covered with a roof, or sometimes with only a big grass umbrella. As we went ashore from the hired boat we found ourselves heading a long procession of priests, beggars, and people, one word at least of their jargon being intelligible—"backsheesh!" One of them fastened himself to us like a leech, in spite of our strong declaration that we needed no guide but the one from the hotel. At every point of interest he was on hand to give us information.

We soon found our way to the sacred well or tank, the most holy spot of this exceedingly sacred city. It is about fifteen feet wide by thirty long, and twenty feet deep; is a little way from the edge of the river, and at such a height that high water fills it, and then receding leaves it full. The missionaries called my attention to this peculiar holy of holies before I had come here. The water yet remaining in the tank was about three feet deep, and so filthy that it was green with dirt and slime; yet walking about in this stuff were half a dozen priests nearly naked, to receive the flowers and pice of the devotees. The surface was well covered with flowers, marigolds and bale, in single profusion or in wreaths. For a pice or two a priest brought a couple of wreaths of the sweet-scented bale flowers for Ernest and me. Groups of women stood here and there on the lower step by which the water was approached, each group attended by a priest who was giving directions for the worship and prayers. They would drink that fetid water, bathe in it, wash their garments in it, and cast flowers and sweets on its surface. A favorite use of the water was to take some up in the hand and let it slowly drip through the fingers. Some sat or stood with strings of sacred beads in their hands which one by one they would slip along, calling on their god, "Ram, Ram, Ram!" As I turned from this sight a snake-charmer stood behind me with a hand-cage of snakes, wanting to show me his cobras. About his shoulders was lying a boa-constrictor full two inches in diameter. The guide had told the crowd we were Americans, and I could distinguish that word as they repeated it to one another. One old fakir was covered from his tall head-gear down to his hips and legs with strings of their beads composed of fruit-stones that they use for saying prayers. It looked like a cuirass of chain-mail. A foot-print of Vishnu, as large as that of a baby, in a piece of marble, was a cause for demanding backsheesh, as also a marble post marking a place specially holy, where a beautiful princess long ago performed suttee. The re-volting, sensual emblems of Mahadeo every-where greeted one on the bases of temples and palaces, on shrines, and at particular spots along the banks, the li-bations of sacred waters, clarified butter, sweets, and ochre showing plainly the wide worship of this dread-fully debasing god.

I wanted at least to bathe my hands in the sacred river, so, selecting a ghat that was not crowded, Er-nest and I went down to the brink, and, as we would do in the Merrimac or Mississippi, washed our hands from the dust and grime of traveling. A dozen or two of the devotees stood looking at the Christians perform-ing what was to them a sacred act, but to us hardly more than a noon-day hand-washing. Even the Mo-hammedan guide, following suit, dipped up some in his hand and splashed it over his face. A fakir close by vociferously set up a demand for something, and on my asking the guide what he meant he said the man urged that as we had bathed in their sacred river we must give him money. I said, "No, no," but he was persistent, and, as we walked away, he followed us, loudly urging his claim. I told the guide to send him away, as I should not pay him any thing, but still he kept on, and quite a crowd collected to see what would come of it all. After a while I stopped, putting my hand in my pocket, and he rushed close to me for the coveted and well-earned money. I stared hard into his gleaming eyes, slowly drew out my hand with a single pice, and, smiling on the persistent beggar, laid it on his open palm. Seeing what it was, and, I think, fully appreciating the joke, he turned grinning away, to the laughter and loud talk of his fellows.

From this fascinating locality we went a mile back into the city to the region sacred to the worship of the cow. After leaving the carriage we walked along narrow, dirty lanes to enter a small court in which was the figure of a recumbent bull cut from a single block of stone, measuring ten feet in length, four in width, and five in height. All about this figure and the court were numerous signs of worship, flowers, sweets, garlands, and the like. Under an open colonnade was the "Well of Knowledge," down which one of the gods had been thrown, but his virtues are not enough to keep the water sweet. Over the mouth of the deep well a cloth is spread to prevent the rice, sweets, and flowers that are offered to the god from falling into the water, but the success being only partial the smell coming from it made me cry, "Faugh!" A priest keeps a bucket of the water fresh drawn for the faithful to drink and get cups of it for holy purposes, but we thought we would not indulge after the odor had once invaded our nostrils. By looking down into the well one becomes very wise. This we did. But if the knowledge obtained is as fetid as the smell then it must be like certain doctrines I wot of. About the walks and lanes were emblems of Mahadeo, as well as many living cows, calves, and bulls. The Golden Temple here, while not a large one, is immensely rich and ornate, its dome, towers, and columns being covered with gold-leaf and glittering in the sun. In the same place is the real "Cow Temple." Being foreign unbelievers, we were not permitted to enter the sacred place by the regular entrance, though possibly our Mohammedan guide was the plague-spot, but we could go into a narrow corridor through a low door by which the dung from this stable-temple was taken out! This we did, to find one of the strangest sights for a place of worship I have ever seen. In the temple area, not large but well attended, were some altars and other paraphernalia of worship, many devotees, and several priests. But the strangest of all were the cows, calves, and bulls walking about, seeming to enjoy their part of the programme, for they were at liberty to go to the altars and eat thence the flowers, leaves, grasses, sweets, and other things offered, and by this had become fat and sleek. Some devotee would approach one of these animals and reach out his hand toward it, when it would open its mouth to have chucked into it fresh flowers or sweets. Water that was holy had been poured upon the altars to run over the floor, and water that was not holy was over it also, and other things, till this precinct of sanctity was as foul and filthy as a poorly kept New England cow-stable; yet here was worship! Far in a recess was a statue of "Saturday," the guide said, but later I learned it was a statue of Saturn. Why Saturn was here I do not know. It was a bright, silvern face hung about with wreaths, but with no body at all. One image of worship was a woman, and many of the devotees were of that sex. A peacock, sacred among the Hindus, wandered about among the people and cows.

Thence we went to the gold-beaters' street, passing

that of the brass-workers, to find offered for sale most charming work, merely ornamental as well as sacred. Into an upper room, along narrowest, darkest passages, the guide brought us to find the people at work weaving their exquisite materials, gold and silver and silk brocades and cloth. Giving Ernest and me chairs, the native trader sat on his haunches while the attendant brought web after web of the beautiful things. One, of five yards, cost two hundred rupees. The colors, besides the gold and silver, were of the brightest blue, green, purple, brown, red, yellow, and so on. I finally bought a short piece of gold and silver trimming, and when only one was purchased the quiet trader wanted to know of the guide if I would not take more—if I did not need some more for others of the wives at home! I held up one finger to the sly rogue.

In spite of the guide's importunities for us to drive direct to the hotel for tiffin and go to the monkey temple the next day, we had the ghari-driver go at once to the latter. It is far in the outskirts of the city, and on the road we passed one of the famous juggernauts, now quietly standing under an open shed. It was about a dozen feet each way, and high enough to have an upper story, where were seats for the priests and a place for the god. Thick wheels supported it, and holes were in the front axle for stout ropes to be tied for the crowds to draw it. Missionaries tell me that the stories of people casting themselves under the wheels are far-drawn, arising, doubtless, from accidents, as in haste and excitement the great crowds draw the huge car through the streets. This peculiar mode of worship is falling into desuetude.

The monkey temple is one of the most noted fanes of this famous city. Beside it is a deep, broad tank, with steps leading to it on all sides, like so many of these bathing-places, and here a boy having been nearly drowned some time during the day the family were all at the temple returning devoutest thanks for the favor of rescuing him. This temple has extensive grounds, trees, and accessory buildings. In front is a corridor where each morning a kid is sacrificed, and we saw the blood and the instruments of sacrifice where its head had been cut off. We gave the guide some pice to buy grain and sweets for the monkeys, but only one or two of these could be called up from their hiding-places, the chilly winter air being too severe for them to be hungry. As we passed the door we handed the waiting priest half a rupee, who in return flung over our hats a garland of beautiful flowers, which we wore about the temple and home to our hotel. It was a kind of devotement to the god, so we thought we ought to be pretty good after all these consignments to the deities of Benares. In the temple we could see from a distance only, being unbelievers, the holy of holies, in which was a figure of Durga, the Pandora of the Hindus, since from her, as from the Greek goddess, numberless ills have come to the race.

A couple of magnificent bells hung in the court, which, on being struck, gave forth a rich, mellow tone. In one part of the grounds stand some grand old tamarind-trees, said to be a thousand years old, able to tell strange stories, if they would, of India's mutations. One hollow one is said to be the lying-in place of all the monkey mothers. Beggars, as usual, followed us with their impudent importunities, and one boy ran far along beside the ghari, as we went to the hotel, trying to extort by his very persistency something from us, but he got no pice at all.

LETTER XXIII.

THE WORK OF THE WOMAN'S FOREIGN MISSIONARY SOCIETY—SCHOOLS—SUNDAY-SCHOOLS.

It is rather a remarkable coincidence that at least three mighty forces for the bringing in of Christ's kingdom should be correlative—Methodism woman's work and the missionary spirit. At Bombay I was introduced to the representative of the Woman's Foreign Missionary Society as a walking interrogation-point, and as I met them I felt willing to ask about this part of the church work the same as I did others. Their toil in most of its results has been a surprise to me, as was that of other departments. It is all better than I had surmised before getting into the field. The mission of Methodism is partly to woman, whether she is found in America or Asia. Her enfranchisement in Methodism began with Wesley's woman leaders and stewards, and its highest gift to her is when it admitted her into the Central Conference in India as a lay delegate, with all the opportunities of work before her which that right gives. The chances in all parts of Asia for woman to be benefited are vast and deep. It is not to bring material good so much as spiritual benefit, but the good done covers woman's whole being—soul and body and spirit.

The work I saw in foreign fields embodies several departments. The great schools built up in India, Burma, and Japan were a joy and wonder to me, who have always believed in woman since I got well acquainted with my mother, sisters, and wife. From these schools are going out the enfranchised Christian young women, thrusting strange leaven into the social, industrial, intellectual, and religious life of these heathen countries. There is vast difference between woman as a plaything or slave and woman as a Christian worker.

Prominent among the first of these schools I saw was the one at Moradabad under the direction of Mrs. Dr. E. W. Parker. A hundred and sixty girls were there, ranging in age from six to eighteen, pursuing studies reaching from primary grade up to those taught in an American high school, and some languages of India not taught in America. In a broad compound, or yard, the buildings are located, put up one story high, of brick, narrow, so that fresh air can easily be obtained from both ways through the rooms; earth floors covered with mats; a protecting veranda in front; one of the buildings adapted for recitation-rooms, others for dormitories, then dining-room, kitchen, and the like. But more interesting than the odd buildings that are adapted to the needs of Indian people and climate were the girls there being taught. As it is partly a high school, to which girls come who have studied more or less in the primary schools founded here and there all over Dr. Parker's large Rohilcund District, these girls form a choice body of students. Only the most promising ones are brought in from the lower schools, and as there is a large number of these schools it can be seen that the selection of those to give the advantage of the higher schools must be very careful.

I saw them at study, poring hard over their books of English, Urdu, Persian; of reading, spelling, writing; of arithmetic, algebra, geometry, at all of which and in others many become eminently proficient. At a chapel service I was present to stand face to face with a prophecy and promise that almost drew tears from my tough eyes. As in any seminary the teachers sat together, the pupils fronting them. A cabinet-organ accompanied the singing, a prayer in the vernacular was offered, my few words of cheer were translated, and they were dismissed to their regular duties. They are a brown-faced, bright-eyed lot of girls, decently clad in the cheap calico dresses and head-enveloping chuddars.

Then I saw them at dinner. In a spacious dining-hall, seated on matting spread on the ground, they were arranged in long rows, each with a plate in her hand. When all was still thanks were sung to the heavenly Father; then the cooks brought a large kettle of a kind of vegetable stew composed of bean-pods and cauliflower, and the matron, assisted by two of the large girls, dipped a plateful out for each one as she came from her place in the line to the side of the dining-hall, where the cook had deposited the kettle. To each girl was given also a loaf of their native bread, looking more like a large griddle-cake than what we call a loaf. These loaves are generally baked by being stuck on the side of a hole in the ground, first heated by burning some weeds or leaves; but in this case they were baked on a broad iron griddle. I tasted the stew, to find it so strong of pepper, or chillies, that one taste was all my Yankee mouth could endure. It was a constant wonder to me that the people of India seemed to need so much pungent condiments in their food, but I have found my own appetite craving sharper condiments here than at home, owing, doubtless, to the enervating climate.

In addition to their studies these girls are taught to make their own clothing, take care of their rooms, prepare and cook their own food, yet so as not to detract time enough from their studies as to injure the mental drill. When through school they must go into native homes as wives of teachers, preachers, government workmen, and the like ; so Mrs. Parker's plan is not to educate them away from the possibility of living successfully in such homes. They are not to be heathen homes, to be sure, but Christian ones, for of all the hundreds of girls who have been in this school and taken in it the full course of five years or more not one has been known to go back to heathenism or to a bad life. It is a marvelous record.

A story they told me of one girl shows the worth and power of their teaching and character. She was from a family brought out of heathenism a few years before, and had spent three or four years in the school, a promising student. Two of her younger sisters were there also, coming in later than she had done. It transpired that the father through some influence relapsed into heathenism, and only waited for vacation to come in order to have his girls return to his home, and then, not permitting them to go back to the school, compel them to enter with him on the worship of the idols. On coming home he told the older one in the course of a few days that she was to be married at such a time to a certain man, though she was but fourteen years old. She pleaded with her father that she wanted to go back to school ; that she did not want to marry at that time; then, finally, that the man designed for her was a heathen, and she would marry only a Christian. But the father was inexorable till she, reproving him for returning to the old idols, told him he might go ahead with the preparations for her marriage, but when the time came she should not be found, and that he might look for her body in some well or tank. This last resort determined upon by the girl called a halt in the man's mind and purpose. He stopped the marriage plans, and then the brave girl urged and begged him to return to the worship of Christ; and so potent were her words and influence that he again threw away his idols and sent the three girls back to school. The oldest one, having finished her course, is now in the Government Medical College at Agra, and the others are doing well in this school. O, women of America, believe that these sisters of yours in India are worthy of your work, your money, your prayers, and confidence!

Schools like this or but slightly modified, all doing grand work for God and humanity, are scattered through India in different denominations, while the government furnishes professional ones for those who wish to take a medical course, and chances for a college course to those who desire to go beyond matriculation, to which grade most of our girls' schools take the pupils. At Lucknow our own Church is commencing, with Miss Florence Perrine in charge, to teach girls beyond the matriculation grade, having already taken a few two years in a college course. I hope the embryo will yet produce a full college course for our Christian girls here. I was delighted with the nicely kept grounds, the commodious buildings, and complete air of comfort about the whole establishment at Lucknow, and Miss De Vine's successful conduct of her variously graded school. Many a point in our property secured in India has come to us in a providential way that is surprising to me; some gift of government, some lease of long standing from a native, or, possibly, a purchase at astonishingly low prices. In this school at Lucknow the expenses for the boarding department are all met by the fees charged, so that the expense to the American Church is comparatively slight. Some of the girls are learning the American mode of working their own way through school. When we think of those girls, at the most but one generation out of the abjectest condition of subjection and ignorance, so eager for an education that they will toil and try to get it, those helping them can be assured that the help is well expended. In all the schools many are converted, just as is occurring in America. As at home, so here, that change often works wonders in behavior, character, and work. Girls from heathen homes, as well as from Christian ones, are led to conversion by their teachers and the Spirit. It cannot be otherwise than that in such work the teachers should be happy and contented as I have found them to be here. Happy the women that can be in such work, and fortunate the girls for whom they sacrifice and toil!

In Calcutta the school-building, owing to lack of space, could not be built as well adapted to native habit and taste as those in localities like Moradabad and Lucknow; hence, here it is of three stories and more like an American school building. It is the same at Naini Tal, in the school under Miss Easton for European and American children; and each house has the dormitories not separate as we do, but so arranged that ten, twenty, or forty girls sleep in one room. The people of India are extremely social among themselves, and especially is this true of the girls; so they desire to sleep and eat together. I noticed in Mrs. Parker's school that two of the smaller girls often ate off the same plate as they held it between them. If they are made to observe rigid caste lines before attending Christian schools, so that only those of the same caste associate with one another, after coming to these schools they generally learn that no caste can be observed here. Dr. Parker insisted, in his school for boys, that in Christianity they are higher than any caste.

The schools for girls in all parts of Asia that I visited are kept separate from those of the boys, and that is as yet a necessity; but there are tendencies toward a condition of things when that will no longer be a necessity. At the great Sunday-school *fête* in Lucknow I saw groups of native girls from our schools going about the park as freely as such girls do in America, but which would not be thought of by the natives outside the Christian church work. Such promise in that to India and to her women! The nineteenth century is truly woman's century, whether woman is white, brown, yellow, or black.

At Moradabad and elsewhere I caught passing glimpses of the primary schools for girls; and while they are crude and strange, when gauged by our notion of a primary school, they are full of promise and prophecy. Under some veranda or tree a group of a dozen or two of girls would collect to read, learn arithmetic and geography, under the direction of a teacher from our mission, or some one selected for this purpose from among skilled non-Christian teachers. They told me that sometimes those who were married would come, bringing their babies in their arms or astride one hip, as they generally carry them. Mohammedans as well as Hindus attend these schools. The Bible is one of the principal things taught, the parables, the simple, straight statements of history, personal life, and doctrine appealing most sweetly to the keen minds of these young Indian girls. Besides their studies they are often taught to work—learning to sew, embroider, knit, and such light tasks. Their attempt at singing was funny, and in many instances most commendable. Their native songs are sometimes changed so as to express Christian sentiment; and then, too, some of the native tunes have had words composed for them by our missionaries. Good translations of our popular hymns have been made, it being a most interesting thing in the schools and churches to hear "What a friend we have in Jesus," "Nearer, my God, to thee," and other familiar hymns sung, not a word of which I could understand, though sung in a familiar tune. At such times I would join in, using the English words, thus singing in the spirit, if not, in that place, with the understanding also.

Another active agency in giving girls and women their place in India is the custom very recently entered upon by our Church, and possibly by others, of admitting girls and boys into the same Sunday-schools, and, in a few instances, into the same primary schools. At Shahjehanpore I saw a hundred boys and fifty girls, not one of them Christians, in one Sunday-school in a crowded part of the city; the boys in two rooms of a mud-house, and the girls in an adjoining room, with two broad door-ways between them. In the reports of the North India Conference there came the fact from all parts that mixed Sunday-schools were going on as regularly as though it had been done ten or twenty years. Of course this has been the case for years in cities, where we have native churches and schools of converted boys and girls; but for it to take place among non-Christian communities was a thing unknown till in the last two or three years. The use of women teachers in boys' schools, the use of American women in projected work, the way the native girls are being educated in schools, both Christian and non-Christian; the genial, helpful, assuring influence of the native Bible women and medical practitioners, all must aid in this elevation of women. God intends the Woman's Foreign Missionary Society, in his beneficent designs for womanhood, to set women at work from races who have had generations of cumulative Christian culture, and to enable them to carry the light to those in the darkness into which heathenism has plunged woman.

LETTER XXIV.

WOMAN'S WORK—MEDICAL, BIBLE READERS, DEACONESSES.

YEARS ago the women of the Christian Churches found that they could reach their sisters in darkness in several ways through the knowledge and practice of medicine. With devoted women to know is to do. Our Church has not been slow to use this means of reaching the homes and women of other lands. So I have found a medical missionary at almost all the great stations, hard at work for the natives at the same time that they stand as guardians of the health of our missionaries. The more scientific development of medical knowledge among Western nations, coupled with the superior skill of our physicians, enables our woman doctors to do a vast amount of good to suffering humanity in those countries.

The general plan of work is to have a dispensary centrally located in a city to which all can come at certain hours in the day for advice, medicine, or treatment. As they gather in the waiting-room, to go in their turn to the doctor, a Bible reader is with them reading of the greater Physician, telling gospel truths and incidents, and singing Christian songs; by this means much spiritual good is done, along with the bodily good. Two or three times I was taken to such dispensaries, to see a few of the poor things waiting for their call from the doctor, or else, in other cases, they had been permitted to pass from my masculine presence to the "pardah" of some of the back rooms. In most cases there is such poverty that they cannot pay, so the medicine and treatment are totally free; in cases of attendance on the rich they are permitted to pay for such service. Now and then some native prince or rich rajah is so grateful for the restoration of himself or some of his family to health that thousands of rupees are forthcoming, and it not infrequently happens that invaluable concessions for chances to preach and teach Christianity are freely given by him.

Superstitions regarding ill health are hardly less pernicious than those concerning idolatry; indeed, the two are closely blended in their beliefs and practices. Even the very medicines given out by our women are sometimes regarded not as things to be taken and used as good ministries, but are kept stored away in the hut or about their persons as talismans. At other times they will take all the medicine designed for several doses and several days at one time and then return for more. Often the missionary does not allow strong medicine to be taken away, but requires her helper to prepare and give it on the spot. In many instances outlying dispensaries are established in some populous district or large town, in charge of a skilled native, some student in medicine under the American doctor or one from the medical college. A judicious issue of medicines is the most to be expected of such establishments, but in India that is much.

Another way our missionaries have of doing good and leading to the truth is to take a medicine-chest with them as they attend a great mela or Hindu religious festival. There as they gather to worship their native gods the children of the true God come with healing for soul and body, and many attend, to receive the double healing. Dr. Christiancy, of Bareilly, who was at the Brindaban mela this year, told me that her medicine-chest from which she was dealing medicine to the crowds that flocked about her, and the teaching and preaching of Christ, kept the masses close about her and her helpers totally oblivious of the passing of Krishna's image, though it was one of his most attractive processions.

Our missionaries at these melas have some rich experiences. Miss Downey told me of the people crowding about her to hear the story of Jesus in such numbers that sometimes she could not go from place to place, and those who had heard once or twice were most eager to hear again. Once a lot of men who had stood apart as she was preaching to the women came as soon as she was done with those, begging her to speak the same things to them. Sitting on the ground and on their haunches, they listened for half an hour to her and then begged her to go on. Dr. McDowell told of her and Mrs. Dr. Scott's being at the Brindaban mela when a man disposed to create a disturbance was stilled by a native policeman, who then said in a low voice, "What these ladies say is true; I am a Christian myself."

Every-where the grosser forms of idol-worship are being abandoned. The game of imposture practiced by the priests upon the credulity of the people is less and less a paying one. The very fakirs under special vows are vastly fewer, they told me, and for myself I saw very little of their peculiar practices. The whole life of India is being touched by the power of Christianity, and even women are coming in for their portion of its benedictions.

It was my supreme joy to see the inside of one of the Lady Dufferin Hospitals, that at Cawnpore, under the direction of Mrs. N. M. Mansell, M.D. It has been established with funds raised at a fair at Naini Tal, and when that fund is exhausted it will be turned over to the American mission. It is in a thickly populous part of the city, where women who have never before been outside their closed homes can easily reach it. In some cases the husbands come as far as the court-gate and there wait while their afflicted wives are being treated inside. By a curious decision of her ladyship, neither the physician nor her attendants in the Dufferin Hospitals are permitted to say one word to the patients on the subject of Christianity. Waiting was the fate of Rev. Dr. Mansell as his wife took me in to see the inside, where he had never gone. Being a passing stranger I could be permitted to see it. Mrs. Mansell's assistant is a native high caste woman, very efficient in her place and duty, whom the low caste people that come there for treatment hold in such veneration that they are said actually to worship her, falling down before her as they come into her presence and when receiving the medicine from her hand. This sacred one, this goddess, was certainly not up to the Greek ideal of the goddess in beauty, judging from their expressed thought in the statues of Venus and Diana, and comparing that ideal with this woman. Through the somewhat spacious court we were led by this sacred one across the wide veranda, where the man of the house, when it was a native dwelling, would receive his visitors, or he might take them into the first room, also spacious, opening from the veranda by two or three doors. In this place was the consulting-room, and on each side of it smaller rooms, in which were operating-tables and other fixtures of a hospital. Three or four rooms farther back were the real living rooms of the women, when it was a dwelling, with no windows, all the light entering them coming from the front room. They are now fitted for actual hospital-rooms, with beds and other necessary furnishings. They seemed to me veritable cells. I was exceedingly glad to see the inside of one of those houses occupied by the rich, and here I had the chance. Mrs. Mansell receives and prescribes for hundreds of the women every week. Her reputation for success has been a benediction to those who by it are encouraged to come to her for treatment.

Not far away from this very hospital where Anglo-Saxon women are doing so much for their Indian sisters was the well made famous in the awful Cawnpore massacre as the place where the bodies of six or seven scores of English women and children were flung after their remorseless butchery in a bungalow near by. I visited the spot with Professor Rockey, to stand in silent sorrow, as I recalled the horrors of that day. It seemed just that no native is permitted to enter the gate-way of the iron fence surrounding the place and the beautiful angel cut in marble holding the palm-leaves in attitude of grief, nor to approach near it. Even the driver of our carriage knew his restrictions, and kept far away from the English soldier at the well. That is the only punishment, and in the crowded city near by English and American missionaries are devoutly laboring for the very descendants of those who did the bloody deed. That is a part of God's revenge.

The stories Mrs. Dr. Mansell told of the suffering of women, the brutal treatment and coarse neglect bestowed on those whom all human instincts should protect and help, the awful showing in her able paper in the

Indian Evangelical Review on "Child Marriage," of the results of this on the deterioration of the noble Aryan race of India, and the suffering and destruction it entails upon the child-mothers, all, and more, combined to give me a picture of India's needs that made my heart's blood grow chill. Woman in heathenism is a pitiable object. The Master who encouraged Mary also to sit at his feet, as well as the twelve, is leading India's millions of women to do the same. Never has the worth of that place seemed greater to me than when I have seen these poor women here receiving its blessings, both material and spiritual.

I have asked many of our experienced missionaries about the probable outlook for Ramabai's movement in behalf of the widows, and the unanimous opinion is that vast difficulties lie in the way of success. That something is demanded to ameliorate the lot and condition of widows is as plain as the sunlight, they say, but the problem is how to succeed. The missionaries have tried to reach them as a class, and so far have met with very indifferent success. Our church at Lucknow has had a home for them of some modified purpose, one at Shahjehanpore, also on a small scale, and a few have found refuge in each, but their number is small, and the class of women entering has not been the child-widows so much as older ones, whose course of life since widowhood has often thrown additional difficulties in the way of their making useful members of society. Child-widows and those younger could be taught and set at work with a noble purpose. They say that the American Board has met with a slightly better measure of success than we have, but in it all the results have been but meager. My heart was deeply moved as Miss Blackmar, at Lucknow, and Mr. Bare, at Shahjehanpore, and others, told of the interesting cases which came under their direction and knowledge. The home at Lucknow has been made into a deaconess home by the action of the North India Conference at its late session, though that need not necessarily change its distinctive help to such as may come to claim its benefits. But such are the notions and superstitions in regard to widows that it is extremely difficult to gain access to them. Often our zenana workers go months to a home before learning there is a widow living there, as she is always hustled out of sight when the women come, since she is the household drudge and actually a slave in the home of her dead husband's relations. By a real exchange of money or presents she had become the property of the husband's family, and after his death can never go back to her own people. It is the belief that through neglecting the gods or other fault of hers the husband died, and now she must suffer to atone for his loss in the household. Half-starved, miserably clad, overworked, beaten, despised, these widows are the most pitiable of objects. Being owned by the dead husbands' fathers they can hardly at all get away from them, hence our missionaries have succeeded but poorly in reaching them. If God has raised up Ramabai to reach this suffering, despised class of India's women the blessings she can bring are numberless. But it will doubtless be a long, hard struggle, with many delays and some mutations.

The devoted wife of President Scott, of the Theological School at Bareilly, is doing a most productive work. Almost all the young men coming there for the benefit of the school are married, and sometimes fathers of two or three children. In many instances these wives have had but limited chances of school, if any, so they must be instructed along the line of rudiments as well as in the Bible to fit them to be workers with their husbands when these go out as preachers and teachers. A few have had the advantages of the high schools for girls at Moradabad, Lucknow, and elsewhere, and such can be utilized at the same time they are taking advanced studies as teachers, Bible workers, and the like. Mrs. Scott told me of her school, of the fifty or more eager to learn, since they see the need of measuring well up to their husbands in mental development; of their coming to the study with one baby and sometimes two in their arms; the difficulties of teaching when crying or crowing babies prevailed in the room, the little plans they formed to have the babies and young children cared for as they themselves came to the school; the eager, hopeful spirit of these young wives and mothers as they caught glimpses of the broad field opening before them and their sex where before all had been almost a total blank. If I had heard of this school before it had not attracted my attention enough for me to remember it, so its worth, promise, and results came to me like a revelation.

Another pleasing phase of work supported by the Woman's Foreign Missionary Society is that of Bible readers. The book is its own best teacher. Scores of native women, mostly the wives of preachers, teachers, and other native Christians, women of educational attainment and converted hearts, are sent out to the homes of the non-Christian natives in the villages and cities, to read to the women and children, and sometimes to the men also, to give them a knowledge of the teachings of the book which has revealed to us eternal life and all its crowd of blessings. This method of work, costing the home society but a few dollars a year for each reader, has proven its worth and wisdom. Usually these devoted native women are directed by an American lady missionary, the one designed for zenana work. Many conversions and much good that is now foundation-laying come in this way. The native women can admirably reach their shy sisters, whose life has been that of seclusion and superstition.

Great hope for the deaconess movement is held by our veteran missionaries in India. Homes have already been started at Lucknow, Agra, Calcutta, and I think at Madras. It has been my fortune to see some of the ladies brought out by Bishop Thoburn to found and direct these embryonic institutions, and their hopefulness and promise seem prophetic for doing much good. Personally I have a bit of undefined fear that these homes may degenerate in Protestantism in the course of years to something like the nunneries of Catholicism, but I greatly hope my fears are baseless. Any way, they seem at once to have an inviting field here, and I am glad to see so good an entrance made. Some way seems to be demanded for supplying workers in foreign fields faster than can now be done with the rather high rates of expense necessary for regular members of the Woman's Foreign Missionary Society, so that if the deaconess movement will supply that demand it will be seen that it is of God and has vast promise.

LETTER XXV.

WOMAN'S WORK—ZENANA, ORPHANAGES.

I WAS exceedingly eager to learn about the practical results of the zenana work, since on its start a class of India's people was reached that could not, at present, have the Gospel carried to them except by this means. I presume the good missionary women of India will recall a wearisome interlocutor, but if so it was to get at as many facts as I could of the system. It is certainly an opening such as is found to present itself to us for God's work if only people are ready to enter it. Here was the problem—a vast part of those benighted millions totally inaccessible to the truth, then the narrowest kind of providential opening to admit that truth, keen-eyed missionaries to use it, and the known results, access to thousands of women and children, limited only by the number of workers that can be employed. In Bombay, for instance, a city of six hundred thousand people, the workers of the Woman's Foreign Missionary Society of our Church have access to a hundred and fifty families, thus meeting about two hundred women; a few hundred more are reached in a similar way by other denominations, so that possibly a thousand families in the city at the most are visited, while they might be reached by the ten thousand were there workers enough to knock at the doors. The missionaries say that the native women and girls soon show the good result of the teaching given them at their homes; the employment in substantial duties, the hope coming to them through the Bible and song, and the touch of modern life, all unite in imparting a brighter, more hopeful look to their very faces. The mental curse of these women whose minds have been left blank all these generations, with an ever-cumulative weight of hereditary darkness, must rest with blasting effect on the men and system imposing this ignorance and imbecility upon them. The workers find interminable difficulties in the families. Often there are two or more wives, and children variously related, so that the question of what these women shall do as they begin to believe in Christ is a perplexing one. The mothers-in-law are often the veriest tyrants, Miss De Line telling of one who brutally flogged her daughter-in-law who was nineteen years old and the mother of two or three children. Think of a young Yankee woman's being expected to submit to whipping by her mother-in-law! But then the sons-in-law! The women in the homes to which access is obtained gradually come to be delighted with the visits of the missionaries and native Bible readers. Sometimes the husbands get alarmed lest their wives may believe in the new faith, which must stand inimical to their practices, and so close their houses to the Christian workers; in some instances the native women assure our people that though their visits must cease they for their part will pray in secret to the Jesus of whom they have learned. It not infrequently happens that if excluded from the houses for a while by the husbands' fears and notions they are heartily welcomed at a later period.

I was taken by Mrs. Bruere into some of the native Christian homes of Bombay, calling at seven and eight o'clock in the morning, which would be an odd hour to call in America. It was in a dingy quarter of the great city, where the dank, slimy water stood in the ditches over which one stepped to enter upon the veranda. Fevers, small-pox, and cholera could not but be engendered in such a vile atmosphere. Most native houses have wide porches, under which the men-folks are likely to sleep. Some little bamboo bedsteads, or "charpoys," were usually set out in these to relieve the one room inside where the family lived. Now and then we found a family able to have two rooms, but whether one or two they seemed to me the poorest places I had ever seen that human beings inhabited. Half a dozen tin or copper dishes, a charpoy or two, a few bits of matting on the earth floor, some blankets folded away in a niche in the wall, in one corner of the room a little fire-place built of mud, as large as a man's hat, over which could be placed a copper kettle, with a little fire under it made of leaves, straw, or dried cow-dung, the pungent smoke from which comes into the room, since there are no chimneys in an Indian house, and you have a view of an Indian home. These are among the homes of the better class of those who do daily labor, since Christian belief and practice show themselves very soon in the care and comfort of their houses. Of course, no man is permitted to enter the homes of the unchristianized natives, no matter how poor they may be. The women, even in Christian homes, are exceedingly shy of strangers, because of the long habit of seclusion, but in this case the presence of Mrs. Bruere was assuring to them.

They told me that a result which was having a good influence among the non-Christian people was the better condition of the homes of those converted to Christ. The poor creatures are not so dull or bigoted as not to notice that when their neighbors accept Jesus they at once keep their homes in better shape and more cleanly.

In Cawnpore a plot of land has been purchased in the heart of the city, where a hundred or so of native Christian families live near each other, and in most cases these homes have only one room. When visiting them with Dr. Mansell, the pastor of the native church, I found them to be clean, well-regulated, and their inmates well clad and cheerful. Such improvement, when seen by those yet in heathenism, cannot fail of being an attraction to the natives. Our women become greatly in love with the zenana work, and no wonder, for they can do so much good.

At the North India Conference Mrs. Dr. Badley told us of being called to visit a Mohammedan girl who had been in one of our Sunday-schools, where she had learned the Golden Text, "He that believeth on me hath everlasting life." She found the girl in a filthy home, on a broken charpoy, dying. The poor thing, drawing down Mrs. Badley's face close to her own so her people would not overhear, told her she was trusting in the Christ who had spoken the words of that text, as Mrs. Badley had explained to her. Then the girl wanted her to sing in Hindustani "Little children, little children, who follow their Saviour;" and asked her if she who had always been in rags would have a white dress like Mrs. Badley's. One more thing the Christian missionary could do, bend down over the wan face as the girl requested and kiss her ere she went away. A few days afterward she called again to find the little broken charpoy vacant; the girl had gone to the Saviour of whom she had heard at the Sunday-school.

Such are the conditions of society in India that those who would do good to the people must do many kinds of beneficent work for them. From the early history of the mission orphanages have been a necessity. Into every school, both for boys and girls, these waifs are certain to find their way, and the missionaries see in every one of those coming to them the possibilities of a good worker hereafter. So they are welcomed, fed, taught, and used. At the girls' school at Shahjehanpore the matron and Dr. Hoskins showed me a little girl whose story they told. She was eight years old, perhaps, but small, like all the children there. Her people belonged to the leather-workers, one of the low castes. One day, not long before, while playing with a little girl of another low caste, the oil-men, she entered the little girl's home and ate with her a bit of bread, not thinking for the moment of breaking her caste by it. But her people heard of it, and so strong and horrible was the feeling of caste in them that they at once drove her from their home into the street, beating her away from them. After a while, crying, hungry, she returned, begging them to let her in, but it was in vain, and they drove her again into the streets of the city. What would be the results? Any one of several. She might gain a precarious existence a while by begging, only to die in the end from want and disease, or soon starve in spite of begging, and her body be eaten by dogs, jackals, and hogs; or she might be picked up by Mohammedans, and brought up for use in houses of ill-fame. This last was what actually did befall the poor thing, and at this juncture one of our native Bible women heard of it all. By a good British law when a child is known to be kept in such a house the missionaries, and doubtless any one else, can, by legal process, send a policeman to take her away. This our folks did, and I saw her a day or two after she had been given over to the missionaries. Think of parents, for their notions of caste, utterly traitorous to all human instincts and affections, turning their helpless girl into the street to starve or live a life worse than death! In the mission the little thing, bright and clean and dressed, was contented already, they said, being better clothed, fed, and kept than ever before. God may have a mission for this waif. As you see a successful Bible reader or teacher, or the happy wife of some teacher or preacher in our Church, who has come to her place through our mission by some such dreadful start, you feel like putting more and more money at the command of the missionaries.

At Bareilly Rev. Mr. Neeld, our missionary, showed me a boy at his house one day whose story, if less pitiful, was still very pathetic. His name is Munglee, the son of a widow, and he is now fourteen years of age. They were of the leather-workers' caste. A boy friend of his had become a Christian and was being educated at the Shahjehanpore Orphanage. During vacation the Christian boy went home, when the two young friends got together and ate together and thus this one broke his caste. As he went home and it was known he had eaten with the Christian boy his mother could not take him to her house, and as she was too poor to pay for his re-entering the caste by a costly feast to the rest of them she turned him away. In his despair he found his way to our native preacher at Bahari, who brought him to Mr. Neeld to see what could be done for him. For his support the missionary gave him two rupees and a half a month and put him with a Christian family in the mission compound, having him attend school, where he has been about eight months. At the end of six months, finding that no one put in a claim for him as a minor, as could have been done up to that time by law, he was baptized in November, 1888. The boy is a fine-looking one, and has learned to read well in the first book of Urdu. Recently his money has been increased to three rupees a month, and should he grow up as promising as now he will doubtless become a valuable worker in the mission and among the people of his caste, as there are many of the leather-workers in and about Bareilly. I wanted to give him a rupee, and on his being called to me and asked what he needed he said a blanket to sleep in, as he now had only one, and the rupee, with a little money he had on hand, would buy him the needed blanket.

At this same city of Bareilly, where our Mission began in India, the Woman's Foreign Missionary Society has now a large orphanage for girls, containing two hundred and thirty, of all ages, from little babies to young women of marriageable age. Standing one day chatting with Dr. T. J. Scott in front of his house, a native approached, made his profound bow, and handed him the following letter:

"AMBALLA CITY, *January* 9, 1889.

"MY DEAR MR. SCOTT: The bearer, from Bareilly, wishes to get married, and for that purpose has taken leave of me, his mother, living at Bareilly, having called him. He wishes to get a girl from the school there.

"Will you kindly assist him in the matter? He assists me in the hospital and has general oversight of my room and house. I would like to have him get a really good, steady girl who can read and write and be of some assistance in the hospital among the women; but that would be only occasionally, when called upon.

"Yours sincerely, M. B. CARLETON."

He handed me the letter, and, on reading it, I asked him what he would do, and he said he should refer the man and the letter to Miss English, the lady in charge of the orphanage, for that was what Dr. Carleton meant. The letter was given to me, with the request that I ask Miss English, as I visited the orphanage that afternoon, what she should do in the matter. On going to that institution she said this request was like many that were coming to her, and that it was in the regular course of the way such things have to be done in India. Girls among the non-Christian people are not consulted about their husbands, but the arrangements are all made by the father or brothers, and as yet much the same course must be followed in regard to the Christian girls; still not wholly, for in many cases the young people see each other in the Sunday-schools, at the homes of the missionaries, and other places, so that there is possible for them a slight chance to get a little acquainted and, at least, to see each other. Miss English said that she should have the man call at the orphanage, talk with him a while, and, using her judgment of the girl who, of her dozen or twenty marriageable ones, would suit him, bring her to meet him in the reception-room, and if the girl and the man were both suited after having talked with each other the marriage would be arranged, in a few hours consummated, and he would take her to his mother's home in Bareilly, preparatory to the long journey back to Amballa, which is near Delhi.

It was to me an odd way of doing this thing, but after all a great gain over the custom savages have of forcibly abducting the girl, yet far behind the Western mode, where the woman has the same right to her wish after years, it may be, of acquaintance as the man has to his preference. To the orphanage many native Christians come to obtain wives, Miss English reporting that during the past year twenty-five have thus gone out.

As in all the East, smoking is an inveterate habit among the women as well as men. Dr. T. J. Scott, president of our theological school, with others, has organized a crusade against it among the native Christians, and at the mela, at Chandusi, I saw the great procession of the "Lal Fita Faj," numbering about eight hundred, all wearing the red ribbon, for the native name of this organization means "The Red Ribbon Army." Some of the Christian men and women who have smoked all their life-time are gladly giving it up, and the students in both the boys' and girls' schools are pledging themselves to abstain or not to begin its use. In the orphanage the older girls to the number of ninety have joined this organization, making quite a division. I went into the mill-room to see them grinding flour and making bread. There are thirty-two sets of stones, the lower one of each set fastened into the dirt floor, the upper one capping down over the lower and turned by two girls as they sit beside this primitive mill, each grasping a peg of wood standing upright in the side of the upper stone. The coarse flour comes out from under this stone, dropping into a narrow trough arranged for that purpose. Two girls were baking loaves of bread over a fire of leaves or dried sugar-cane on a large iron griddle, much as flapjacks are made in America. The griddle was dry, instead of being greased or buttered as with us.

Not the least interesting part of Christian work in the city of Bombay is the private hospital of Dr. Armstrong, a sister of Rev. Dr. Armstrong, pastor of the Methodist church in Nashua, N. H. Trained in her school and medical course for work in the Woman's Foreign Missionary Society, but not being sent out by them she came out here on her own account, began practice, and in the two or three years since has become well established in her work and is justly attracting attention to her skill and success. But her purpose is to work along missionary lines, since she has an organized private hospital in which are six wee waifs, both native and European. Associated with her are her sister, an English woman, and a native Christian woman as a medical student. The expenses of this novel venture amount to two hundred rupees a month, and are met entirely by the lucrative practice of Dr. Armstrong. Mr. Stuntz, Mr. Delamater, and I rode to her home in a bullock-cart, which is not a "tony" way to ride in Bombay; but we got there all the same, safe and sound, to enjoy a pleasant breakfast with these elect ladies, and then went to look into their nursery and hear the ways of thus bringing the blessings of Christ to India's needy ones.

LETTER XXVI.

THE QUESTION OF CLOTHING AND HOMES.

WHILE these people, brown, and oftentimes almost black, present, in their features and skins, a very dark aspect, they frequently dress in white. They have come to a conclusion that white better resists the awful glare and heat of the tropical sun. Not that all dress in white, or that all those who have clothing once spotless keep it so, but a majority dress in white cotton. Colors used are bright ones. Under our duller skies this glow of coloration would seem gaudy, but under the bright sun and high tints of nature in this country it seems all proper in taste. The working classes, when their clothing is composed of white cotton, get it greatly begrimed, so that its dirty hue might be supposed by its wearers to add color more cheaply than dye-stuffs. But when they have on really white, clean garments their graceful way of wearing them loosely about the form, the slender build of the Hindus, their jet black hair, whiskers, and eyes, form a contrast and create an effect that are very fine and seem the perfection of ease and grace. There being no prevailing style, as in America or Europe, much latitude is used by different races, different castes, occupation, and ability to dress. Though the beginning of winter when I landed in Bombay the air was scalding hot in the day-time, and not very cool at night, so that many of the working-men and boys could, and did, go with almost no clothing, none, indeed, save a little about the hips and loins and a cloth bound about the head. The poor women would usually have on a skirt and a loose cloth about their shoulders and head. Of course, I could not see how the rich women were dressed save now and then a glimpse obtained as they would get in and out the special zenāna compartments prepared for them in the rail-cars. All who are able, both men and women, make frequent use of shawls. The women envelop the head in these, while the men wrap them gracefully about the shoulders. One of these Indian men, in a faultlessly white turban, a waistcoat of some bright-colored silk, a white or colored shawl or chuddar so thrown about his shoulders that one end is flung backward over the left shoulder, a peculiarly folded cloth so arranged as to wrap around each leg separately, makes a most interesting native dude. The Bengali people seemed to me to be more set up in fine clothing than those of any other part of India. It does seem queer to see them almost entirely go barefoot. But in such a burning climate the need of shoes is not deeply felt. From constantly going barefooted the under sides of their feet become almost as hard as sole-leather, so that they sound hard and dry on the street or pavement. A few wear loose coarse slippers, especially in the cities. It was told me of one of the new lieutenant-governors that as he came to Calcutta and saw the people all going about the streets barefoot he said to one of his council it should be the object of his administration to enable these people to have shoes!

The richness of the shawls, silk garments of one kind and another, cloaks for the children, and other clothing of those who are very wealthy, is most fabulous. They told me at Moradabad of a small boy only three or four years of age that I saw playing in his grandfather's banking-house, who had made for him a cloak of gold-cloth which cost a thousand rupees, a sum equal in purchasing power to a thousand dollars in America. When we saw the boy he was inclosed in a cloak that was stiff with gold and silver thread.

The ways of washing their clothing were strange and funny. I first noticed it in Bombay. Beside some pool or river they will place a rock or block of wood made rough; the washerman, standing in the water nearly up to his knees, will souse the garment around a while, then with both hands whip it down over his shoulder on the wash-block. At each blow he emits a stifled grunt. Indeed, the India people, as they do any work requiring an effort of muscular power, give forth such a grunt. These washermen, called in the native tongue "dhobies," while not boiling their clothes, manage to get them quite clean. They use a coarse kind of native soap, and for drying the clothes lay them out on the sand or grassy banks. They will return to you a washing well done up and costing so little that you are at first half ashamed to pay it.

It is a curious necessity laid on one traveling in India that he must carry his own bedding. So in Bombay I purchased a pillow stuffed with cotton and some quilts adapted for one, and these, all of them bright-colored, rolled up in a mat, formed my "resai." I am going to take them home as mementoes. Later I have added a thick woolen blanket of coarse native work and of ample dimensions. When I have stopped at a hotel or missionary's home the servant at once has taken these things and made up my bed on the small single bedstead, or charpoy, assigned me.

To me, fresh from the comfortable homes of New

England, their homes seem exceedingly poor and inadequate. Outside the great cities, and often in large sections of these, the house-walls are built of mud and then thatched with grass or leaves, or else covered with bamboo first and then a coating of earth. If among these huts of the poor there are two rooms it is the exception. One room in such a mud hut forms the home of most of the families in this country of vast populations. A few rude pieces of furniture, a charpoy or two, a bench or other primitive seat, a dish or two for boiling the rice and vegetable food, are about all the things they possess. In one corner of the room, with no chimney to carry off the smoke, is a little fire-place made of burnt mud, as large as a man's hat, over which the cooking is done. A bit of fire is made of leaves, grasses, weeds, or more often of cakes of dried cow-dung. The mud of India, owing to so much lime being in it, is very tenacious, and well mixed can be laid into walls or fire-places and last a long time. Brick walls, laid only in such mud, if kept away from the rains, will last many years. These mud huts at the best are poor apologies for a place in which human beings can live. Their earth floors are dirty and form a harbor for vermin, the walls are liable to totter to ruin in the rainy season, the roofs frequently fall in, and yet so costly are other kinds of buildings that these must be made and used. In the better part of cities and larger towns brick buildings are not uncommon, while others are built of wood and bamboo. One sees here half-deserted villages, the walls and roofs of the mud houses falling to utter decay. Such ruins form the best kind of refuge for the terrible serpents of this country. As I am here in the winter they are dormant, and I am glad of it.

The homes of Europeans and of the American missionaries that I have seen are generally of better make. Usually ample grounds are secured and houses of wood or brick are put up, so that they can approach to something like comfort in this terrible climate. I am glad I am not here in the summer to endure the sun, when in its full ray the thermometer rises to 160 degrees Fahrenheit. But no homes I have seen thus far around equal for solid comfort those of eastern United States. Houses for Western people to live in have to be built with reference to shielding them from such heat, walls thick, roofs in the one-storied ones high, the windows small, to keep out the glare.

But these people, inured to the climate, sit or stand about in such a sun as now compels me to cover my hat with a "puggery," and over that carry an umbrella. They must scald in the sun and shiver in the night's chill. In the streets of Benares I saw children totally naked playing like puppies in the dirt, heat, and grime when the thermometer registered in the sun 135 degrees. Such naked or half-naked creatures then must endure a fall in temperature at night to 38 or 40 degrees with but scanty covering on their mats or charpoys. I am amazed at the way these people can sit down on their haunches. Their legs, almost as thin as sticks, seem to get used to being doubled up in this way and sustaining their weight.

Their love of finery is most surprising, and the customs guiding in its use are so funny! Nose ornaments of one kind and another abound. Sometimes it is only a bit of silver with the poor, or with the rich a gem stuck in the outside of the nostril, while some wear a slender ring of brass about three inches across, pendent over the mouth from one nostril. Fashion makes fools —in India! The bracelets worn seem almost as strange to us Western people as the nose ornaments. You will see some low caste women, when engaged in the dirtiest kinds of work, have their wrists and arms covered nearly to the elbow with bright metallic bracelets. They are cheap and tawdry, but doubtless yield their wearied, burdened wearers some comfort. At a station in the native State of Rajputana I saw a woman, who had just thrown off her head a pile of dried hides, have on her arms bracelet after bracelet till they reached nearly to the elbow. It is also quite common for them to wear great rings of silver or other metal above their elbows. The men put on these armlets as well as the women, and they often furnish all the clothing, besides the cloth they have about their hips, that workmen, or coolies, will wear. Many of the women wear on their thumbs an immense ring with a small mirror in it, just as the Greek and Roman women did two thousand years ago. These Indian women also wear great massive anklets, sometimes solid silver, sometimes hollow ones filled with small beads of glass that rattle as they walk. Then the end of ornamentation does not come until the end of the foot is reached, for on the toes of many of the working-women one sees thick, stout rings of silver. As they always go barefoot these rings make a comical showing. Sometimes they are only plain and broad, others have large rosettes on them. Three or four will be crowded on one toe, put on when the woman was a child, and, being allowed to remain, grow tight on. Now and then you will see some bit of colored glass or a poor native stone put into these toe-rings. The whole effect of these white silver ornaments, about the ankles and on the toes, placed on feet that are bare and brown and dirty, is to us practical Western people thoroughly laughable. So wide-spread and costly is this use of finery, since all, whether coolie people earning two or three cents a day or richer ones rolling in wealth, indulge in it, that much outcry is being made against it by Western people interested in the welfare of the natives, and is also attracting attention from some of the educated native gentlemen. It is known that India is the vortex which is swallowing up much of the gold and silver of the world, and while great quantities are hoarded and buried, more of it goes into these ornaments.

LETTER XXVII.

AT THE BENGAL CONFERENCE.

HAVING greatly enjoyed being present at the North India Conference, now grown to grand proportions from our first mission, I was eager to visit one of the other Conferences to see how this class of work was succeeding. Here the self-supporting plan of William Taylor has had a trial of several years, though now the work is being partially taken under the wing of the Parent Board, with some grants of money to aid it. The Bengal Conference met this year at Allahabad, a city at the junction of the sacred Ganges and the hardly less sacred Jumna, and also at the junction of two or three important railroads. I am the guest of J. P. Flemming, Esq., a prominent English official, the father of Mrs. Dr. Dease, of the North India Conference, who is present. The station of Dr. and Mrs. Dease is far among the Himalayas. Half a dozen of us were entertained through the Conference by this man, the men of the party having a large, splendid native tent of canvas to sleep in, lined with purple, red-trimmed, with hangings and other elegant accompaniments.

Bishop Thoburn came fresh from the North India Conference, full of the spirit of work and devotion. He is a kind of father to this Conference, and I could see at a glance that he felt this paternal relation most fully. The majority of the preachers are young men, but all—Americans, English, and natives—are full of promise and capacity for work. The sixteen of last year have been increased to nineteen by the transfer of three from America—Henry Jackson, P. M. Buck, and W. N. Brewster. One, W. F. Oldham, has come two thousand miles from under the equator at Singapore to be present. I think this Conference must cover the most territory of any that has ever been organized, being from Singapore to Mussoorie, more than thirty degrees of latitude, with a population of over one hundred and thirty millions of people. These missionaries, counting opportunities as God's calls, should be exceedingly happy in their very extended call linked with God's promises.

The growth of this Conference during the year, while not so fine as the North India, has yet had an increase of ten per cent. Such an increase, however, all over Methodism, would in a year give us a gain of two hundred thousand. The general plan of this field, taking in Central India, Burma, and Singapore, is to use the English-speaking churches, mostly founded by William Taylor, as centers and supporters of evangelization among the natives. The work has been going on for about ten years, though this is only the second Conference session. There are four districts—the Calcutta, Ajmere, Mussoorie, and Burma, the last including Singapore. During this session, however, Singapore has been set off into a separate mission and Burma made a district alone. So small is the Conference that the routine business has not taken up all the time, and Bishop Thoburn has thus been able to give several admirable talks on questions of prime importance in the mission field.

On Sunday, January 20, Bishop Fowler, who in his tour of the missions of our Church has been making his way from the east, was present and preached in the forenoon, and in the afternoon Bishop Thoburn did the same. It was apparent from these two sermons that bishops differ in their modes of work as much as other preachers. Both were uplifting sermons. Though granted correlative powers by the Discipline, when present, the full-fledged bishop, while in this field of a missionary bishop, did not exercise his right save when invited by Bishop Thoburn to take the chair in his necessary absence from it. Possibly a precedent was made in this quiet gathering that will be used hereafter.

The reports of the English churches, the native ones, the Sunday-schools, hospital work, day-schools, seamen's work, women's work, and other fields were almost everywhere encouraging. Bishop Thoburn, for one, has great expectations of this Anglo-Indian work. It has certainly opened and sustained stations at many points that would not have been entered by us save through this means. It must assure these timid natives to find the men in the English churches, often their very employers and directors, interested in their salvation. Doubtless with the episcopal oversight that Bishop Thoburn can now exercise this work will receive new impulse and enlargement. I am so sorry not to see the South India Conference, the third one of this vast country.

Four men have been ordained, three as deacons and one as elder. A fine class of men is being raised up all through our India missions from among the natives, and to these in the long run India must look for its Christianizing workers. The natives of every country have in the past formed the final corps of evangelizers. The women had their Conference here the same as at

Bareilly, and the reports show successful, aggressive energy. Woman's systematic relation to the evangelizing duties of our Church in India is a step or two in advance of what is accorded her in America. The vexed question of her place in the General Conference and other higher councils of the Church may here find its solution to show the mother-Church at home how it can be done. They are admitted as lay delegates into the Central Conference. I thought as I saw them in these Conferences that in the way of doing business even the men might catch some insight.

Mr. Flemming was permitted by his official duties to have some time in which he could grant favors to his guests, which he did in part by taking us around this beautiful city. One day he drove me to the junction of the Ganges and Jumna, a spot held especially sacred by the Hindus. It was two or three miles to it, the drive being through the English quarter of the city, to find the same magnificent streets of crushed "kunker" that they build every-where and call metal roads. On every hand were broad yards, or compounds, full of Indian trees that retain their large leaves all winter, as our pines and firs do. Fine residences in which officials lived were embowered among the groves, orchards or profusion of vines, roses, bignonias, flashing bourgainvillias, and other flowers. Green vegetables, fresh fruit, and sweet-scented flowers were in abundance. Among the fine buildings was the Government House for the official business of this province. Out across the plains was the fort in which an English garrison remained during the mutiny, while the city, a stronghold of Mohammedans, was held by the natives. This fort is an old one, but sufficiently strong to protect those men through those dreadful months. Just below the fort is the junction of the rivers, the Ganges flowing from its start far in the Himalayas, the Jumna from its source north of Delhi. On the sand fields, which in the season of high water are covered many feet, but now are dry and pleasant, the Hindus were already gathering preparatory to the great mela to be held a month later, when a hundred thousand or more will be here. Grass huts were scattered over the fields and already filled with devotees. In some instances pretentious booths or tents had flying over them a flag or pennant to distinguish the abode of some priest of peculiar sanctity or influence, preempting locality and claims for service against the time of greatest influx. The scene reminded me of the age of chivalry in Europe and the preparations for some great tournament. I should like to be here at the full season to see the crowds, the bathing, the strange phases of Hindu life, manners, and devotion.

On the great bund or bank raised to keep the mighty Ganges within limits, on a line with which stands the fort, is a thing of special interest. It is a brick platform, about six feet square and two feet high, on which was sitting till two months ago, when he died, an old fakir who claimed he had sat there eighty years. Mr. Flemming and other residents of Allahabad said there was no doubt but he had been sitting there fifty years, as he was a very old man. His place was soon occupied by another, who will seek to emulate his predecessor. It is a strange way to win salvation. This one was sitting cross-legged, surrounded by half a dozen people, who seemed only listlessly standing about while he was busy writing, making selections from his sacred books. I begged a bit of his writing, and on a piece of brown manilla paper I had in my pocket he wrote some Sanskrit sentiment—a direction, he said, of how I could win the favor of the gods. This I have treasured up among my choice mementoes. As I gave him a piece of money to pay for it he told me to lay it on the platform on which he was sitting, having refused to take it from my hand, and then peremptorily warned me not to touch the platform lest I should besmirch his sanctity. Under a small tree near by was his charpoy, or little bedstead, on which he slept at night, and also a few signs of something to eat.

Not far away, almost under the walls of the fort, was a prostrate image, of peculiar sanctity to the women desiring offspring, the most horrible of any I have yet seen. Whether it has always lain prostrate I did not learn. It is where the water flows over it at every inundation, but each year at low water it is dug out of the sand by the priests and then worshiped by devotees. Over it was a rude roof of grass and reeds, and near by shrines with Mahadeo's peculiar emblems. Some priests were preparing this gigantic body, the "Mahabeer Khoond," ten feet long by six wide, for worship by oiling it and coloring it afresh with red ocher. Steps of stone led to it from the level of surrounding sand, and down these they would not let us unbelievers go. The image holds in its left hand the figures of two newly-born infants, one in its right hand, and has its feet upon another.

For another drive Mr. Flemming took me to the banks of the Jumna, and into the ample grounds of the Presbyterian mission. Here are the usual accompaniments of a great mission, homes, schools, gardens, a church, orphanage, and the like, while in the heart of the city, among the bazars, they have just completed a fine brick church for the native Christians. This denomination, like others from the West, is doing grand work for Christ. From the high grounds of this compound we could see a curious sight—acres of the sand-banks and low places along the Jumna planted with melons to ripen in March and April before the rains raise the water to cover those spaces. The ride through the native portion of the city was another of those trips of sight-seeing that have fascinated me all along, the strange shops, the vast variety of odd things offered for sale, the kaleidoscope of faces, costumes, races, conditions. Here was a native theater built of grass-mats and poles, the audience being left to stand or sit on the ground. Thence we drove through the public gardens just outside the old city walls, to find flowers in a profusion that astounds me as I think of the snow-drifts and sleigh-rides of New England at this very time. To find the Conference rooms and the homes massed with banks of luxuriant flowers in the dead of winter tends to daze me. Yet but a month ago I felt the snow crisping beneath my feet as I stood on the top of Cheena Mountain above Naini Tal, more than eight thousand feet higher than the sea, while beyond the mighty Snowy Range was in plain sight, from which the snow never departs.

One morning I arose early to write and was treated to a serenade as daylight came that to me was most interesting. It was not light enough to stop the numerous screech-owls from their piercing notes; it was light enough for cocks and crows to awaken and seem determined that all else should awake. The apex of the tent proved a favorite place for the newly aroused crows, and they evidently meant that the Yankee below should recall their sweet songs as he went to his native land. I do. Then the children in one or two of the servants' houses in the compound vied with the other noises, so that the notes taken together made a medley such as only the abundant life of India could furnish.

A beggar came one day while I was busy writing in the tent and sat down, nearly naked as he was, in front of the door. If I looked up from my work he would begin to talk. Those in the tent could understand his jargon and told it to me. It was that this poor beggar was very hungry, and, rubbing the part mentioned, said he had had nothing in his belly since yesterday morning. From his lankness I could half believe him. If I could give him a pice or two, since I was rich and he was poor, he hoped I would get on well in the world, would be the happy father of sons, and would rise till I was made the governor of the province. By this time I deemed the poor fellow deserved a handful of pice, and when I gave them to him his blessing on me, in which he hoped God would grant me long life and the desires of my heart, was sweet and pathetic. One feels at first, on seeing the biting misery and want of these people, as though he would like to empty his pockets among them. But that would be only useless.

If such scenes tax one's sympathy till his heart aches there is in India many an ameliorating scene to gladden the heart. To say nothing of the thousand ways in which English rule is bringing peace, protection, food, education, Christianity, and other elements of a better civilization to India, the homes of many of the Europeans and Americans are a constant object-lesson to the keen-eyed natives. At levees and receptions they meet women from the West who are considered the equals of the Western man, and who are paid a deference that is most bewildering to the high-toned native gentleman. Music in the homes seems a most fitting accompaniment of the tropical luxuriance that can be made to abound. The piano-playing by the expert Misses Flemming, and singing by them and their mother, aided one in interpreting the natural beauty around him. It seems strange to me that the Indians do not produce better music. They are imaginative, poetical, but appear to fail in having preserved a high style of music. Possibly their racial deterioration has in it the cause of this lack and others.

LETTER XXVIII.

MEANS OF LOCOMOTION.

THEY call me a "globe-trotter" here, and if I am one the means of getting around are important considerations. Riding on the cars, in spite of the crowds of natives and the glare of the sun, is pleasant. Certain compartments are reserved for Europeans, and in these one can usually find ample room and good accommodations. There are really four classes of cars, first-class, of the palace-car pretensions, the second-class, "intermediate," and third-class. I found that most of the officials, missionaries, soldiers, and other Western people ride in the intermediate; so I have generally done the same. The cars are after the English style of compartments, with an overhanging roof to shield from the sun's glare and heat. If only two are in a compartment for a night-ride they can spread out their "resai," make a cozy bed, and sleep more comfortably than in the crowded sleepers in America. In the intermediate class your fare is about half a cent a mile. I believe these trains are the best served of any I have ever seen. Usually the engineer, or driver, as they call him here, and the conductor, or guard, are British, all the rest of the attendants native. It takes almost an army of people here to run a train and attend a station, but then labor is cheap and people numerous. They say that during last year the railways of this country carried over fifty-one millions of people, and only two were killed besides those suffering from their own carelessness. The train never leaves a station till the guard gets a telegram from head-quarters to go ahead, so that collisions are almost unknown. I am constantly amazed at the solidity of railways, stations, and other British work. The Anglo-Saxon evidently builds and plans to stay. Whether the national congresses they are having, with representatives from nearly all parts of this vast country, will have any effect on the future of British control remains to be seen.

But railways are not native modes of locomotion. I was more interested in the latter, if they were not so much used as others. In Bombay I noticed, in addition to carriages, or "gharis," and the street-cars, that many people rode in bullock-carts. I wanted to ride in one, but was almost unconsciously kept from it by Mr. Stuntz, one of our pastors there, till, on pressing the matter, I was surprised to learn that it was not a "tony" way of riding, and that one other than a native indulging in it was likely to be despised. That made little difference to a peregrinating Yankee like myself, so one day Mr. Stuntz, with Mr. Delamater and me, climbed into one to go to breakfast at Miss Dr. Armstrong's. With horror Mr. Stuntz saw one of his stewards gazing on his audacious pastor, but with true republican grit the latter declared he did not care. The bullock-cart is on two wheels, the top covered with cotton-cloth to keep you from the sun, the driver sitting almost on the tongue of the cart between the hips of the bullocks. He drives in a slow trot by cries and beating the bullocks with a short stick, first on one side and then the other, but in case you cry out "Chalo! chalo!" which means "Go! go!" he will catch hold of the bullocks' tails, giving them a sharp twist to hurry them along. Since then I have ridden several times in bullock-carts of one kind and another. These beasts are the small white cattle of India, with a hump on the shoulders, and though worked in this and other ways are considered sacred, so that a constant outcry goes up from the natives against their being killed to meet the wants of the beef-eating British. They can despise and neglect even to death in the street a man of a different caste, but carefully tend and savagely protect their sacred cattle. In addition to these light carts designed especially for travelers there is a very heavy, cumbersome two-wheeled one, drawn by the huge, slow, thick-bodied, domesticated buffaloes. The clumsy wooden wheels, the vast cart-body of bamboo timbers reaching between the buffaloes almost to their heads, the great loads they can take, the slow, snail-like movements of the team, the dumpish driver seated on the tongue of this vehicle, combine to make a most interesting sight. Some of the earlier means of locomotion among the missionaries was by these mortally slow buffalo-carts.

The horses of India are not numerous, and you are glad. For some reason those you do see are miserable things, owing to the climate, poor breed, poor care, or to some other causes. If you take a carriage in Bombay or Calcutta, so as to go in "tony" shape you are easily ashamed of your horses. In the northern parts of India little scrawny horses are hitched into a light two-wheeled vehicle called an "ekka," which is designed to carry one person besides the driver, but in which two or more can ride. Like the bullock-cart, it is covered with a cotton awning to guard the passengers from the sun, and there being no springs the sharp jolting keeps one from getting asleep. The American gig may have been fashioned after the ekka, as it is very like the Indian vehicle. The latter has the horse close up to the driver, the seat for the passenger being a little platform about three feet wide, as high as the wheels, where one sits with his feet curled up under him, or he may let them hang off one side. The means of attaching this odd carriage to the horse are of the most primitive kind—grass or cotton ropes that are liable to snap at any unusual jerk or strain. The ekka is balanced in such a way that a passenger of considerable weight raises up the thills so that they must be kept in place by a broad, loose band under the horse's belly. The horses seem to be used to this odd arrangement, hence if the thills stand at quite an angle upward, as high as the back, they do not get nervous about it. For a cent or two an hour among the inland towns and cities one can ride in a swift and commodious manner, only it is mostly patronized by the natives, so that this is not considered tony, especially for Western people. Indeed, the only American I have seen riding in one was Professor F. W. Foote of the Boys' School at Naini Tal, whose back during the ride was supported on the other side of the ekka by mine!

Allied to the ekka is the "tumtum," or dog-cart, as they called it in English, that I found in Delhi. It is a more pretentious thing than the ekka, since it has a seat facing frontwise, and one backward, but it is on two wheels all the same. In such a one I rode from the city out twelve miles to the famous Khutab Minar and back, and as it had springs it was not an unpleasant mode of riding. But the driver of such a vehicle in this country will not care for his own horse, so in addition to that man, who sat beside me on the front seat, another one rode on the rear seat whose duty it was to hold the horse and feed him while we examined the Minar.

With real Yankee curiosity I am seeking a chance of trying all modes of riding that I can find. One day at the Chandusi mela I saw an empty palanquin being carried by, and begged of our missionaries to secure a ride in it for me. So for a slight consideration the four men bearing it gave me a short ride. Much talking was done to them by the missionaries, the purport of one part at least being unknown to me until later. As it was set down on the ground I crawled into it, and the men, two at each end, putting their shoulders under the long bamboo pole on which the box was suspended, lifted me up and started off. They were to carry me to a certain large mango-tree in sight, and back again. With an habitual sound, combining a sing-song tone and a grunt, they kept a kind of mixed time of stepping so as to break the dead jolt that would occur if they all four kept the step together. It was not a pleasant mode of riding in such a narrow box, in which one as long as I am could neither stretch out at full length nor sit upright. The mango-tree was reached, and they turned to go back. It was rougher than the journey out, so I inferred they had got a little tired with the weighty Yankee; then they jolted as they did not before, till, had I known the call to go easier, I should have suggested it. To add to the situation, one or two of the slats under the bamboo-netting on which I was reclining broke, and I was heartily glad when they finally set me down among the missionaries again, who appeared quite inquisitive as to how I liked that mode of riding. Well, I liked it moderately! It was a week before I learned that they directed the coolies to jolt me well, but then the palanquin was broken by it.

The boats of India, judging from the little that I saw of them, are most cumbersome, awkward things. On the Ganges at Benares the boats in which they take a single passenger to see the burning ghats and other sights are large enough to bear up several tons, requiring the work of half a dozen oarsmen, and then move so slowly as to give just the chance of seeing the wonderful river scene that one wants. To cross the Hugli at Calcutta to the Botanical Gardens a boat almost as cumbersome as the double-decker at Benares had to be chartered. It was longer, and had in the middle a bit of cabin six feet square and only four feet high, in which one could crouch away from the sight and sun. The captain, the steersman, and two oarsmen were the crew of this "dingi," and the pay for all this outfit for three or four hours was no more than twenty-five or thirty cents. The Indian people do not take as naturally to water as their conquerors, the British, though a brave and efficient lot of sailors, called "Lascars," have grown up at Madras and other ports of the country who are used on all the ships in those seas. I saw one of them in his scant clothing hang for two or three hours at the very top of the main-mast looking out for some sunken rocks on the run between Singapore and Hong Kong.

I have found that the people of Malaysia are better boatmen than those of India. At Rangoon there is constant demand for the small river-boats to carry back and forth to the ship as they lay in the stream. In all this country the oarsman stands and pushes his oars from him instead of pulling as we do. This enables one to look out the way he is going. All about the peninsula of Malaysia they call their boats "sampans." Like the Chinese, they paint great eyes on each side of the bow, and explain the reason to those who seek it thus: "No have eyes, how can see? No can see, how can savey [know]? No can savey, how can sail?" The Burmese boats are flat and shell-like; those of Singapore are more sharp and graceful. The Malays, now that they have been compelled to give up their piratical practices, take to boating of various kind about the harbors that are every-where to be found among their islands, inlets, and the peninsula. They told me of a boat-race by these lively boatmen in the straits between the island of Singapore and the main-land. At the appointed time they started out with a brisk breeze, and in a sudden squall two of the ten or a dozen capsized, but in a few moments the crews had them righted, bailed out, the sails set, and the keen racers came in but a short way behind their more lucky competitors.

LETTER XXIX.

IN THE MATTER OF SERVANTS.

I AM constantly wondering, as a wandering Yankee can be allowed to do, about the servants. All the way from home to this country servants, good, bad, and indifferent, have waited on me, and a gradual decrease in efficiency and an increase of numbers have been marked as I have passed into Southern Europe, Egypt, Palestine, and now here. You would be much in doubt whether the many that hang about you and your room in Italy were there to serve your wants or to expect tips. Here they are multiplied beyond all conception, and one needs to be posted to know what to let them do. Then a stranger is constantly making mistakes, asking one to do something that he neither can nor will do. A division of labor is reached in India of which we in the West could never have dreamed, and which could be reached only by a long civilization and in such a teeming population as that with which this country is burdened. Some writer on ancient customs has suggested that the beginning of the system of caste might have been in this very division of labor, and thence at a later period been carried into religious practices. I half think now that caste practically has more to do with labor than with religion. As generally known, a caste of men do one kind of work and that only. Such are the customs and notions that one in his plans of life-work never rises out of his caste and trade. If his father belonged to the caste of cooks, he must be a cook, and never know or practice any other duty. If the father was a barber, the son must be one; if a sweeper, the son must be that. Hence it happens that to complete the necessary lot of servants to keep the house and its surroundings in order every Western family must have five or eight of them. One must be hired to do each kind of work. A cook can cook, and do nothing else. Another can wait on the table, and do nothing else. The "bheestie" brings the water, the sweeper carries off the offal and sweeps the rooms and walks, the gardener tills the yard and garden, the butler is a kind of general overseer of all, and purchases provisions. Thus, because Western women cannot work at housekeeping here, owing to the enervating heat and ignorance of ways and utensils, and in the case of missionaries their time can be more valuably used, it happens that all Western establishments, British officials, missionaries, men of business, teachers, and others, have what seem to us a very large corps of servants. The people on the ground declare that it is a necessity. It is impossible to get one's house and food kept and prepared in any other way. Now and then some one coming from republican America determines that he will get along with one man or at the most two; he begins in this way, but things are illy done, or not done at all; one more is hired; later, after some further chaos, another; then in despair, all that are required to make the establishment progress in the usual Indian way. To listen to these experiences is to hear a funny chapter in one's change of country. Only men do work about a Westerner's house. Women never cook, wait on a table, or make one's bed. The women may be used as nurses in Western families, but in no other way.

But this corps of servants costs little if any more than one or two in America. Each one gets two or at the most three dollars a month, from six to nine rupees, and on such pay boards himself. In rare instances one of special worth and trustworthiness will be paid more. In our country a girl to do housework costs more in a week, including the board, than a good Indian man-servant for a month; hence the question of money is easily solved by comparison in the two countries. Here it takes two men to care for a horse and carriage, since the coachman will never get the feed and care for a horse, nor tie it when waiting on the street. This is all the duty of the "syce," a caste looked down upon by the drivers. The syce must always go out with the carriage to care for the horse, and usually rides standing at the rear of the carriage-box, to cry out to the people thronging the streets to get out of the way. There being no sidewalks in the native cities, and the streets being narrow, a team, owing to a habit many of the people have of wrapping their turbans close about their ears, is constantly in danger of running over some one. The syce, in thick-crowded streets, keeps crying out. But these two men cost one much less than a coachman in America. It is related to me that a few years ago one of our ministers was being driven through the streets of Moradabad, not by the native coachman, but by a well-known evangelist, who has since been elected Bishop of Africa. The team, taking a sudden fright, ran away. Down through the crowded streets they went at full speed, the stalwart driver, who had learned some native terms, crying out in the vernacular, to those likely to be run over, the idiom, "Save yourselves," while the minister sitting in the carriage was wringing his hands and praying, "Lord, save us!"

These men make good servants, docile, obsequious—too much of the latter to suit one fresh from home. But, having been in subjection for twenty or thirty generations, and in the case of many of the low caste longer still, it is no wonder that their spirit and subserviency are so debased. These lithe, agile little men make graceful-looking help about a house. Their picturesque costumes, added to their intelligent brown faces and eagerness to serve, leave a pleasant impression on you. But, after all, they are often unreliable. Being taught from their childhood's earliest impression to steal, they are slow to get over this vice when in Western families. One of the favorite gods for children to worship is a diminutive figure of Krishna crawling out of his mother's pantry, when a child, with a ball of butter represented in his hand, which he had stolen. A necessary servant of every considerable establishment is a night watchman or policeman, who, having slept during the day, keeps awake during the night to watch the house, barn, garden, and yard against thieves. But for such a policeman every thing movable would be stolen. These watchmen keep up a loud calling out through the night to scare away the thieves. The one at the establishment of Rev. A. J. Maxwell, our Book Agent at Lucknow, had his mat spread under the porch against my door, where I could hear him coming and going at all hours of the night.

In addition to these things Indian servants are so slow that they tax most severely our Western patience. A thing needing to be done about the house that in one of our homes would take but a few minutes here will take five or ten times as long. If one is in a hurry to get started away, or to have a meal prepared, it is almost impossible to obtain quickness of movement.

Those long in the country get used to it, but such of us as are freshly here are sometimes much annoyed. If something arises that is out of the usual course of things the cook or butler or coachman can by no means meet the emergency. They have been so used to doing things a certain way and at a certain time that they cannot well do it at any other way or time. In spite of all these drawbacks, however, the general impression is of good service done by these people. They are capable of strong attachments, and often inspire much love and respect from their employers. It is said that English officials become so pleased with these servants, and find so great difference between them and those in England when they return there, that some of them throw up their home establishments in disgust and return to India, where they can get better service. This I have noticed, that they are not willing to have you do any thing. At the hotels they do not want you to roll up your bedding; before you know it one is on his knees in front of you to tie up your shoes; in your room, at the table, everywhere, they watch your wants and desires and try to forestall your doing things for yourself. They are jealous of your reputation as a gentleman, even declaring, as you try to carry home a bundle, that gentlemen do not do such things as that; so you must allow them to do it.

But these very fellows who are so obsequious to you are keen and sharp about their own place and precedence. The caste system is carried into all of these Western homes. If the servants are not converts to Christianity the bother of caste is sometimes very annoying to the family. One will by no means do the work or service belonging to another. Then they are quite apt to assume importance from the supposed dignity and importance of the one they serve. While a guest at Bishop Thoburn's, in Calcutta, I wanted a dozen oranges for use on the ship to Rangoon, and Mrs. Thoburn sent her butler with my money to procure them and at the same time to buy herself a loaf of bread. He bought both, and there was no lowering of his dignity or place to bring home the oranges, but there would be such degradation if he brought the bread, so he hired a coolie, always to be found waiting for such jobs, to carry the single loaf home in the big basket on his head.

From the first I have been greatly interested in the water-carriers or "bheesties." They are a separate caste whose industries consist in furnishing water to houses and for other needs. They carry the water in skin bottles, slung across the back. This bottle is made of a goat-skin, the body having been taken out through the neck, so the skin is nearly whole, and has the hair left on till it wears off with use. At railway stations, in the cities and houses, every-where, you will see these men. They sling the goat-skin across the back in such a manner that the neck, which forms the place for putting in and letting out the water, is held on the left side under the arm, and this neck orifice is grasped by the hand or tied up with a string. If you want water they loose their grip or the string and give you a cupful or a pailful. The water for the American houses and mission establishments is all brought to the house by these bheesties. If water has to be brought from a well half a mile away, as is often the case, the work of the water-carrier can be seen to be no light duty. Attached to every sleeping apartment is a bath-room in which sit two or three great earthen jars of water, kept full by the industrious carrier. The water in such jars becomes very cold during the chill air of the winter nights. It is a pleasant disturbance in the early morning to hear the gentle bheestie come into your bathroom and pour this out, and then, as you are dozing, to hear the silvery gurgle, as it is emptied from the water-skin into the jars, of some warmer water that he has brought from a deep well in which during the cold night it has retained much of the heat poured upon it by the hot sun through the day before. These men have another duty that is interesting. None of the cities have sprinkling-carts, a thing greatly needed during the rainless winters, but compensate for such lack with the bheesties. They become street-sprinklers. From some tank, well, or water-pipe the bheestie will fill the water-skin, then hurry to his appointed spot, and with his legs bare, to endure the wetting better, swing the bottle under his left arm, and, holding the neck with the left hand, flirt the water one way and the other with the right hand. In this way they sprinkle the streets very effectually and rapidly as things go in India. As you pass along you are safer from a shower-bath than you are in America with the huge "monitors" in use.

The carpenters, furniture-makers, weavers, blacksmiths, and other crafts do their work in little shops open to observers or on the very edge of the narrow streets. Here you will see a turning-lathe worked by hand with the motive-power sitting on the ground pulling ropes back and forth, while on the other side sits the turner, with his diminutive chisels. Axes are almost as thick and cumbersome as the stone ones made by our prehistoric ancestors. Short crooked saws are used, and to saw planks they set up the log on one end, leaning over, one man sitting on the ground below it, the other standing above the slanting side. Many of the kinds of wood are highly colored and capable of fine carvings and polish. In some cities they do most beautiful brass-work, Moradabad being noted for its elegant designs worked in brass and jet. In many places cotton and paper mills and other industries after European methods are being established, with much advantage to the poor people.

LETTER XXX.

THE FUTURE OF METHODISM IN INDIA.

To meet our missionaries in India is an inspiration. They are boundless in hope, and point to what has already been done. They talk about seeing tens and hundreds of thousands of native Christians, and men use these numbers who have already spent here half of the possible years of their labors. Such men as Parker and Thoburn and Waugh are the ones most assured. After looking over their reasons for these expectations I think them sound, and place my hopes along-side theirs.

Look at their successes—not an unbroken course, to be sure, since some mistakes have occurred, as is common to things human. Thus, at the beginning of their work in North India they adopted opinions from missionaries already a long time in the field, that to break up idolatry, caste, and prejudice, they must get the high caste people converted first, and that the lower castes, always influenced and directed by the upper ones, would then be certain to follow. But their success among the Brahmans and other high caste people being poor, the same as other denominations, they are turning more to the low castes, whom for some years, especially in the North India Conference territory, they have found accessible. They tried to found Christian villages, buying or getting the grant of a piece of land, and gathering the families of the converts there in order to protect them from the persecutions of their neighbors when in a village only one or two converts had been made. But these villages all perished, save one, Panahpur, not far from Shahjehanpore. Now they find that it was doubtless God's design to leave these converts among their heathen friends in order to open new places of work and to be an attractive light in the darkness and unrest. By this means a vast number of new places are now opening, many more than they can enter. And having got started with preaching, schools, hospitals, and other means in some caste, as farmers, leather-workers, or sweepers, the work is rapidly spreading through that caste until, in some instances, great sections of them seek Christ. It is not uncommon that twenty or forty seek baptism at one time. It is like the success of the Baptists among the Telugus and Karens. Our missionaries in the North India Conference are now reaching a high caste with much success, the Thakurs, a caste of former warriors. But this they have learned, which they did not think at first, and which some in the United States have not yet learned, that these low caste men and women make as good preachers, teachers, helpers, Bible readers, and the like, as the high caste, for their hard work and sharp struggle to live seem rather to have developed their faculties, instead, as might have been supposed, of lowering them in the intellectual scale. They now think India is to be regenerated from the bottom upward. Sir W. W. Hunter, long in India, and whose many books on this country compelled him to study India in special ways, has recently said, in an address delivered in Great Britain, that there are about fifty millions of these low caste people in India, and that these, being specially susceptible to missionary effort, should be directly sought after by the missionaries. When these people of the low castes are converted to Christ and educated and sent out to do various kinds of missionary work they are respected by the natives of all castes.

All the missionaries, both American and native, consider the presence of a national bishop one sign of future success. Though the matter was proposed and agitated at least a dozen years ago and since, possibly God and the Church were waiting for the right time and the right man. It seems as though these had both come. Methodism here is wise, strong, successful, and is getting intrenched all over India and beyond in Malaysia, there being now three Conferences and one organized mission. Other denominations are looking upon us as having in our movements "the swing of conquest;" they are coming to respect our plans of working among the low castes as well as high castes, and our splendid schools, among both native and English-speaking pupils, are their admiration; the natives appreciate the push and hot-hearted ways of the Methodists. Then there is a universal feeling that in Bishop Thoburn they have the right man for success. He is pious, simple, intense, has had very great success among the English and natives, having won a place in their esteem and confidence that would take a new man long years to gain, while to the two southern Conferences and the Malaysian work he already held a paternal relation. His welcome is deep and unfeigned. With such an episcopal supervisor on the ground all the time, mistakes in debts, neglect of entering on new work, the admittance of inefficient men, and other elements of weakness and disaster can, it is hoped, be reduced to a minimum.

The work of the women is carrying assurance that

they are to have, most wisely, a prominence in our church development here not accorded them in other than missionary fields. The Woman's Foreign Missionary Society workers and the wives of the missionaries are proving their call of God. It is probable that Paul had organized workers among the women, and in this respect, as in others, Methodist missions are getting up to apostolic heights. The American and English-speaking women are organized for business into a Conference sitting while the men have theirs, hearing reports, planning for new work, and doing many things that carry forward the grand advance of the cause. The deaconess homes are already in operation here, with hopes in the hearts of the most experienced missionaries as well as others that this experiment is fraught with vast good to Christianity in India.

A spirit of unity can now be fostered among the scattered Conferences and stations that could not as well be pressed before. There was a chance that the two methods, self-support and heavy help from the Missionary Society, might breed petty jealousy; comparisons not in the right spirit could be made, one section of the work being old and organizing grand success, another crude and not so brilliant in immediate results; little causes of fretting and friction might grow up with no one who was looking over the whole field to point them out and successfully suggest their removal; the change of American and native workers from one part of the field to another as the exigencies would seem to require; the inability to settle questions at once that sometimes require immediate action—all these things and others can now be adjusted and corrected as never before. There are at least fourteen nations besides tribes in India, and our work is already being carried on in nine different languages, but the work of a General Conference—as the Central Conference, now held every two years, must some time come to be—will always be conducted in English, so that this wonderful language is to be a connecting bond among the diverse nations, peoples, and Conferences of our work. The future of that Central Conference in India, acting as a unifying power in educational, publishing, and other interests, must be very important. The whole situation is somewhat like that in England during the seventh century, when Archbishop Theodore was sent from Rome to Canterbury, whose synods and councils of a unifying Church led the way to a national unity in speech, life, and law not before possible. It may be that God has much future good to India's national life along the lines of our church unity.

The press also bids fair to be a potent good in the field of our unity and usefulness. Methodism at home knows too well the worth of this agency to question its importance. More than ever the three presses here can work together and flood the country with products along evangelical lines. The schools are full of encouragement, growing every-where, almost every one a success in conduct, numbers, and work done, while those in debt are generally successful in prospect of getting out of it. While some other missions are questioning if they will not give up their system of founding schools our own is founding new ones and wisely making them centers of broad beneficent evangelism. The two colleges at Lucknow, the one for boys and the one for girls, are certain to pass soon from the embryo stage to one of lively usefulness.

The missionaries speak with modesty of another phase

of work which was sadly lacking among other denominations until we came on the ground—the revival spirit. But genuine old-fashioned revivals such as are common in America have for years been accepted by several of the other missions as well as ours. In our own they are sought for every-where. When I saw at one altar service at Chandusi camp-meeting thirty-three forward for prayers I knew that Methodist ways of salvation were in good use. The work of William Taylor was in this way, among others, of immense worth. This shoot of Methodism does not fail in producing fruits of the genuine American and Wesleyan kind.

The question of English-speaking work is an important one. It touches the English and Anglo-Indian alike. In it those people of greatest experience here see great promise of success. These people need salvation as much as any others, but they had been sadly neglected till our advent. They usually speak the vernacular of the region in which they grow up as well as English, and by that are fitted to become grand helpers. English speech is to be more and more important as a general language in India. All college-educated natives speak and read it. This work has given us some splendid workers, with promise through our schools of many more. Such men and their wives have come from the English work as these: Oldham, superintendent of the mission at Singapore; Gilder, Curties, Morton, Dennis Osborne, Meik, De Souza, Jeffries, Dr. Dease, Knowles, Plomer, and others. It has given us several strategic points over India, besides Rangoon and Singapore. The policy will yet prevail of uniting the English and native work at the same station, a policy not yet made very successful, but sure to come. Already the opening English work has made native work possible at several points, though kept under different control.

Above all, Methodism must keep full of the spirit of the Master. With the love for souls that he had, with a love for one another and for God that is a consuming power, the future of our work in India has sublimest prospects.

LETTER XXXI.

THE METHODIST PRESS IN INDIA.

AMONG the forces wisely set at work in India for Christianity is the press. Perhaps every body at home, excepting myself, knew how great and important these plans had become and how successfully they were being carried out, though they do tell here of one of the bishops who came, held Conferences, and returned home to say that we had no mission press in India! I suppose I had glanced at the reports made in the Methodist papers of America, or the glowing words of Dr. Butler and others who have descanted upon this phase of our work; but its greatness did not become apparent until I saw it with my own eyes. At Lucknow, instead of seeing a set of three or four rooms with a dozen or fifteen men at work, as I supposed, I found I stood in a building having a wide front on the most beautiful, important business street of the city, two of its entrances being leased by our Book Concern for retail purposes, the other three rooms in front being rented to native gentlemen for stores, by which an income of one hundred and forty rupees a month is realized. As you go from the front of our building toward the rear you enter a second suite, in which the agent, Allen J. Maxwell, a graduate of Boston Theological School, has his business offices, in which alone he has to use nearly as many clerks and accountants as I expected would number the whole establishment. Further back one begins to get a sight of the reaches of store-rooms, press-rooms, type-setters' rooms, and so on, until the vista is extended across a whole block, where there is an entrance from the street on that side also. Possibly the new buildings of our parent Book Concern recently completed on Fifth Avenue, New York, have less ground-space than our Book Concern at Lucknow, though those run up more stories than these, since in India few business blocks do transactions save on the ground floor. The force of workmen Agent Maxwell now uses is about one hundred and twenty-five. This corps of men is not as efficient and productive as the same number of workmen would be in America, though it gives a glimpse of the large amount of work to be done; and the work of the press is so increasing that even this number must constantly be enlarged.

There are printed and issued books, periodicals, pamphlets, tracts, school-books, hymn-books, Sunday-school lessons and helps, and the like. The demands on such a publishing house by the acute, awakening Indian are very great. It is a critical time to the people of India, as, brushing against Western ideas, spirit, and civilization, they begin to think and act more for themselves. Consider the Brahmo-Somaj, the Arya-Somaj, the National Congress, and other mental and spiritual ferment. Just now the masses of pure, right, and instructive literature poured out by our India press is of special worth. India can be mightily moved in this way. The common people are learning to read. Mr. Prautch, of Bombay, sold tracts the past summer by the ten thousand on "The Resurrection," "The Christ," and kindred themes, by hawking them through the streets, which the people read with avidity. As a help to our missionaries the press is taking a prominent place. The early workers felt this, and with a hand-press, setting the type themselves and doing the press work, they began by counting their issues by the thousand pages where they now count them by the million.

In Lucknow our press puts forth its products in six tongues—Hindi, Arabic, Persian, Sanskrit, Urdu and Roman-Urdu, and English. India must be largely Christianized through the native speech; hence the English yields to the vernacular in importance and in the amount put forth by the press. Much lithographing has to be done, that process as well as type being used in Persian, Arabic, and Urdu. I have among my choice things a Church History made here by the lithographic process.

The buildings and land, stocks, books on hand, presses, type, and other things, unite in making a property worth about one hundred and thirty-five thousand rupees. Most of this was accumulated by the business tact and push of Rev. Thomas Craven, now stationed at Naini Tal. A part of it is in the form of endowment, which, judiciously invested, enables the press to scatter free at least two million pages of Christian literature a year, besides helping the other publications. The output during the year past has been more than twenty-five million pages. Owing to cheap labor books can be produced at the lowest prices. A compositor can be had for ten cents a day. The sales of books amount to twenty-five thousand rupees a year. The prospect is for enlargement every way. The periodicals take a prominent place. The *Woman's Friend* is printed in Hindi and in Urdu in this press, in Bengali at Calcutta, and in Tamil at Madras. It is endowed with $25,000. The *Children's Friend* and *Star of India* are also successful. *India's Young People*, illustrated and issued fortnightly, is on a paying basis, and has the largest circulation of any paper in India save one.

The Calcutta press has not been so successful financially as the one at Lucknow. Its central purpose was to publish the *Indian Witness.* This valuable paper, with a list of over a thousand, is doing much good. Unfortunately, a debt has accumulated until its weight is now most crushing. Efforts recently made to sell out the press having failed, those in charge think Providence is clearly pointing to its retention, and so are trying otherwise to pay the debt. A sum covering a third of the debt has been borrowed at a low rate of interest; about twelve thousand rupees were pledged at the late session of the Bengal Conference, so that light appears ahead. A plan is being pushed to endow subscriptions for the *Indian Witness* at one hundred and twenty-five rupees a copy, and as many of these are coming in their products are aiding at this pinch.

A dream of the Methodists of India was to found a great publishing house at Calcutta, as that city is the commercial and political capital of India, with the one at Lucknow and at Madras as branches. If this dream is realized it must be in the distant future. In the meantime, by careful internal management, by rigid reduction of expenses and wise business conduct, the press can be made to pay its own expenses and possibly aid in reducing its own debt. The business insight of Agent Maxwell, of Lucknow, is being called into use in giving direction and skillful business methods.

The work done by this press is quite extensive. Besides the *Witness* it publishes two papers in Bengali, one of them being in the interest of the zenana work; Sunday-school lessons and helps, also in Bengali; all kinds of books that it can secure contracts for, school-books, dictionaries, and others in English and Bengali. If the debt were paid the property owned would be worth full thirty-five thousand rupees, and it has ample room for all the work likely to arise for some time to come. They employ about seventy men, though that need not convey the impression any more than at Lucknow of the amount of work seventy men would do in an American publishing house. They have five steam presses, and some lithographing is done in Bengali. For some time they have had a permanent job of printing tracts for European societies, and still have it. If the present plans to pay the debt succeed there is a fine prospect before the mission press at Calcutta. The business of the city is immense, and, being what it is, the city must carry along with its growth any successful business enterprise in it.

The Madras press, the smallest of our plants for press purposes, has a history such as the other two might envy. Dr. Rudisill, being a practical printer, bought a small press four years ago, and set at work himself. It appears to have been his purpose to do two things at least in the management—first-class work, and keep out of debt. Persisting in these admirable purposes, the results are most cheering. The press has a name for good and reliable work. It has not done as much printing as the other presses, and does not now. It has twenty or thirty men at work, with a steadily increasing outlook for future and greater success. The Sunday-School Union and Tract Society of our Church at home has made Dr. Rudisill grants of aid to produce their publications in the vernaculars, which have greatly aided the press. Just now it is getting recognition at home, so that some important help toward its endowment is being secured. Besides English this press puts out its products in Tamil, Telugu, and Kanarese. It prints books, periodicals, Sunday-school lessons and helps, with many other things. Each of these vernaculars is spoken by a dozen or twenty millions of people, these three nations being of the Dravidian stock, one of the aboriginal races of India. They take kindly to Christianity. The success of the Baptists among the Telugus shows what other Churches may accomplish among the millions of this and kindred races. The question concerning the future of these aboriginal races in India is a curious one. These outcasts, pariahs, low castes—for all these are mostly of those races—have been before the Hindus in accepting Christianity with great alacrity, so that they are getting nearly all the benefits of Western civilization, while the Hindus of high caste are getting only a small part by refusing the Gospel of the New Testament. Will the aboriginal Turanians yet take precedence in this wonderful land of races and changes? So hopeful is Bishop Thoburn of those three peoples in South India and of our work which is spreading among them that he begins to talk of the time when we shall have three Conferences there, one in each—Telugu, Tamil, and Kanarese. God grant he may live to see his hopes realized! He says of the press, "I consider that the most transcendently important interest next to preaching the Gospel is the press in our mission work."

LETTER XXXII.

AT CALCUTTA.

The run from the Allahabad Conference to Calcutta used twenty-four hours, but it was in good company. Bishop Thoburn, Superintendent Oldham and wife, McCoy, Warne, Craig, and their wives, Mr. Brewster, Miss Wisner, and others made up a charming party. The country down the Gangetic valley was level, with some of it wild, but much of it green with growing wheat, and other parts fixed into rice-fields. These are made by forming a small dike or bank on all sides, so that the water necessary for this cereal to grow in can be retained. Palms of two or three species increased, and also impenetrable thickets of bamboo. After a chilly night-ride, in which our ever-attendant roll of bedding, or resai, was a most valuable accompaniment, we came at early morning to the city of Kali and were soon at the various places to which we were assigned in the homes and hearts of the missionaries.

Methodism has a strong hold in Calcutta. There is the English-speaking Methodist Church, the first to be started in this city under the labors of William Taylor and Bishop Thoburn, now with a membership of three hundred. This has proved the parent of all the rest. There is a hopeful work among the Hindustani people; one very successful among the Bengalis, the main part of the natives in this portion of India; the Seaman's Bethel, doing a grand work for Western sailors;

a boys' school that should be more successful than it is; the largest of all the girls' schools of the Woman's Foreign Missionary Society, and a printing-press, with the *Indian Witness* as its principal issue, that is doing good work for Christianity. Last of all, the deaconess home is just beginning its existence, with much hope that this and kindred ones established at different places in India will prove a pleasing success. This is a most hopeful start for the Church in the capital of India. My first anxiety was to see all of these things possible in the three or four days before sailing for Rangoon and Singapore. After that I ran around to see other sights.

The first was to the temple of the goddess Kali, after whom the city is named. The drive, with three other Americans, Misses Black and Wisner and Mr. Brewster, was across the wide park surrounding the English fort, which is situated on the bank of the Hoogly River, the park being kept free of houses the better to use the cannon of the fort in case of need. Thence we went through the native part of the city, along crowded bazars, narrow, dirty streets made muddy by a recent shower, to the south part of the city. As we came near the temple the bazar was full of flowers, sweets, and other things for selling to those going into the temple. Half a dozen temple attendants ran officiously ahead of our carriage as we approached to secure the job of showing us around. We selected two of them, while the attention we attracted was extensive. As we entered the temple area I noticed the headless bodies of kids being carried out, having been offered at the shrine of the bloody Kali. The natives, who eat no other meat, do eat these kids and other things offered to this goddess. We were shown first an almost unnoticed image of Shiva the Destroyer; but this being located in a deep recession of the building, and not being permitted to approach nearer than the first steps of the portico, we could see little of his lordship. A lone worshiper or two, an attendant priest, a few flowers and sweets were all the signs of interest.

But it was all different at the contiguous Kali shrine. As in the other temple, we were not permitted to go very near the figure of this deity, but were granted a view from a distance. A continuous stream of devotees, men and women, was going in at one side of the shrine, passing in front of the image, and going out at the other side. Loud screams and supplications by those passing the goddess were joined with the half-frenzied cries of those about the paved yard, till a din was made that heightened the strangeness of this scene of active heathenism. That the noble Aryan race could descend to such abject worship as this was a great surprise to me. Possibly our ancestral worship of Woden, Thor, or Freya was as strange as this. We unbelievers could see only glimpses of the goddess through the passionate throngs crowding and praying in front of her, though our two guides would compel them to stand aside once in a while to let us see. She was hideous, black and red, with three eyes, as the guides kept telling us in their imperfect English. We could also see two hands reaching out. When we essayed to join the throng which passed in front and close to the goddess we were peremptorily forbidden and hindered by the guides. Priests were beside the image to receive the presents of money, sweets, flowers, and other things. As the devotees came out of the temple each was adorned with a wreath of bale and marigold flowers hung around his neck, and these, I noticed, were worn about the streets of the city. As I was getting a position for better observation under an arched space my shadow came near being cast on the food of a dirty fakir sitting on the floor to eat his dinner, when he yelled loudly to me to look out lest my shadow should defile his food.

After being shown some of the sights, and every-where being pestered for money by the crowds, we found that in another part of the court preparations were made to sacrifice some kids. The rest of the party did not want to see this, but I did, and so watched the proceedings. Two or three priests, each holding a kid securely under his arm, came to the place already soaked with blood, where the deed was done. The head was inserted into a forked post, a pin slid above it, the body of the victim drawn back, making the neck taut, which was then cut off with a single quick stroke by a priest who used a long hooked knife almost as heavy as a butcher's cleaver. They said it was considered a bad omen if the head was not severed from the body with a single stroke. Here was a concourse of the thugs, the priests of Kali, looking like a villainous set indeed, whose highest wish would be to offer better things at the shrine of their deity than goats and sheep, no less victims than human beings. But for the strong arm of relentless British law they might have offered us that day instead of kids. For these priest-thugs, as late as the time of the Sepoy rebellion, did offer such victims, but this being proved against a group of them they were executed like common murderers, since which time they have mostly given it over—mostly, I say, for the missionaries and residents surmise that even yet some of the dead bodies found in secluded nooks are human sacrifices made by the thugs in spite of law and modern light. It was with a sense of relief that we came from that spot of din and blood, which had also such awful associations and memories.

A drive alone to the well-known Zoological Gardens of Calcutta was one of the rich afternoons to a transient sight-seer. The assistant superintendent, a native, Mr. B. L. Dutt, on my asking in vain for a catalogue of the animals and birds, kindly went with me several hours, explaining much that I could not otherwise have known. In this garden I found a very full representation of the fauna of rich tropical Asia. Here was the white peacock, as fond of his faded feathers as those who retain the brightest tints ; strange monkeys—one, the Hoolock gibbon, from Assam, whose exceedingly loud cries could be heard in the farthest corner of the garden ; the nylghau, or "blue cow" of India, a thick, heavy deer common in the jungles ; a curious cow from Chittagong called the gyat ; the hog-deer, as thick-set as a goat, or more swine-like ; the wild hog, black and heavy-built, and the two-horned, hairy-eared rhinoceros. The birds were also fine. The famous mandarin duck from China was the most gorgeous of its kind I have ever seen. Toucans, cockatoos, herons, red macaws, the argus pheasant, jungle fowls from which our common barn-yard fowl came, and many others were there. In a pond was the snake-fish, from Lake Baikal, that would swim around on the top of the water, with its eyes out of it. Some Bactrian dromedaries, patient and evidently of the most hardy endurance, as their country would demand, slowly munched the hay given them. A department was given up to the cat family, and in it were various species, from the possible wild progenitor of the house-cat to the royal Bengal tiger and majestic African lion. Among the tigers was one that had a bad reputation. He was accused of having eaten three hundred people before he was captured. His capture was accomplished by luring him into a pit, where he was wound up in nets and ropes till he could be handled with safety. The native prince in whose dominions he was taken presented him to the British authorities. He was a gigantic fellow, about twelve feet long, a breast fully twenty-four inches deep, and a forearm that would girth twenty inches. His dulled teeth showed his great age, and his fierceness was awful. I stayed till the time of feeding the animals their meat. Most of them ate it at once; but this aged sinner crouched over his food and would not eat it while people were looking at him. He would now and then rise, and with terrific growls, his battery of glittering teeth all uncovered, suddenly dash to the front of his cage and strike out through the bars with his mighty paw as far as he could reach at the people looking on. All would scud backward from the iron rail that kept us three or four feet from the cage, and I did so once or twice; but when I saw he could not reach as far as that I stood still to mark his rage and actions. Finally the crowd went away, and I lingered to see those fine beasts that I should never see again. The old tiger wanted me to go away so he could eat his beef, but I still stayed. I thought, too, that I could stand there and gaze at him no matter how sudden might be his useless spring toward me. Growling at me in deep but moderate basso, he suddenly sprang with but a step or two full at me with a withering snarl, dashing against the iron bars, and reaching one of his great paws through them, and I, with all my self-congratulatory nerve and certainty that I could endure any menace as long as I knew I was absolutely safe, suddenly jumped back, with a big, dismayed thump in my heart. A fine black bear from America looked good to me, and such was my patriotic sentiment toward any thing from the great republic that I wanted to hug his bruinship, and I have no doubt he would have been fully willing to reciprocate the act, seeing I also was an American.

Another day was spent in the Botanical Gardens. These are on the west side of the Hoogly River, while the city is on the east side. As the draw-bridge was open I had to cross far below the city on a "dingi," or small ferry-boat, directly into the gardens. If the day before I had obtained extensive knowledge of the fauna in the Zoological Gardens I here added to my knowledge of the flora. This garden, founded by General Kyd, of whom there is a fine statue in the middle part of the grounds, is located in a tropical forest, the great native trees, palms, bamboos, vines, and the like forming deepest mazes and most entrancing drives, while the places cleared away for flower-gardens, parks, ferneries, and imported species of plants, are like open fields in the woods. One of the palms brought from tropical America had a body shaped like some Greek column, and almost as smooth as polished marble. An avenue of these was like a long colonnade. The mahogany trees, also imported from America, have already become a hundred feet high and two feet in diameter. In these damp tropical forests the trees and plants seem to grow the year round, since they never shed their leaves like trees in a temperate climate, but broad-leaved foliage, looking like maples, basswood, and elms, remaining green during the winter months the same as the pine and spruce in America. Arbors for ferns, orchids, bignonias, dwarf palms, and the like were made by being lightly covered over with boughs and bamboos.

The great banyan tree wholly took me. Every traveler seeing the sights of Calcutta is cited to these gardens, the most attractive feature of which is this tree.

Of course, I followed the wake of other people and saw it. I had seen other banyan trees, though none very large, yet was not wholly prepared for this one. Being alone in the wide gardens, with no bothersome guide or good friends determined to show all the sights, I came upon this giant fig-tree unexpectedly; so I had all the sensations of a genuine surprise. As I passed up a long, straight stretch of wood through tall trees, the banyan, a hillock of green, stood in an open space before me. The general outline of the top was oval, the branches from the main stem reaching highest, with a gradual shading off toward the outer edges. All the branches are gnarled, huge, crooked, the whole impression being of gigantic force pressed into the growth of this strange tree. I first went to the main stem, and there posted up was a statement of its dimensions. It is over a hundred years old; the body, not a solid stem, but an aggregation of sections, is forty-two feet in circumference, the crown eight hundred and fifty feet around, the aerial roots numbering two hundred and thirty-two. This enormous growth has come to pass by the branches, when a distance from the main body, dropping down the aerial roots, which, becoming fastened to the soil, grow vigorously, thicken fast, and act in the double capacity of a brace below and the beginning of a growth above into the body and branches of another tree. In this way a large number of new trees seems to be formed, so that in a sense this tree is not one, but many trees, though starting from one original stem, and all these side branches retaining their connection with the main body. I started from the main stem and paced one way of the extended branches, finding it to be one hundred and forty feet, and by another direction one hundred and sixty-five feet. Then pacing around the outer branch tips, I found it to be actually eight hundred and fifty feet, as the descriptive placard said, considerably over one sixth of a mile. It is estimated that ten thousand men could stand in the shade of this monster tree.

The branches ran out at no great elevation and in a line nearly parallel with the ground, so that one walks under a continuous canopy of limbs, leaves, and parasites only a dozen feet or so above him. Some of the aerial roots have become of great size, forming the body below of the tree-growth above them; others are small and of recent beginning. One not thicker than my finger had apparently been rooted only a few years, but was straight and taut as a fiddle-string. It is a botanical peculiarity of such roots, as it is of tendrils, to shorten when firmly attached. Near the main body was one as thick as a man's coat-sleeve, dropped, straight as a line, from fifty feet above. Under one great branch, where the aerial roots had perished, two thick buttresses of brick had been built to support it.

On many branches and stems was a luxuriant growth of parasites. This one tree, at least, seemed capable of the most vigorous growth, and at the same time of supporting a heavy load of parasites. Orchids were sticking to the branched stem, slender vines hung in festoons from the limbs, large epiphytes swung gracefully from the thick arching sections. On one side was a growth I had never seen parasitic till in India, a cactus extending along the branches forty or sixty feet, and dropping down from its elevated perch in long loops far toward the ground.

The old growth of leaves from the banyan was falling, and the natives were sweeping them into great piles to carry away. Like the pine-leaves in New

Hampshire, these do not fall till a year old, so the tree is evergreen. The vast crown, heavily loaded with the large, oval, thick leaves, smooth and entire, made a sight as the tree stood alone never to be forgotten. A small fruit, at this time, in January, the size of large bullets, grew on short stems out of the branches direct, in the usual way of the fig. This tree is the Indian fig —*ficus Bengalensis*—brother to the sacred peepul-tree, the *ficus religiosa.* Both are wonderful trees; the latter, when it can find another tree for clinging, will act as a vine and inclose it in a lattice-work clasp all around the body, and in time kill it. The fruit of neither is worth much for eating. Seeing the great banyan of Calcutta was more instructive than a lecture on botany.

LETTER XXXIII.

METHODISM IN RANGOON, BURMA.

Among the places where mission work has been successfully set in motion through English-speaking beginnings and the self-supporting plan that at Rangoon takes a prominent and hopeful position. This city is the commercial and political capital of British Burma, a fine sea-port on the Irrawaddy River, about thirty miles from the coast, where the largest ships can run to superb docks or find safe anchorage in the wide stream at all conditions of tide and weather. It is already a city of a hundred and fifty thousand inhabitants, rapidly growing, and destined, owing to the overthrow of King Theebaw and the opening of all upper Burma to European trade and enterprise, to become much more important in the near future. A railway now runs from Rangoon to Mandalay, two or three hundred miles, and is to be pushed much beyond this to tap the large Chinese trade of rich stuffs from the great inland city of Yun-Nan and the country about it. Burma itself is rich in tropical products, the valuable teak-wood, the most remunerative ruby mines in the world, petroleum wells that are already productive, rice-fields that are ever widening, pine-apples growing as wild as raspberries in America being a few of the prominent yields of this prolific country. As a strategic point in this vast country where British rule and industry are swiftly developing a vast future, Rangoon is an important point at which to plant the beginnings of a glorious work for Christianity. It has in the Great Pagoda, the largest Buddhist temple in the world, a marvelously great and rich foundation. The Baptists here have had abundant success with an aboriginal tribe, the Karens, and also some advance among the Buddhist Burmese themselves.

Eleven years ago Bishop Thoburn, with Rev. R. Carter, began a work among the English-speaking people here, and out of that beginning has grown already a mission with several departments and much promise. A church building paid for, capable of holding three hundred and fifty people, and a devoted membership of one hundred and thirty form the center of the activities. They have a good parsonage also, the church property being near the center of the city. These English-speaking people all over this East country have a way of giving money to support church work that astounds a Yankee. One on a salary will sometimes give half his yearly income, and Bishop Thoburn, acquainted with both peoples, declares that in India they beat America by far in giving. The regular services of a Methodist church are carried on in a Rangoon congregation, including old-fashioned altar services, at one of which, improvised when I was there, two soldiers and four leading people of Mr. Long's parishioners came forward for prayers, making the heart of the pastor jubilant.

Under direction of Rev. S. P. Long, the pastor of this English-speaking church, quite a group of other mission activities are set in motion. A Seaman's Rest, occupying two leased buildings, one for refreshments, reading-room, chapel, and the like, the other for lodging, is a full course of benefit to this class of people in this large port. It is time we had one, for another

Church, sustaining one there, has opened sales-rooms for liquors! The city government pays ninety rupees a month toward the expenses of our Rest, the remainder of the expenses being met by subscriptions among those interested. Evangelistic work, in charge of the superintendent, Mr. Hailstone, is carried on every night in the chapel, save Thursday, when services are at the church. Many sailors are converted, the weak are strengthened, and backsliders are reclaimed. They find that during the past year between fifty and seventy-five have been led to a Christian life, while nearly four hundred have signed the pledge. The design is being reached to make this institution self-supporting, and also to use it as a base for other mission work. Mr. Hailstone now has charge of a large Sunday-school class among the soldiers in Rangoon, evangelistic work in two hospitals, and in other fields.

Another thing under the wing of this strong Church is the girls' school, one of those grandly successful undertakings in this line that are placing our Church in the front rank in the East and yielding assurance to all interested in the Master's cause. It was organized seven years ago by Miss Warner, and is now under the efficient management of Miss Julia E. Wisner, Ph.B., who three years ago entered on her duties under appointment by the Woman's Foreign Missionary Society. She has as her first assistant Miss Files, also a Woman's Foreign Missionary Society appointment from America. They and their seven helpers in the corps of teachers are making the success of the founders enlarged and assured. A good building, paid for, accommodates the one hundred and fifty pupils, half of whom are orphans, or at least utterly homeless, the other half, including thirty boarders, paying their way. Misses Wisner and

Files, while sent out by the Woman's Foreign Missionary Society, have their salaries paid out of the income of the school; so that, save a grant of two hundred dollars a year toward the support of the orphans, that Society has no money in the school. In it are taught English, Latin, French, and Burmese. On the grounds owned by the school Mr. Long has finished building an orphanage, ample sized, two stories, of the beautiful teak-wood, the upper part to be used for teachers' and children's dormitories, the lower part for dining and recitation rooms. It will accommodate seventy children, and they already begin to plan for more than the two buildings can accommodate, so rapid is the growth of the school. Pupils range from kindergarten age to those prepared to enter the Calcutta Government University. Several of the older girls speak Burmese as their vernacular, so that a good chance is presented for workers to open a mission among that race. The orphanage is costing ten thousand rupees, and plans are perfected at Rangoon to pay it.

The inhabitants of Burma include, besides the native Burmese of Mongolian origin, many Tamils and Telugus from the region of Madras, who are at work in many ways about Rangoon and elsewhere. Under direction of Rev. Mr. Long's church a promising work is begun among the two latter peoples. Mr. Colly, an Anglo-Indian, holding a good government place, devotes the hours before office-time and after that to guiding a school among the Telugus now having sixty scholars; on Sunday he preaches to them in the vernacular, and on Wednesday evening he has a class-meeting. There is a membership of over twenty. Mr. E. Peters, also in government employ, has a work among the Tamils, having a membership of over fifty, a good school, Sunday-schools, two points of work besides the city, one at Toungloo, a hundred and twenty miles up country, where there is also a small English congregation. Both these men preach in the open air to such as gather to hear street-preaching, and often good results are seen. The Tamils are very apt to stick when converted, and, being less migratory than the Telugus, the work is full of promise. Native catechists and teachers aid them. It is no infrequent thing for the native Tamil people to bring one of their fellow-countrymen to Mr. Long for baptism, so earnestly are they succeeding in leading others to the truth.

Not the least among the plans carried on in this new station for doing good is the woman's workshop. An elect lady of the Anglican Church, Mrs. Hodson, having opened a place where native women without means of earning any thing could do sewing to help support themselves and families, prepared to leave Rangoon a few months ago, and offered to turn over the institution to our Church. Mrs. Long, assisted by Mrs. Nesbitt, has entered on the work, so that now forty women get employment in it. The building is leased, the furnishings belong to the ladies, the expenses are provided for by reliable subscriptions, and evangelistic work is carried on in connection with the other duties, so that much good is done. Besides these things several other points are occupied and others opening temptingly. Rangoon is made a district of the Bengal Conference, and Mr. Long, in charge, needs men and money to enter these openings. At a village nine miles out of Rangoon, which is fast becoming a place of country residences, two or three Methodist families reside, a Sunday-school of a dozen scholars is opened, and Mr. Long preaches there twice a month. At Toungloo the outlook is promising both for Tamil and English work. A promising chance presents itself by an incipient flame among the ten thousand Chinese in Rangoon, but it cannot now be followed up. The girls in the school speaking Burmese could wisely be utilized to start a mission among that race, of whom not one is a member of the Methodist Church. Possibly a deaconess home will soon be set up in Rangoon for this special purpose. It makes the heart of the missionary sick to stand face to face with so many rare openings that seem the beckonings of Providence and for lack of workers and money not enter them. The heathen world is ripe for Christ, but the Church cannot occupy. O, for a baptism of the missionary spirit to furnish money and men!

LETTER XXXIV.

THE GREAT BUDDHIST PAGODA AT RANGOON.

THEY said in Calcutta that I must see the Great Pagoda, and I did. Its golden dome could be distinguished several miles down the river long before any other object of the city was in sight, rising in glistening brightness above the green trees that shut in all other views of Rangoon. We went to see it early the second morning after our arrival, driving to it a mile or more from the heart of the city, to find that a continuous stream of worshipers was already coming and going along the main avenue of approach. The extended precincts of this great temple were made into a fortification before the advent of the British, and at this place it is said the natives vainly made their final and most determined stand against the invaders. A deep moat crossed by a draw-bridge is first passed, then strong brick walls in two lines pierced with musketry loopholes run completely around the conical hill half a mile wide on which the pagoda stands. At the entrance across the moat stand huge griffins on either side, between which one must pass, big enough, open-mouthed, and so fierce-looking that they might be supposed to strike terror into the hearts of passers. They sit reclining on their haunches, being in this posture full forty feet high, twenty-five feet long, and fifteen wide. They are evidently built of brick, coated over with plaster or stucco, and seem to be conventional figures set as a guard to the entrance of most of similar pagodas in Burma.

Passing these, one comes into a long, narrow-roofed passage-way with steps, such as are necessary to ascend the slope, the roof being supported by columns on each side, and along these colonnades huddle beggars, lepers, deformed people, and also hucksters selling candles, flowers, fruits, sweets, and the like, for offerings, and other small truck not so designed. The physical and moral lepers alike sought the sacred precincts. Doubtless the latter were as hopelessly incurable in that place as the former. A book-stall yielded me a Buddhist catechism, translated into the Burmese from the English, in which it was first written, both texts being in this novel tract. This covered passage must be at least a hundred yards long, finally landing one, after having passed many small shrine-pagodas, a hundred feet higher than the street, on the broad level platform from whose surface rises the Great Pagoda. If one was surprised at the outlook before, of colonnades, beggars, shrines, painted and gold-covered columns, he is now struck with amazement at the wonderful sight that bursts on his view. Before his eyes is the gold-covered pile rising in easy gradations for the first hundred feet or more, then growing rapidly smaller, forming a graceful, strong spire, or tower, at least two hundred feet higher yet, till the entire altitude is greater than St. Paul's, London. There is no interior, this vast structure being solid, it is supposed, though rumor says it is built above a sacred tank. On every side of this huge pile covering the seventy-five acres or more of the hill-platform are smaller pagodas, shrines, summer-houses, and other buildings, of every shape and size, probably private donations to the strange collection. There are four entrances to these grounds, only one being much used, the western one toward the city; and at the base of the Great Pagoda, facing each entrance, is a smaller shrine-pagoda, in which the principal part of the worship was going on. Huge images of Buddha, six or ten times as large as life, are sitting with the peculiar calm face of all the Buddhist images. These are covered with gilt, while one or two of them are of brass or bronze, with the face freshly brightened, presenting a curious appearance. Before these images were placed multitudes of little candles lighted, whose glitter in the dark inner court of the temple served to give light. The worshipers were satisfied in most instances only to present their offering of fruit or flowers, but some prostrated themselves on the pavement and muttered prayers. One old man thus praying had beside him a little boy who repeated the words of the old man after him.

Every Burmese boy at about the age of eight must spend several months in a novitiate attending on some Buddhist priest, repeating prayers like this boy or beating the peculiar bronze gong they use to call for alms, as we saw another boy doing, or at some other service for the priest. Thus early in this way the young Burmese boy is preempted for their own religion. Missionary success among them is slight, but they are a race to make good Christians—docile, truthful, and smart. The priests and worshipers before these images did not object to sight-seers wandering among them as they were busy here and there, appearing pleased rather at seeing Western travelers. There were Chinese, Burmese, and a few without the Mongolian cast of features, though representatives of that race were by far the most numerous.

The columns supporting the small pagodas are like

those by which we had passed in coming, covered with gold-leaf. In some of the poorer work the size of the square pieces could be distinguished as it was laid on the side of the columns. On each side of the entrance to the small pagoda were kept burning, by attendant priests, roaring fires of prayer-paper, and further around, in another shrine, I found one lonely old devotee using only an iron kettle in which to burn his messages to the gods. I begged one of these sacred scraps as a memento. Lights were kept going also in porcelain or cut-glass lamps hung from the ceiling of this first shrine. One altar was very rich in inlaid work of choice cut stones. The smoke of the candles, of the incense, burning paper, the queer genuflexions, the muttered prayers, the pictures and things, the devout faces of the worshipers, made in the busy movement and change a most interesting picture. Here paganism was active, a living force, to which men were devotedly attached. I had seen only two or three such aggressive sights before, one at Benares along the bathing ghat, another at the Kali ghat in Calcutta. Christianity is in contact with living forces of opposition in this east country. Here were multitudes of worshipers with the accumulated force of a cult unquestioned by these people and their descendants for fifty generations, their images, temples, rich altars, shrines, all showing the hold of their faith on them.

After watching these things for a while we wandered about the court to see other sights. Beggar-priests could be found here and there beating a small crescent-shaped gong, asking for alms. The gong was suspended by a cord that twisted and untwisted as the gong was struck, adding a wavy cadence to the tones as it swung thus loosely in the air. We approached one of these mendicants with some rupees in our hands, telling him by signs we wanted to buy the gong. He would sell it for four rupees, and we knew we could buy a new one at the bazar for two; but wanting this one, worn by long use, we finally struck a bargain at three rupees, and went off happy with our purchase, as he no doubt was also at getting a clear rupee out of the trade.

The court is paved with square, finely made bricks, having trees and palms growing here and there in its area. A space is kept open about the base of the Great Pagoda, while the outer limits of the platform, next a wall, are covered by a vast number of shrine-pagodas, the idea being not unlike that of chapels added to a European cathedral. Most of these side pagodas were unused, falling into decay, or at least neglect, while others were elaborately bedizened with gold-leaf, white paint, or very fine white plastering. In all of them were images or statues of Buddha in many different postures, the favorite position being a sitting one. In one small pagoda a reclining figure of Buddha was full thirty feet long, the half-closed eyes, placid face, and position on the side, with the head raised, all suggesting the meditation for which that saint was renowned. In the same pagoda were a couple of large figures in a sitting posture, made of beautiful white alabaster, and most exquisitely polished. The mouth, eyes, eyebrows, and hair were painted on the images. About many of these figures in most of the pagodas and on the columns were bits of mirrors, usually of glass, put in by the hundred at all angles, trying, it would seem, to suggest omniscience. The effect of these numberless little looking-glasses was very striking. In some of the shrine-pagodas the images were of brass or bronze, like those in the first place of worship, the faces also brightly polished, as in that case, suggesting the faces of the Bible saints that shone with the glory of God.

Another attractive feature of some of the small pagodas was large masses of most exquisite wood-carving. The strong mahogany-colored teak, which abounds in Burman forests, is the wood used for this, its firm fiber being as good or better for it than the oak of England. The whole front of some small pagodas would have a lot of this carving, representing flowers, fruits, animals, leaves, birds, and the like, in fine taste, or in fantastic figures and grouping. In some instances a single piece would cover a front of twenty-five or forty feet. Some of it was lately cut, showing the recent color of the timber, other was old enough to have imparted to it that nearly black coloring so much prized by connoisseurs and skilled purchasers of old carving. Doubtless some of those pieces would have brought a fabulous price in London or New York.

Bells of heavy pattern and rich tones hung here and there in front of the shrines, for any one to strike who would in order to call the attention of the Buddha god to the act of worship about to be performed. Beside each of these would lie some heavy sections of deer-horns for the purpose of striking the bells, which, of course, all our party did, if not to call the god's attention, to test the tone of the bell, and to do any permitted thing in a strange situation and place. We came in our wanderings to one bell that is a marvel. It is at least twelve feet high by eight across the lower side, and the lip is more than a foot thick. It is hung by a massive attachment taller than itself to a thick beam resting on the top of two stout columns. The whole appearance is that of gigantic weight and immense stability of frame-work for supporting it. Like the smaller ones, it is struck only from the outside by the conventional stag-horn. It is engraved in native characters, probably with the sayings of the saint, and is said to have been cast out of the free-will offerings of the devout, who gave their gold and silver ornaments, rings, ear-rings, and bracelets, and these can be detected in their only partially molten condition in the body of the bell. It is said that the British in capturing Rangoon deemed the wonderful bell a fit trophy to ship to England, and, having conveyed it to the river for embarkation, on attempting to raise it to the ship's deck the means proved inadequate, so that the mighty bell dropped into the river and sank to the bottom. All their efforts to raise it proved futile, and the precious relic was left to its watery burial. After some years the Burmese sought and obtained permission to raise it, if they could, and restore it to its place, which they succeeded in doing. Great flakes are broken from the edges of the bell, showing rough usage sometime. It was a masterful instance of a people doing for devotion what another could not do for thieving. In another part of the court was also a bell of similar size and mounting, but lacking the interesting history of the former one. Tall poles stood here and there, on which was hung a curious devotement, a hollow net-like thing made of party-colored tassels, thirty or fifty feet long and a foot in diameter, kept stretched with small hoops. These, slowly swaying in the breeze, with their many bright colors, were attractive and odd indeed. Pennants and other fixtures were also sometimes flaunting from the top of these poles. One thing surprised us, that among the lesser shrines stood a number of small crosses, perfect, and having a rude crown set on the top. How these came here and how set up we could only guess, but there they were, possibly owing to the influence or acts of Catholic priests. It is said that the Buddhist worship has been influenced by its contact with Catholicism.

In front of one pretty, adorned shrine two women were kneeling, who would each lift up the figure of a turtle cut in stone, the wooden box on which these lay showing much wear where the attrition of raising and putting down the stone had been going on doubtless for years. Probably some legend connected with Buddha would explain this odd worship. They seemed pleased that we were interested and wanted to raise the same stone figures. We could not mutter the prayers they had been using, so there was probably no efficacy in the act, as there must have been in theirs. At the base of one great peepul-tree a platform was raised, such as the Hindus frequently have for worship at the base of that tree, and in this one were recesses in which sat statues of Buddha. The lively roots of this wonderful tree had broken the platform as well as some of the images in pieces, one of the latter having its head knocked off by a huge root, and about the head and neck of a second image some small roots were coiling and twisting like vindictive serpents. One of the pagodas seemed to be a kind of storehouse of images, for it was dark, dirty, deserted, but packed so full of its peculiar treasures that there was not standing-room left either for man or another image of the great teacher. I wondered if they were kept there for use on state occasions; or were they obsolete and going to decay, like the system they represent? Among the thicker trees and palms of the rear part of the great area the cawing crows and screaming scavenger kites made the court hideous with their cries, seeming sadly out of place in that spot devoted to the calm meditation of the contemplative Buddha.

There seemed to be a few favorite haunts of beggars beside the covered colonnades of approach. One of these was a raised platform, where, under cover, hung the second great bell. A poor blind fellow with his wife and child sat on the plaster pavement, he playing three kinds of instruments at one time, while she sang a not unmusical song. It was different from the India bhajans, less monotone and more melodious. The entirely naked baby was cunning and pretty as it nestled in its mother's arms, and when she was asked by the woman of our party if she would give her the child she slowly answered, "No." The blind man played a rude violin with his hands, out of which he drew many sweet tones; then, moved by the toes of one foot, was a pair of jangling cymbals, and by the toes of the other foot a pair of bamboo clappers, making a noise not unlike the bones used by negro minstrels in America. It was a unique concert, and of course drew some pice from our party. On another part of the same platform sat two men, one playing a triple set of instruments, like the blind man, while the other kept time with him on a set of sounding bamboo slats struck with small wooden hammers held in each hand, the slats hanging loosely above a covered wooden box, shaped not unlike a narrow baby cradle. It was rude, barbarous music, indeed. In another small pagoda a huckster awaited buyers of fantastic bamboo and palm-leaf umbrellas, several of which we had seen over the images of the saint in different parts of the grounds. He is supposed to need these in his spiritual peregrinations. Paper flowers and elaborate peacock fans were also on sale at the same stall. In front of the entrance-shrine we found a group of Chinese, many of them being about the pagodas, since it was their New Year festival time. These were clad for the nonce in robes kept there to hire out, of the richest brocades and most fantastic patterns. Each of these dozen celestials had the most extensive beards and mustaches hung on his face by wires and other attachments, just for that occasion, like the robes. They would change the beards to masks, while some discordant horns and other instruments were giving forth unearthly noises, the men thus robed going through motions as fantastic as their dress, the last position apparently being to cast themselves on the pavement and touch it with their foreheads. One of them kept grinning through it all because we and quite a crowd of other people were standing by to watch the curious dress and antics. Another took a small brilliantly clothed doll in his hands, and, having laughingly held it out toward Buddha's image, prayed, and then laid the precious thing down on the pavement as he prostrated himself there also.

Entirely around the immediate base of the great pagoda were two rows of adornments. These were composed of miniature pagoda-shrines, of griffins similar to those at the moat entrance, only smaller, and stone elephants of one third size, kneeling with their heads toward the pagoda. So great is the extent of this base that there was a vast number of these adornments. Interspersed with such conventional things were a few lamps, crosses, and other things, but they were mostly of those named. Only by going entirely around this immense pile could we form any notion of its vastness. Where the real base begins inside the double row of elephants and griffins it must be about four hundred feet each way on the ground. Its ground-plan is square, each of the corners being cut off, making the whole outline rather octagonal. From this ground-plan it recedes as it rises, by gradual steps and pyramid-like recessions, growing smaller and smaller. On one of the platforms thus made, a hundred feet higher than we stood, some monks were repairing the gold covering, and to shield them from the awful glare of such exposure and such a light they had mats resting on a rude frame just above them. To these places they had ascended by bamboo ladders that hung from their lofty perches back to the base over the polished surface of the pagoda walls. Above this the structure grew rapidly less to a slender column, and was entirely surrounded by an elaborate bamboo scaffolding, reaching to the top of the spire. The crown of the whole structure was shaken off not many years ago by an earthquake, and at much cost and labor the fine piece of workmanship, enriched by choice stones and gems, was remade below and raised to its place again by means of immense hawsers, some of which, at the backside, yet remained. The scaffolding remains, also, as some work is yet to be done along the spire. All of it, from the broad base to the pointed top, is plated with gold. How much is used to cover its acres of surface?—tons? I should not wonder. It is vastly rich.

The whole effect of this huge structure is almost as overwhelming as that of St. Peter's or the Coliseum. Standing on a trap-rock hill, that rises a hundred feet or more above the surrounding level country, it is an object of attraction whichever way one is from Rangoon. It is seen above the trees and buildings from any part of the city. From the river far below and above the city its golden spire can be caught gleaming in the tropical sunlight. It stands thus as a natural landmark, but also as a monument of that belief which, next to Christianity, has the most of humanity under its control. The people who worship here are not barbarians, but a people with a civilization old when our Anglo-Saxon civilization was crude and heathenish. What will be the future of the temple and the cult it represents? Who can tell? Christianity is mighty, but it wins few converts from the Buddhists. They try to match the noblest teachings of Christ with those of the pious Buddha. Their faith makes them better people in many ways than the Brahman faith that in India it vainly sought to supersede. One can depend on the word and character of the Buddhist Burmese more than on those of a Brahman Indian. The Baptists, who have had a mission long years among the Burmese, find it hard to change them, under the shadow of this pagoda, to a belief in Christ. Our own Church in Rangoon is preparing to enter the lists, and let us hope that Pagoda Court may yet yield a place for the erection of a Methodist church.

LETTER XXXV.

AT PENANG.

Do you ask where Penang is? I should have had to do so before visiting it. Look for it three fourths down the Malaysia Peninsula, on the south side. It is situated on the north side of an island two miles from the mainland, the channel between the island and peninsula forming the harbor. The city lies on a low tongue of land with high hills back west of it, and contains about eighty thousand people, mostly Chinese, Indians, and Malays, but having enough British to control the other thousands. Our ship from Rangoon to Singapore has stopped a day to change freight and passengers, so in company with Rev. Mr. and Mrs. Oldham I have been ashore to call on Mr. J. R. Macfarlane, of the Chinese Protectorate, and see the city. It is midwinter, the first days of February, when the deepest snows and drifts are likely to prevail in New England; but here we have to carry an umbrella, besides wearing protected hats to keep off the terrible heat and power of the sun.

As we came ashore we found the birds and trees were tropical as well as the scalding heat. While waiting for breakfast, that came at ten o'clock, after an early cup of tea on the ship, I wandered out along the curious streets as the others lounged and talked in the house. Here were the almond-eyed Chinamen, poor and rich; the dark Tamil from South India, doing much of the menial work; the Malay, as dark as the Tamil, but a stronger, more self-reliant race; then a few of the dominant British in their white cotton suits and pith hats. As varied and strange as the people were the trees and flowers. All are tropical. There were the palms, cocoa-nut, areca or betel nut, travelers', and others; the tamarind, tamarisk, mango, and bread-fruit trees, some of them, as well as the brilliant poinsettas and bourgainvillias, being covered with flowers; gardens of fresh cucumbers, radishes, turnips, and lettuce—every thing, in short, that a tropical country could produce in midwinter. Bananas, pine-apples, and other fruits were fresh for the table. The "jack-fruit," growing on a coarse, thick tree, attains a weight of thirty or forty pounds.

Captain Macfarlane took us in his carriage to one of the attractions of the city, a fine waterfall, four miles back of the town, where the hills rise abruptly from the plain. For two or three miles we rode through almost continuous plantations of cocoa-nut palms. They are not as graceful as the date or areca palm, but are very valuable, being rated at five dollars each. They are set out about twenty feet apart, so that on an acre or two a man can have the worth of a small fortune. All the feasible sections of the island away from the city, and the main-land opposite, are covered with this highly remunerative palm. On each tree twenty or fifty huge nuts in their light green husks cluster among the wide, coarse leaves that crown the columnar trunk. Like a few other tropical fruits, they are continuously productive. The fruit of the areca palm, a small nut, is used by the Indian people, together with the betel-leaf that grows on a vine like a bean, to chew as some Americans chew tobacco. A bit of slacked quicklime is used with these things to aid in some chemical changes. What strange stuff degraded man will eat and drink! The areca palm is most graceful, a trunk eighty feet high being not more than six inches thick at the base, with a smooth tapering growth. As we came nearer the foot of the hills the palms ceased and mango orchards took their place. Quarries of a coarse light granite were being worked, the chips from them being laid into the roads. Along the foot of these hills beautiful gardens had been laid out by the city authorities, in which shrubs, trees, flowers, and fruits from all parts of the tropics were being reared. Growing in a small pond was a single root of that gigantic water-lily, the *Victoria regia*, the round leaves four feet across, the blossom but half open to-day, yet full seven inches wide. In the same pond was a real lotus, of the genus *Nelumbium*, the flat leaves lying on the water, but the pink blossom five or six inches across, raised on a stem about sixteen inches above it. Some of the peculiar seed-pods, shaped like a pepper-box, were just ready to shed the nutlets for a new growth. Another lily was very like our white lily.

In a fernery, a slight shade being made by a roof of palm-leaves, were many native and imported ferns. The famous maidenhair fern, the *Adiantum*, that I have found in all the countries visited thus far, was here in great abundance, both in the fernery and in the jungle. In this fernery were eight or ten species of it, some small, others large. Other species that were strange to me exceeded in size and beauty the ostrich fern and osmunda of north United States. An orchid-house had those beautiful parasites by the score. Some were hung up with their roots attached to old pieces of wood, a few were growing in pots filled with broken charcoal and pebbles, while others flourished in coarse, dry soil. Their strange forms, with leaves wide or narrow, spiked or lily-like, their odd way of parasitic clinging to almost any thing, the exquisite perfume of their fantastic flowers, and the exceedingly varied coloration, cannot fail to attract and fascinate those who cultivate them. Begonias of many kinds, and other plants, such as temperate countries can keep only in hot-houses, were produced here in great profusion.

Having left our carriage, we climbed up a zigzag path through the jungle to the falls. It was a real tropical jungle. Here and there huge trees, looking like the hickory, grew to the height of a hundred feet or more, while shorter than those was a dense growth some sixty feet high composed of broad-leaved trees, with palms, creepers, and vines; and then for a few feet above the ground the third growth made such a mat of bushes and small prickly vines that a man could force his way through it only by cutting a path. We picked some lycopodiums of a finer growth than I have ever seen in America. The superintendent of this garden and park is classifying the flora of the island of Penang, and sending pressed specimens to the National Museum at Kew, England. For penetrating these prickly jungles he is compelled, they said, to be leather-clad from head to foot. Very few blossoms were found to-day among those wild tangles, whether out of season or a tropical lack I do not know. Monkeys were said to abound about the falls, but we did not see any. The gardeners, early in the morning, killed a wild boar that had been making havoc among their tender plants. Neither tigers nor leopards are supposed to be on the island, but both abound on the main-land opposite. The cobras, dormant in India at this season, are not so here, and I greatly desired to see one in its native state, but was denied the privilege.

At one shot, not long ago, Captain Macfarlane killed two. There is no known antidote for their bite.

We found the falls in the deep recess of the hill-side, and thick jungle on every side, to be quite a beautiful thing. The water, a large brook, tumbles in white noisy cascades for three hundred feet over the trap-rock. It forms a delightful place of attraction to lovers of nature and those from the city wishing to find a quiet hour. Beside the foot of the falls is a bit of a Brahman temple, ten feet square, devoted to one of Vishnu's incarnations, where a priest in attendance presented us each a glass of the clear, cool brook-water on a tray covered with flowers. As we returned by another path down the hill-side the delightful odors distilled from the jungle by the sun's heat partly atoned for the way that burning orb beat upon our heads. More blossoms appeared on the slope toward the south than on the slope northward, where we went up to the falls.

The Chinese at Penang seem settled for staying. They are in many kinds of business, and numbers of them are becoming rich. One of the most elegant houses in all the city is owned and occupied by a Chinaman. The red lanterns and paper pasted about the gate-way leading to his house showed the national taste. They thoroughly despise all but their own race. Captain Macfarlane told us of amusing encounters with their impudence. Here I have seen my first jin-ric-sha. This novel carriage is two-wheeled, light, something like an American gig, but lower, covered with a real buggy top, and between the slender thills, almost as long as those for a horse, slowly trots a strong man, who is fully contented if he gets five cents for drawing you an hour. I shall try one at Singapore. Chinamen hucksters carrying a large basket of garden products at each end of a pole over their shoulders; Indian coolies, with immense loads on their heads; hats as large as parasols; men with only an apron about their loins and limbs; carriages double-roofed, to protect from the sun, the shutters of the sides all open, are some of the odd things to be seen on the streets of Penang. Above all was the hearty hospitality of the Macfarlanes, and the gift to me of a peculiar cane made from the young shoot of a palm, called a "Penang lawyer," and from its great weight and heavy knob most admirable for a knock-down argument, which I mean to bring home to show to my legal friends in New England.

LETTER XXXVI.

ACROSS THE TRACK OF MRS. LEAVITT'S WOMAN'S CHRISTIAN TEMPERANCE UNION WORK IN INDIA.

HAVING known something of this lady's work abroad before I left America, I was much interested in crossing her path in this country and observing the results of her labors. From Bombay to Singapore I found she had created a deep impression. In some instances good results and successes continued; in others, suspended action, but doubtless in no case an utter failure; for if Woman's Christian Temperance Union local unions have not continued in all cases the valuable influences of a course of lectures as able as those Mrs. Leavitt gave could not fail of leaving lasting results for the good cause. In numbers of instances the unions have been kept up, and in their particular fields are hard at work. Possibly enough remain to enable a permanent growth yet to cover the whole of the land.

Temperance agitation in India has to work under special difficulties, some of which are of a nature not known in America. There are great prejudices yet existing among the English and Scotch people against the women doing public work, like lecturing, and also many of those duties expected by the different departments of Woman's Christian Temperance Union organization. Nor do they believe at all in woman suffrage, and its advocacy is certain to bring down gentle maledictions. These things in some instances may have hindered Mrs. Leavitt's success, and it is certain that they have hindered many of the European women from becoming active members of the local unions. Then, too, the customs of the government officials and the army officers are generally opposed to teetotalism. No public or social dinner is considered a proper one by these men without wine or other liquors. It is said that a Presbyterian minister in one of the Indian cities who is an active temperance man invited a lot of English officers to dinner, and of course he did not furnish any wine or strong drinks. A second time he had a dinner, inviting the same men, and this time they brought to his table their own wine and butlers, who were required by their masters to pour out wine for them at the table of their host. This impudence, very properly, kept the minister from ever inviting those officials again.

Then there are objections among the European women in the East against being associated in any such organization with either Eurasians or native women. They cannot understand the readiness of American women and missionaries to work with any body along such gospel lines. This has proved an obstacle in some places that has hindered an extension of the work, but possibly this and other obstacles will be surmounted in time, so that the hopeful, magnificent results reached in America by the Woman's Christian Temperance Union will be equaled in other lands. There is also need of work being done here to prove that all alcoholic drinks are physically injurious. Many of the people are either unaware of the scientific developments of the matter in these times or will not give due weight to the scientific and medical testimony brought forward to prove it. They affect to pass by such medical authorities as Richardson, Carpenter, and others, and quote against these sentiments medical authorities opposed to teetotalism. Doubtless a thorough discussion of the authorities and proofs of the physical injuries produced would be a valuable one for them to listen to.

To me it has been immeasurably sad to find that among the English clergy there are yet practices and principles opposed to total abstinence. Some of them urge that drunkenness is a weakness against which one should guard himself the same time that he drinks as much as he chooses. A clergyman called on one of our missionaries not long ago, and proved to be in so intoxicated a condition that the woman was about to send him away and scold her servant for permitting a drunken man to come into the house, when the husband came in, who knew the poor fool, and saved his wife from her mistake. I was introduced to a missionary to China from the Methodist New Connection just returning to the field with his new wife, and he had a cigar in his mouth, and at the table of the steamer took his wine regularly. Judgment must begin at the house of God.

Oddly enough, a peculiar condition of things exists in most of these heathen communities. The Mohammedan is prohibited by his religion from drinking spirituous liquors, and this precept he observes as a rule, though he may be a bloody cut-throat, as the Bedouins. The high caste Hindu considers it a sign of low caste if he sees one drunk, and the mark of a degraded character. The Burmese are opposed to drinking on religious grounds. The anomalous spectacle is presented of a Christian government encouraging and fostering the license and out-still systems for the purpose of revenue, by which drunkenness is increasing among temperance pagans at a fearfully cumulative rate. Mr. W. E.

Caine, M. P., has been in this country the present season lecturing on temperance and trying to organize parliamentary opposition to this kind of thing, and, while attacked by the administration press as opposing the government, he is most cordially welcomed and recognized by the educated natives and by the American missionaries. The troubled waters are beating against the shores of Hindustan. Wherever Christianity is a power, there the cry for total abstinence arises in this age in which science, history, and medicine join hands with the Master's teachings.

At Bombay the Woman's Christian Temperance Union is kept up, though languidly. Some unfortunate misunderstanding seemed to hinder a hearty co-operation on the part of British missionaries, but the American ones are doing what they can. Something was being done at Moradabad; at Agra a profound impression was created, and many joined, but there was hardly found the self-sacrifice needed to continue. They were more successful in keeping on at Cawnpore, the meetings evidently doing good. At Naini Tal there was exemplified a misfortune attending much of the Woman's Christian Temperance Union interests, the migratory demands of English occupation. The ladies at a station or city are not at all certain of being at the same place the next year. While a large union was organized there, the season at the Sanitarium closing, the officers of it mostly had to go away. At Bareilly, in addition to lectures in the regular course, Mrs. Leavitt gave one to the soldiers and one in the city hall before a large gathering of educated natives, to whom her address was translated, who were greatly pleased and deeply impressed. So much temperance work had already been carried on there and at many other places, as the

Blue Ribbon movement, the Good Templars, gospel temperance meetings, and others, that it was not always found possible to put in another organization, and this place was left to form a Woman's Christian Temperance Union organization later, if found best. At most of the smaller stations only a few European families live at all, and it frequently happens that as the American women have so much on hand already they cannot well assume any more duties. Then, too, every mission founded by Americans is a temperance organization in itself, since all those belonging to the mission must pledge teetotalism. So, as it is almost impossible under the present conditions of India society to form unions containing natives and Europeans, the limits of the work must be mostly among the latter. Much temperance work is done by the press, missionaries, lecturers, and by other means.

I found the union at Lucknow active and busy; so, too, at Allahabad. At this place a local organization was transformed into a Woman's Christian Temperance Union, and to perpetuate and extend their influence they have public meetings. I had a pleasant chance of meeting the union at Calcutta, finding it active, well organized, and hopeful. At Rangoon I found also an active Woman's Christian Temperance Union, mostly sustained by the American missionaries, with much general temperance sentiment being fostered by them. This station is fortunate in having recently received two or three active Woman's Christian Temperance Union women from America. Among the large numbers of converts in this country gathered by the Baptist the work of temperance is urgently taught, and among the Karen women the names of twenty-two thousand petitioners were appended to the world petition. What a record for these twenty-two thousand Karen women! Among the Burmese there is very little drunkenness, as one of the five great rules in the Buddhist faith is not to drink. There are four unions in Burma, with a prospect of more, and an increase in the Bands of Hope is expected. As in many other parts, those who have a disposition to crowd temperance work have so many missionary duties already that they can devote but little time to this. I had the pleasure of addressing a large audience at Rangoon on temperance.

At Singapore is a vigorous union, started when Mrs. Leavitt was present. They seek by social means, addresses, public meetings, and the like, to extend their influence. They have gone two by two on the streets and among the liquor-shops getting the soldiers and sailors to gospel temperance meetings held at the Sailors' Rest. Something has been done to arouse public sentiment; a Band of Hope has been organized, and progress is observable. Here, too, the most of the pushing has to be done by the missionaries. Not far from Singapore is the native Malay-Mohammedan State of Jahore. Mrs. Leavitt visited the sultan, explaining to him the object and work of the Woman's Christian Temperance Union. He was much interested and pleased, especially as he is greatly plagued with drunken Europeans coming into the precincts of his capital city.

LETTER XXXVII.

A WEEK WITH OUR MISSIONARIES AT SINGAPORE.

At high noon, Thursday, February 7, we had taken a pilot and were slowly steaming through the narrow western entrance between the islands into Singapore harbor. A battery of big guns frowned down upon us at the right, not more than three hundred yards from the channel, while the hills back of the city at our left also bristled with the grim dogs of war. To the south the harbor lies open and wide, much like that of Naples to the west, but lacking the high rocky capes in the offing. Scores of ships were lying here and there about the capacious anchorage, some tied to the docks, some close to the shore, others far out; many of them were native coasting-boats, in such marked contrast with the large steamers that now do most of the world's carrying. They told of two or three ships that were flying the Stars and Stripes; but I did not get time to visit them. I was in company with Rev. W. F. Oldham and wife, superintendent of our newly organized Malaysia Mission, having come with them from the session of the Bengal Conference at Allahabad, and I found them the most agreeable of traveling companions. From Calcutta to Rangoon two other missionaries were along—Mr. Brewster, from Cincinnati, to the English-speaking church at Singapore, and Miss J. E. Wisner, for some years principal of our girls' school at Rangoon.

We were soon ashore, Mr. and Mrs. Oldham being heartily welcomed by the rest of the missionaries and a group of his parishioners. We were driven to the commodious head-quarters of the mission in the new house purchased since Mrs. Oldham's leaving six months before, for a health-lift, so that she had the sensation of a new home. One half of this new property, costing twelve thousand Straits dollars, was paid for by the Chinese whose sons are in our school. It is one of the anomalous things of this mission that the Chinese contribute their thousands of dollars for the property of our school and church. They find that the Americans come seeking their good; they wisely believe in Mr. Oldham's right spirit and great ability as an educator; they are acute enough to see the difference between our work and that proposed by some other people; hence their good-will, their money, and their children in our schools. It is proposed by our mission authorities to make appeals along similar lines to the Chinese at other points in the boundaries of this mission.

The region easily reached from Singapore as a strategic center for planting missions is very extensive. The whole of the peninsula south of Rangoon is accessible, also the great islands of Sumatra, Java, Borneo, Celebes, the Philippines, and groups of smaller ones scattered through these seas, including a million and a quarter square miles and thirty-five millions of people. Most of this vast country has inviting doors. Singapore, where we have a good start, is the commercial and geographical center of all this region. It is the purpose of our authorities here to open new stations at once in several of these inviting fields.

Work was begun in this city four years ago, when Bishop Thoburn and Mr. Oldham came here, hired the city hall, and held revival services. Numbers were soon converted of the English-speaking people and Europeans, a Methodist church was organized, Mr. Oldham left in charge, and progress has ever since been made along all lines. Now, by action of the General Conference, this point is set off from the Bengal Conference, with which it had been connected, into a separate mission, having already a good right for a hope of its own. The English-speaking church has a membership of about eighty and an audience of a hundred or more devoted, liberal people; a fine Sunday-school, good social meetings, a newly organized mission band for work outside, and all the plans of a vigorous church. There are now the following American missionaries: Mr. and Mrs. Oldham, Dr. and Mrs. West, Mr. and Mrs. Munson, Miss Blackmore, and Mr. Brewster. To come here during the year the following are under appointment: Mr. and Mrs. Gray, and, for work on the Dutch Islands, a German doctor, whose wife is a dentist, and a young German tutor from the Kiel University. The mission also employs eight or ten teachers and Bible women obtained here.

One of the trophies of this mission is the splendid school built up largely by Mr. and Mrs. Oldham. The school-house is located on land beside the church, the plot for both having been given by the city government for mission purposes. It is commodious, but not large enough for the rapidly increasing school. At one time the past year two hundred and ninety-seven pupils were in attendance, and the present year has opened with over three hundred. In addition to three American teachers they use five or six others. The pupils are Europeans, Eurasians, Chinese—all who care to go. The income of the school has largely aided in defraying the expenses of the mission. At the same time they teach, the missionaries are learning the Malay language for a mission to that people, and Dr. West is just now beginning Chinese. Our Anglo-Chinese College at Foochow should send a preacher or two for opening up the Chinese mission at once.

Schools are already started among the Tamils and Chinese, under the direction of Miss Blackmore, the appointee of the Woman's Foreign Missionary Society, who came here for mission work from that younger America, Australia, and is very successful. She has a Tamil girls' school of over twenty pupils, most of the expense being borne by a Tamil merchant. There is also a Tamil church of twelve members, for which we use a native pastor educated by the Lutherans, who also conducts our Tamil boys' school of over fifty pupils. These people are numerous at Singapore, and when led to Christianity from their heathenism they are very hearty in their service.

Miss Blackmore also has an interesting work going on among the Chinese girls, one part being a school taught by a native, with nine pupils; besides these about thirty pupils, considered too old to go to school, are taught at their homes. One girl, eighteen years old, has just become engaged to be married, and has left off study to spend six months at embroidering a fancy waistband for her betrothed, as is the custom among Chinese girls. Miss Blackmore, with her assistants, visits about forty families, doing a kind of zenana work among them, reading and telling Bible stories, singing hymns, and trying to teach the women of Chinese and Tamil homes the truth of Christianity. This is all done with only the expense to the Woman's Foreign Missionary Society of five hundred and fifty dollars, I believe, the year past for assistants.

Work among the Malays has been begun by the missionaries with street-preaching, and by Captain Shellabear, of the Royal Engineers, who, having learned the spirit of our work and workers, uses his leisure time helping our mission. With a hand-press he is also printing bits of tracts in that language, which the people are eagerly accepting and reading. Possibly our Church will hear more about this cultured Captain Shellabear as time goes on.

An incident touching this Malay race is curious. Not long ago an Englishman on the island of Sumatra had some dealings with a man of that section of Malays called Dyaks, and found that in a feud one family had killed all of another one, and probably eaten them, save one young girl, whom the victors held as a slave, the owner being the Englishman's trader. He persuaded the native to give him the girl, whom he brought to Singapore and put into the family of one of our native Tamil people, where Miss Blackmore found her, and whom she found eager to accept Christianity, after the girl had been somewhat instructed in it by the Tamils. Not long ago she was baptized by Mr. Oldham.

The whole outlook for Singapore is very fine. Property to the amount of thirty thousand dollars is owned, only a moiety of which has been of cost to the Missionary Society. It is mostly self-sustaining, the fifteen hundred dollars appropriated last year having been put into property. The success with the Chinese in starting English schools here encourages the superintendent to think that at other places, as Malacca, Parak, and Penang, success may be reached the same way. The peninsula is vastly rich in tin mines; much gold is found, and other minerals, the mining of which is done by great colonies of Chinese, some of whom grow rich, and are eager to learn English and have it taught their children. Work can also be set going at once in Batavia, in Borneo, and the Celebes. God has a duty for Methodism to perform in Malaysia, and a good beginning has been made.

This point, almost touching the equator from the north, and just half-way around the world from Washington, is thus penetrated by our Church. What is this region? It is perpetual spring-time; green grass, rich foliage, brilliant flowers, singing-birds, dense woods, wonderful ferns, palms, bamboos, rattans, rich timbers, tropical fruits and plants. It rains about one hundred and ninety days a year. It is seldom scorching hot, and never cold. The island of Singapore, bought of a native sultan in 1819, is fifteen miles by forty, the city having about one hundred and sixty thousand people. The harbor is a most commodious one. It is probable that our missionaries from America can endure this climate better than that of India. It escapes the extremes of that country, the clouds and rains making a grateful relief from the glaring heat, while the nearness to the sea cools the air. The English flag pledges protection to missions.

LETTER XXXVIII.

A DAY UNDER THE EQUATOR.

BEFORE I left India I was promised a ride from Singapore to Jahore by our genial superintendent of missions at the former city, Rev. W. F. Oldham. To-day I had it, and am now cozily resting at his quiet home as I write of the new and interesting things seen. A coach runs once a day, and two of us succeeded in getting a seat with the driver, so that we could see every thing as we passed. Since Singapore was bought of the sultan of Jahore a great sea-port has grown up here, and the island of fifteen miles diameter is partly reduced to parks, fields, and plantations, though much of it is also covered with the wild luxuriance peculiar to the tropics. A superb road runs fourteen miles from Singapore to the water of the channel separating the island from the extreme southern tip of the Malay Peninsula. The British make good roads. In all their colonial possessions where I have been this is apparent. The old Romans were not better road-builders. The poor horses to-day went slowly, which was all the better for our sight-seeing. Along the first mile the strings of Chinese houses lined the road, their vegetable-gardens being the perfection of promise, the rows and beds and patches of one kind and another of products telling what the citizens of Singapore could depend upon to eat. Almond-trees, peepul and other fig-trees, bananas, cocoa-nut, betel-nut and travelers' palms, and others were along the road, also great plantations of the first and second palm. Besides their rich yield of nuts and oil I saw some cocoa-nuts that had sprouted, the incipient growth showing through the hole in the end. Several coffee plantations were just yielding their rich fruitage, the trees, about six or eight feet high, having a rich, glossy foliage like the orange, the fruit the size and color of Cape Cod cranberries, growing along the larger twigs and red when ripe, which the workers were now picking. Orchards of the very fine fruit mangosteen were also along the road, the trees the size and shape of New Hampshire apple-trees and the purple fruit not unlike smaller Baldwin apples in size and color. Under a thick rind is just a mouthful or two of the most exquisite creamy food. One of the acacias, the "flame of the forest," had great showy red blossoms, in some instances on branches from which the leaves had fallen, in that way presenting a most curious appearance. The almond-tree is very like a rough-bark hickory, and the green rind of the nut is like that inclosing the hickory-nut. Pine-apple gardens were here and there, the plant growing like the yucca, the fruit inclosed in the center of the mass of thick, prickly leaves. How odd the arrowroot was, looking for all the world like a castor-bean plant, only the stem is jointed and crooked.

The bamboo, at least three species of which we saw to-day, yields a succulent shoot—"greens" we should call it in America—the young shoot of the large roots, when a foot or so high, being most deliciously edible. We saw baskets of this peculiar food being borne into town strung across the shoulders of the coolies. At the stalls of hucksters was lying the wonderful jack-fruit, a huge green prickly thing as large as a pumpkin elongated, that grows on a tree looking like the American birch. The inside, clustering around great nut-like seeds, is a rich creamy product that one wants to eat again when once tasted. The durion and soursop, allied to this, are also huge, delicious fruits. Many of these torrid fruits have an acidity that is just enough to please one who likes that taste. The only tropical fruit they attempt to put into rivalry with the American apple is the mango, and as that is a summer fruit I have not had a chance to try it, but then I know it could not equal our Yankee product! People in India from America declare that, on the whole, American fruits are superior to those of this Eastern country. The oranges of Calcutta were most delicious, better, I think, than those of Florida; but that was the only locality where I found them superior. The papaya is a fruit almost exactly like a good-sized musk-melon, from a coarse tree like the American papaw. Bread-fruit grows sparingly here, of which I have not obtained a taste. It grows on a coarse tree resembling the papaya.

The flowers seen to-day were not many or brilliant, save the "flame of the forest." Some creepers, the sensitive plant with little balls of deep pink blossoms the size of a bullet, then a plant blossoming like the laurel, the wild white jasmine, and a few others, made up the list. Roses do not flourish here, the growth all going to stalk. Such huge leaves as some of the trees bore I had never seen. I saw them, not of the palms, either, that were three feet long by a foot wide, and one from a teak-tree in a yard at Jahore was twelve by sixteen inches. The leaves of tropical forests are nearly all thick and pulpy, to protect the trees from the intense heat. They are also very glossy.

The ferns took me a complete captive. Such luxuriance of these I had never before seen. The maidenhair, or *Adiantum* in America, is here represented by a dozen species, and is highly prized and constantly cultivated for its beauty. One like the American brake, another like the shield fern, were common, though of larger growth than in New Hampshire. Another, with a beautiful frond much divided, had become a vine, so it crept up twelve or twenty feet among the lower branches of the trees, as did a second species of smaller leaf. In some cases great banks of ferns would override all other growth and make a pile of luxuriance that would be very fine. Huge fronds in other cases stand six feet high. Some were entire, yet six feet high by six inches wide. Numbers were epiphytic, clinging to the sides or forks of the trees, thus making great masses of verdure high away from the ground. One of this kind, the stage-horn fern, is especially beautiful in the branching of its fronds. A few of the great tree-ferns, spreading ten or fifteen feet with their divided leaflets, I also saw. But this climate does not seem fully adapted to them. One is constantly surprised at the vast number of plants growing on the trees as parasites, creepers, or epiphytes. Here and there some giant creeper will cover a tree completely, so in the column of green you see not the foliage of the tree but of its enveloping addition. The rattan, though having leaves like some of the palms, is an arrant thief of this kind. Having hooked prickles on the lengthened midrib of its leaf, it can hook to leaves and trees, and so in time completely overpower its supporters. I saw them cut off at the root in some of the forests today to save the good trees. It is reported that not far from here they pulled one down that they traced for half a mile. They are very much dreaded by gardeners. As we passed an inlet of water I saw how the space of water was crowded upon by the strong growth of plants, for the roots of encroaching trees pushed far out into it. The large trees of the wild forest grow very tall, with long stems like those of rock-maple in a primitive American forest.

Not many song-birds enliven these deep forests and shadowy orchards. The temperate zones furnish much finer singers. Still a few sparrows, now and then a hawk, some starlings and others were flitting about. Just at night, on our return, we heard some with notes that were strange to me. After dark some kind of a bird had a far-reaching note that was not unmusical.

At Jahore in the native sultanate we visited a mill run by Mr. Rajah Meldrum—a prince from Scotland, made nobleman by the sultan. This mill runs seventeen saws, has two hundred and fifty men, mostly Chinese, and cuts out lumber from the tropical woods, heavy, tough, strong, aromatic. Rajah Meldrum's home, built on a gentle hill overlooking the straits between the main-land and Singapore, is as pleasantly situated as could well be imagined. About it is a growth of palms, bananas, bamboos, teak, and other tropical trees, while inside are the amenities of European comfort and civilization. After a dinner the more enjoyed for the ride of sixteen miles to reach Jahore, Mr. Munson, of the mission, and I returned. What did we have of tropical fruits to eat? Pine-apples, bananas, soursop; and to drink, the water from cocoa-nut, with rice, not dry, but soft and mucilaginous. It was a day for learning things such as seldom comes to a Yankee.

LETTER XXXIX.

QUALIFICATIONS FOR SUCCESSFUL MISSIONARIES.

WHEN among the missionaries I was told many things I ought to remember, and among the most vivid things impressed upon my mind was the opinion of those longest in the field as to the kind of men and women the work wanted.

There was great urgency that the people sent out should be those designing to devote their whole life to the missionary field. Only by such a consecration could they make efficient workers. It takes several years for any one to become familiar with the native tongue of the country or tribe to which he goes, very few indeed being able to teach or preach effectively in less than three years, and more often five years are passed before one can do effective work. Besides the language it takes years to learn the spirit and beliefs and habitudes of the people so as to do most efficient work among them. In India a few English-speaking congregations need pastors in that tongue who can as readily enter on successful work at once on getting there as can be done in America, and while such pastors are rated as in the mission field they are really only in contact with the work, not fully in it. William Taylor, when first organizing these churches, considered them an entering wedge to further work among the natives, though the people generally reached by our Church in such congregations were at the first in a most lamentable religious condition, having been neglected by the people of other missions until their case was almost as bad as the natives themselves. Bishop Thoburn, writing of the difficulty to get pastors for those congregations, as many have gone out to India, served these places a short time, and then returned, says he considers the English-speaking work to be the most important.

Those who consider their consecration to mission work perpetual are not so easily discouraged by delays, poor apparent results, sickness, or the uncongenial surroundings. Of course, a few people cannot endure the climate of those countries, that of India and Malaysia especially being very exhausting, so that in some cases the only hope of saving one's life is permanently to leave the country. He who finds himself devoted to such a work falls into it so easily by the grace of God that the enthusiasm and passion for his glory among the heathen lift him far above the lesser issues.

Another condition named was people with the presence and power of the Holy Spirit. The minister at home lacking these does not succeed in building permanently in the Lord's cause, nor does the one without them succeed in the mission work. There are hard conditions in the heathen world to be overcome, long hereditary beliefs to be changed, firm crystallized prejudices to be broken up, a terribly depraved human nature to be met and dealt with, and in most races to whom we go a subtle power and habit of deception that appalls one as he learns its strength. Here mere human power can with some success deal with ignorance and some other elements of heathenism, but it fails ignobly when alone it tries to deal with these spiritual depravities. Only he can succeed whose highest powers and hardest work are multiplied and directed by the Holy Spirit. To the missionary the Spirit is truly his sword and aggressive weapon. In all Asiatic countries he is to meet men of subtile reasoning powers, men skilled in defending their own beliefs and ways. The missionary working with much of the Spirit's enduement can best lead the convicted heathen to accept the care and help of God that he so much needs in his passage out of darkness into the light. The Bible can best be taught and its teachings best received under the power and light of the Spirit. All the benefits to a teacher or preacher in Christian countries coming from a great and full baptism of the Spirit are also fully given to the missionary.

The superintendent of the Malaysia Mission assured me one day what successful men in India urged upon me before, that there was little use to have any but kind-hearted people come out. There is such an easy chance to be domineering and to grow harsh under the exhausting climate and irritating conditions of the work and people that one to succeed must be saved far enough to make him sweet-hearted toward all men. The natives are very susceptible to kind treatment, since they receive so much of the opposite kind from most of the civil and military officers. Some of the brutalities practiced upon them by both men and women that I saw during my few months among them made my republican Christian blood boil. The natives can easily see the difference of treatment accorded them by the missionaries and by others. From what I saw and heard I judge that there is room for improvement in some cases even by missionaries themselves in the treatment of those people. But they have come to know that they are receiving the best treatment by far from the missionaries that they have ever obtained.

High culture is an important factor in a successful missionary, but of less demand than any one of the qualifications already named. If one has studied a language or two besides the English it will, in addition to the culture obtained by it, help in learning the vernaculars. Yet one can succeed if he has other necessary elements of success who has only a good English education.

THE END.